The Newfoundland

Emmy Bruno
translation by Louis Palmisano, M.D.

Published by Doral Publishing, Phoenix, Arizona

Printed in the United States of America.

Copyedited by Ellen M. Young
Drawings by Enrico DeCenzo
Cover design by Amy Antonio

Library of Congress Card Number: 96-84684
ISBN: 0-944875-47-5

Second Printing   2003

This book is dedicated to my mother who taught me to know and to love this splendid breed.

Acknowledgements

I wish to thank all those who by their counsel and moral support have contributed to the realization of this volume and in a special way give thanks to the friend and artist, Enrico DeCenzo, whose art graces these pages.

Foreword

Mrs. Bruno has written a first class, well balanced book full of information on the Newfoundland. Her chapters on type, structure and movement should be included in every student judges' library. Especially interesting were her theories on how the early formation of the breed developed as a result of its various uses.

An extensive section on breeding and rearing is also included that is full of common sense information.

Along with the chapters on the history of the Newfoundland on the continent there is much new information that readers of only English-written books will enjoy.

I believe this is the only foreign language book on the Newfoundland ever to be translated into English. My compliments to Dr. Palmisano, who translated from the original Italian, on an excellent job.

Judy Oriani
Breeder in England

Author's Preface To The American Edition

"Read not to contradict and confute; not to believe and take for granted; not to find talk and discourse; but to weigh and consider."

—Francis Bacon

When I began to write this book, I wanted, above all, to offer a contribution to the knowledge of the Newfoundland, but my greatest hope was that of being able to open a more ample dialogue with all of the lovers of the breed.

To broaden the technical bases, to exchange other opinions and experiences, to follow the methods of research and investigation, these are the only routes capable of reaching a more objective and unified vision, and I wished to follow these paths to meet with other researchers and devotees. On this path, however, I found a great barrier-that of languages.

The American edition, which follows the recent German edition, is for me a cause for great joy because it overcomes such obstacles and enlarges the horizons of dialogue.

I have never believed that distances, orientation, or the lack of exchange should result in differentiated types. I am, on the contrary, convinced that beyond all the possible individual variations, the science of breeding can be oriented to a unique type-that type which all of the standards describe-an ideal type in which the functional characteristics of the breed are expressed with the maximum of equilibrium and harmony.

I shall forever be indebted to Doctor Luigi Palmisano who made this realization possible. To translate a book is always a delicate undertaking. Thanks to the ability of this eclectic man, who knew how to blend his medical experience, his passion as a breeder and is expertise as a writer, each sentence and each definition have found their true meaning.

My thanks to the artist Enrico DeCenzo who with his works changed words into pictures.

If a greater number of people can understand better and work together for the welfare of our beloved Newfoundland, we will have achieved our goal.

Emmy Bruno

CONTENTS

PREFACE

Italy, a natural harbor, deeply hidden within the Mediterranean Sea, has thousands and thousands of miles of coast. Every year we read about people who perish in the waters, while the people responsible for taking care of the bathers become more rare. Thus, the Newfoundland could be of great help along our coasts. Let's hope that this book will contribute to their diffusion and utilization as lifeguards.

I met the author of this book in 1968, at the Monte Carlo Exhibition; I was immediately struck by her passion for the Newfoundland, a breed that I adored as a child, even before dedicating myself to the St. Bernard. On that occasion, though Emmy was a young woman and dealing with her first experiences as an exhibitor, she demonstrated such knowledge about the breed to allow me to predict a brilliant future as a breeder and judge. Even then, one could notice between her and Cora, her Newfoundland (who later became Italian and International champion), an extraordinary feeling; dog lovers know that there is often such a feeling between dog and owner that they end up resembling each other. Beyond these considerations though, there is no doubt that Emmy has always had a "Newfoundland personality" as evidenced by her will power , patience, care and courage with which she persevered in her breeding and research programs.

Reading these pages, the reader will notice the deep level of understanding of the dog, both as a historical subject and a canine subject, with particular care for its morphological and functional character. Her standard comments represent a classical example of applied canine studies, the first ever written regarding the Newfoundland breed. One must keep in mind that the Newfoundland standard published by the FCI (based on British criteria) is quite imprecise and different from the "typical portrait" described by modern zoological science. That is why there is the need for comments based simply on general canine knowledge that can be applied to, and answer the questions that lovers of the breed, breeders and judges may have. With a simple style, understandable also to those who are not experts, Mrs. Bruno answers the numerous questions regarding the standard. For example, the description of the head—so typical and different from all other breeds—is conducted in a very precise and technical manner, as is the description of the anterior limbs with their relationship between shoulder, arm, and metacarpals that contribute to giving to the Newfoundland the appearance of a bear.

The Newfoundland is examined in this book, from every possible point of view and in such a deep manner as has never been seen before, even in foreign publications. To achieve this the author was aided not only by her passion for the "magnificent bear" but also by her solid scientific background, which one can clearly perceive in every page of the book. Emmy Bruno is, in fact, a veterinarian.

It must be specified that books about dogs are often put together in a haphazard manner, with bits taken from various other writings. This causes mistakes to pass unnoticed. In this book on the other hand, aside from the historical aspects described with criticism, and an ample supply of bibliographical material, everything is original, personally tested and lived. It is also interesting to notice the author's remark about constitutionalism which is the foundation of every classification, which is, for us judges and breeders, a very important point that must be expanded upon because, as said by the great judge, Robert De Santis, who sadly for us died prematurely: "the study of the constitution allows us to pass judgment and make evaluations about the biometric character of canine breeds."

The portrait of the Newfoundland that emerges from this book describes both an exposition and a working dog. This is an important point because the "lap dogs" or the so-called "Ballerinas," bred only to dance around a circus ring, possess great elegance, but have lost every contact with the zoological reality of their breed. The Newfoundland is a utility and water dog, and its type, so strongly characteristic, was created both by nature and by man for water rescue. I must add that every part of its body is created so that it can achieve the most with the minimum effort. "Durch Arbeit zum Typus" (meaning: through work, one can perceive typology) wrote Prof. Heim, one of the founding fathers of the continental Newfoundland in the twenties, and he added: "Ignoring the work, to make out of this breed a toy only to show, denaturing it, would be both absurd and negative." I would like to add to these words that only a working dog can become a show dog. Personally I believe that writers and judges must first demonstrate what they are able to achieve in a reasonably long time span (ten, twenty years or more) as breeders, before giving an opinion. Too often one sees people talk about a breed without having been a breeder or having been a bad one first. This is most certainly not the case of Emmy Bruno who has demonstrated what one can achieve by knowledgeably managing blood lines. This passion as a breeder now involves her whole family: mother, husband and son. The results are important, as seen by the many champions she has created. Though at times she used foreign dogs, the genetic base remains hers, to indicate that she follows a very personal road in the breeding of the Newfoundland. One must also say that the Newfoundland is a part of her family. Her grandfather and uncle owned several, and her mother also passed this passion on to her.

It would be too lengthy to indicate all of the champions bred by Mrs. Bruno in many years, but it is necessary to specify that after the breeding of Aar, Amanda and Baia degli Angeli Neri, Italian and International Champions, Emmy bred in 1972 that which she considers her masterpiece: Ch. It. Int. Rip. Christian degli Angeli Neri. This great dog, whose pictures appear in many publications, had a noble head and expression, a return to the Swiss prototypes of the past, which many consider the most typical Newfoundland ever bred. I am talking about the dogs of the 1930s through the 1960s , before the use of foreign bloodlines that somehow modified a great work of selection done by breeders such as Burkhard, Buchner, Toppius and others. Emmy always used those dogs as a reference and in her career as a breeder, aside from Christian, she was able to produce other dogs with those characteristics. In fact, after the breeding of Ch. Ethel, Harold, and Felix, she tried, not without hesitation, to couple Christian with his daughter Flora. The results were positive because one of the puppies, the female Suomi, later coupled with Ch. World Erasmus Graf v. Luxemburg, gave birth to the most beautiful Newfoundland litter ever seen in Italy, the famous "letter Z" which had five high class champions: Zeder, Zenith, Zeus, Zingarella, and Zelda. The combination was later repeated creating other champions such as: Dilys and Debbye. At the moment other dogs carrying the name of the "Angeli Neri" are winning, all with very distinct characteristics that allow them to be recognized from the others that appear in shows.

Emmy Bruno hides a bombproof efficiency and a great willpower under a delicate and genteel appearance (I believe she would even walk to the North Pole for her dogs). In 1976, she was elected president of the Club Italiano del Terranova, founded by her after forty years of the club's inactivity. She later became a specialist judge. Today, after a career of twenty-three years and honors given by the dog world, she really has much to say, and she offers us this book, which is not only a historical-scientific study of the Newfoundland, but something more, because it holds in its pages a human experience lived day after day for the love of a breed.

—Antonio Morsiani

THE LEGEND OF THE NEWFOUNDLAND

There in that land where the ocean waves explode upon the reef in a boiling foam, this legend was born.

As the story is told, God turned one day to contemplate all of His creations and saw on that Newfoundland Isle, flailed by storm, a small nation of fishermen, whose rough, weather-beaten people fought courageously against the impervious elements of nature as the freezing cold winters and the unforgiving coastline took its toll, and the sea often asked its sacrifice of human life.

Nevertheless, they remained deep rooted, these men of Newfoundland, with a stubbornness as great as their courage.

God saw, and in His infinite compassion, thought how He might alleviate their suffering. He searched among all the creatures of His creations, but He found none that would serve. It was then that He decided to create one anew!

He took the body of the Bear; whose bone structure lent well to such arduous labors and whose thick fur would resist the bitter Newfoundland Isle cold.

Then He thought to sweeten this silhouette with the lithe, limber lines and movements of the Seal, with all its prowess to swim and speedily slip between the waves.

Now turning to face the sea, He saw the playful Dolphins, happily following the ships. Their sweet, joy-filled eyes revealing their serene temperament, and more; they so loved man that they often rescued them, saving them from the sea. Yes, they too would be part of this new creature.

When He was done molding and casting, there suddenly appeared in His creative arms, a superb animal with glistening black fur, powerful and sweet in the same moment.

This new being, however, had to have an allegiance and faithfulness, tried and true, to be able to live beside Man and be ever ready to offer his life for his master. It was at that moment that the Lord placed in its chest the heart of the Dog, and the miracle was complete!

From that day onward, those men of the sea had beside them their courageous companion, ever strong, ever faithful, the Newfoundland!

Emmy Bruno

I. ORIGINS AND HISTORY

Rebuilding the remote origins of a breed of dogs, beyond its written and documented history, is not an easy task. The things we know for certain do not go further back than the last century when modern canine science was born, illuminating the importance of the dog, outlining, classifying and recording data.

In any case, this time span is too short to satisfy our curiosity. Consequently, we search through the niches of history to find clues that show man's early involvement in the selective breeding of dogs. It's like trying to focus on a picture in which the dog is part of the landscape, but rarely the main subject. One takes a page of history, a few lines of literature, an image from a painting, and then one considers natural science and paleontology and takes long imaginary trips on a map.

All of this is extraordinarily fascinating, but reaching certainties is as utopian a task as trying to complete a puzzle with many missing pieces. It is for this reason that I choose not to state conclusions, but rather to present the existing material as is in order to give readers the opportunity to make their own deductions.

Some of the various theories about the origins of the breed appear more believable than others, but don't be horrified, nor smile, nor shake your heads in disbelief when you read of the strange theories. There could very well be a small part of truth revealed by genetics and then manipulated by man. Thus, a wavy coat, a curving tail, a thin muzzle or a falling lip is rarely the product of change, but the remainders of an ancestral memory, partly hidden, but carried forward for many generations.

Remember that in the past, breeds of dogs were less unique than breeds of today because of the lesser possibility of specialization and exaggeration of physical characteristics. Before the appearance of specialized genealogical texts and standards, the descriptions of various breeds were mostly superficial, often confused, and most certainly the number of those who bred purely was smaller than it is currently.

Today's crosses between two breeds are mainly caused by accident, and the lack of a pedigree constitutes the biggest problem in crossing two different breeds; however, we can easily imagine how two or three centuries ago, hybrid crossings were a common way to bring out the best of two breeds in one animal. At that time, the dog's ability to work significantly affected the life led by colonists, for whom the dog's abilities meant security, increased physical strength and the difference between having a full or an empty basket.

Today, we know traditional breeds with well-defined characteristics: the setter and the pointer, the Great Dane and the Mastiff, the St. Bernard and the Leonberger, but to achieve this, years and years of selection were needed, and their formation left a trace of lesser breeds, some later recognized but not well known, others now extinct.

There is an essential current that runs from these origins like the source of a river. As different sublines meet, some aspects fuse with the principal ones, but at times, some sublines remain hidden only to reemerge much later.

It is this method that breeders use when trying to create new breeds, and it is to these "hidden" characteristics that one must pay the most attention so as not to create new variations in an already homogeneous breed. It is necessary to slowly filter out those characteristics that do not fit the standard instead of involuntarily fixing them in the bloodlines of the breed. Consequently, it is of the utmost importance to be able to perceive these characteristics immediately, when they are still barely perceptible.

At this point, the importance of being fully informed about the genetics of the breed and its history becomes quite clear. Before going back in time though, it seems necessary to introduce the island to which the history of our breed is so closely related.

Newfoundland Island

Newfoundland is a large island situated in the Atlantic Ocean at the entrance of the St. Lawrence Gulf, where Canada protrudes north through the Labrador peninsula, leaving Nova Scotia at the south. The Island of Anticosti and the Belle Isle Strait, which is about 15 to 40 kilometers (or 9 to 24 miles) wide, separate it from the North American continent.

It is about one third the size of Italy and almost half of it is covered by water. The coasts, full of bays and fjords, have a menacing aspect, and where the rocks leave space for vegetation, various types of evergreens are found. The island climate is humid, with abundant rain and fog that lasts throughout the year. Following a summer so short that fruit fails to mature, there comes a harsh winter that ices the bay and covers the ground with snow until April.

The island's fishing grounds in the southeast are rich in sardines, cod and salmon, and because of this, after the arrival of the Europeans, the island's nationality was claimed by many countries.

Around the year 1000, the Vikings, or Scandinavian pirates, had come to these coasts. After touching Greenland, they moved south to visit Newfoundland and then worked their way further south around the southern tip of the American continent, or Cape Horn, all the way to Peru. It was only in 1497 though, that the island was formally discovered. In that year, the Italian sailor John Cabot was given five vessels by the British Navy in order to find a northeast passage that would lead to Cathay. He never arrived in China, but instead discovered the coasts of Labrador and Newfoundland.

In 1498, his son, Sebastian Cabot, visited the island and declared it uninhabited either by men or domesticated animals. Presumably these coasts were, at least between April and September when the climate was somewhat less harsh, inhabited by the same indigenous populations that lived in Quebec and Labrador. Here, as on the rest of the American continent, these indigenous populations probably withdrew at the arrival of the Europeans, who likely came for the abundance of rich sea life.

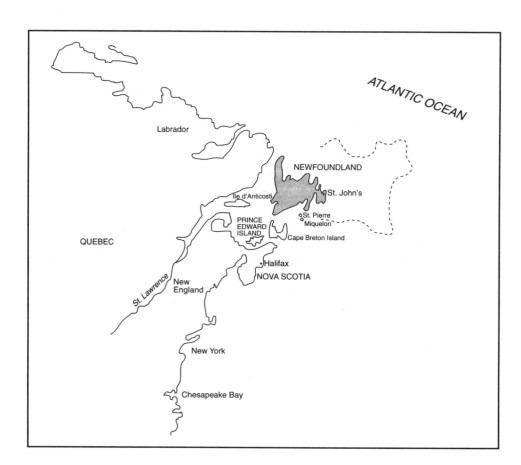

The Island of New-foundland.

Basque, Briton and Norman fishermen frequently visited, and it is likely that by 1504 they tried to make settlements on the island. In 1524, Verrazano took possession of it in the name of the King Francis I of France, but it was the British who took definite control in 1615.

The island passed from French to British possession through the Treaty of Utrecht in 1713, and it later became a dominion in 1917. In 1949, Newfoundland, along with the northeast part of Labrador, became the tenth Canadian province.

Understanding both the geography and the history of Newfoundland is necessary to comprehend what gave birth to this breed.

Theories Regarding Origins

Various theories about the origins divide into two groups: those who want the Newfoundland as a native of the American continent, and those who want it as a cross between breeds imported from Europe.

From the *Neufundlanderhund* of Dr. Heim (1952), we learn that when the famous naturalist Th. Studer examined the craniums of the Newfoundland dog, he found a bone structure similar to that of the Canis Familaris Inostranzewis, descendant from the strong Northern wolf, with its powerful head, and predecessor of the Tibetan Mastiff and the molossus in general. He affirmed that the Newfoundland belonged to this group and would not have been able to develop independently on this island; rather it must have been imported, and once there had undergone processes of natural selection because of physical conditions and the intense cold. There remains doubt, however, about how predecessors of the Newfoundland could have initially arrived.

Eben Hosford, of Harvard, wrote in 1888, that during the expeditions to the American continent, the Vikings used to bring along their domesticated animals and in particular their "bear hunting dogs." These were surely descendants of the Mastiffs, which they used as guard dogs and to pull sleds. There is mention of a great black dog named Oolum that the chief Viking, Leif Ericson, had brought along on one of his trips. These animals are ancestors of dogs that Norwegian farmers used in the nineteenth century for protection against wolves. Wearing collars with spikes to protect their necks, even the bears retreated when faced by them.

In the Italian Encyclopedia of 1940, at the word "bear dog," we find the following: "Breed of dog principally used in the hunting of bear; large and squared head, short muzzle, thin and small ears, short and muscular neck. The coat is reddish brown with white patches and black shadings. The hair is long and solid."

This description talks about the Pelshound, the famous molossus coming from Asia and descendants of the Tibetan Mastiff, which spread throughout Europe giving origin to the various mastiff breeds.

The Viking incursions in America have been documented by Doctor Helge Ingsted of Oslo who recently discovered in Meadows, on the island of Newfoundland, the remains of a Viking camp containing, among other things, the skeleton of a dog.

Viking contact with the Indians could also be demonstrated by the appearance of children with blond hair and fair skin among the Inca population. Because the Vikings likely abandoned animals in the places that they visited, it is easy to believe that some of their dogs were left behind and then crossed with indigenous breeds. Additional proof is suggested by the presence of an embalmed dog, similar to the Scandinavian dog, found in the tomb of an Inca prince of the twelfth century.

This theory, aside from demonstrating the links with the origins of the molossus, allows for a time span long enough for natural selection to occur. More recently Fred Stubbart, during a reunion of the American Newfoundland club, espoused a theory based on his studies of the bone structure of Indian dogs, that the Newfoundland is originally of American descent. He assumes that the Tibetan Mastiff or his predecessor, the molossus, would have come to this continent through the Bering Strait, the Aleutian Islands and Alaska, along with ancestors of the American Indians.

Theories of the origin of the Newfoundland

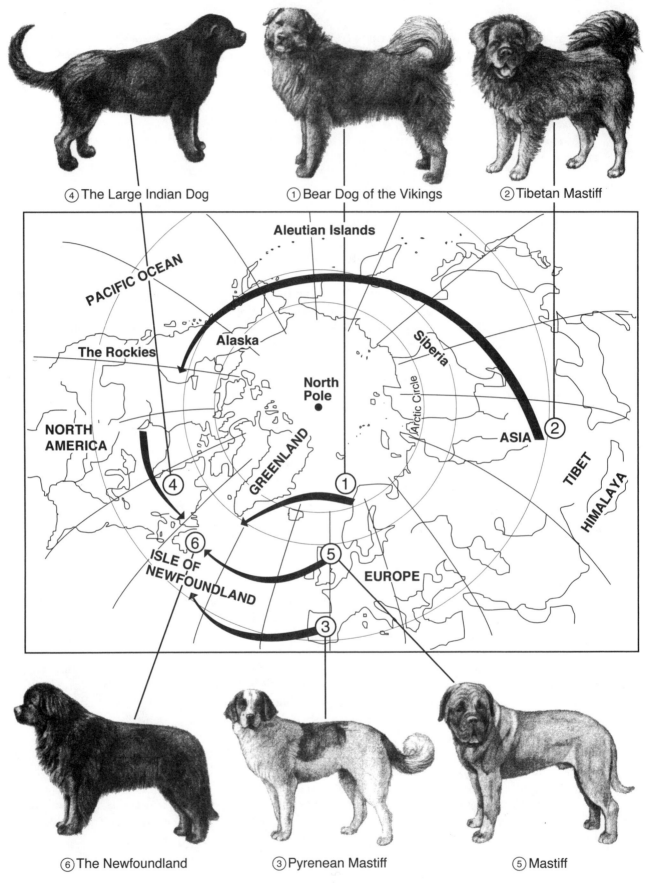

④ The Large Indian Dog

① Bear Dog of the Vikings

② Tibetan Mastiff

Aleutian Islands

PACIFIC OCEAN

Alaska

Siberia

The Rockies

North Pole

Arctic Circle

NORTH AMERICA

GREENLAND

ASIA

TIBET

HIMALAYA

ISLE OF NEWFOUNDLAND

EUROPE

⑥ The Newfoundland

③ Pyrenean Mastiff

⑤ Mastiff

The Newfoundland would thus come from the "great black dog" of the Algonquin and the Sioux. The former lived in Ontario and Quebec up to Labrador; the Sioux, after coming from the north, occupied all of the central zone of Saskatchewan, Arkansas and the Rocky Mountains up to the Allegheny Mountains. The Indian dogs were thus spread throughout the area of the Great Lakes, the Central Plains, and from east to west down to Mexico.

Professor Otis Mason, in his *Handbook of the American Indian*, tells of how these animals were used for hunting, fishing, guarding, working or simply as companions to the elders and the children. During the changes of location they were used to carry part of the load, or to pull a sort of sled made by teepee poles and deer hide. When the Indians used their canoes, the dogs ran along for many miles on the banks of the rivers accompanying their masters. They were very useful and adored, so much so that they appear on some totem poles.

This occurred before the Spanish invasion, when the horse was imported, and took the dog's place in helping man. Slowly the dog began to disappear, remaining mainly in those places where the harsh climate and terrain made it difficult for a horse to work. This hypothesis, as well as others, leaves ample space for the genetics to be strongly imprinted allowing the breed to maintain its basic characteristics despite the various crossings between breeds that were imported in the sixteenth and seventeenth centuries. Notwithstanding this, little prevents these two theories from being interlaced, so that the bloodlines of the Tibetan Mastiff brought forth by the "great Indian dog" and by the "Viking bear dog" could have fused together to create the ancestors of the Newfoundland.

Other theories refer to a cross between the Indian dog and the black wolf of America. This breed of wolf, which is unfortunately extinct, presented very particular traits. It was different from other wolves in its color, the position of its eyes, the quality of its coat, and a greater predisposition for being domesticated. Typical and unique to the female was a white star on the chest.

J. Godman in *American Natural History of 1836*, and J.G. Wood in *Illustrated Natural History of 1865*, told of this being very common in the great plains, and the explorer Samuel Hearne described a habit the Indians had for play of taking young wolves from their caves. Therefore, we cannot exclude that the two species had contact. We should also keep in mind that even the ancestor of the Tibetan Mastiff was a wolf, and that in this case, because of the enormous time frame, species modification appears credible.

Other hypotheses include crossings between Nordic dogs from Alaska and Greenland. In 1820, Scott described a great resemblance between these two breeds, with the greatest difference being that the ears were carried straight in the Greenland dog. Interestingly, representations of the Newfoundland in the eighteenth century show ears semipending, straight or cut.

Goodman describes the Greenland dog as similar to the Newfoundland, but, he adds, "[T]he nose of the Newfoundland is wide, like that of the Mastiff." He also states that the Newfoundland was more domesticated than the Greenland dog, which was mainly used as a pack dog.

Completely different from the other two theories is the opinion of Hon. Harold MacPherson of Newfoundland (1937) and Johan Pietersee (1932), breeder and president of the Netherlands club. Both believe that it was European colonists who brought the ancestors of the Newfoundland to the island. These colonists would have brought dogs from their countries of origin to the New World.

At that time in Europe, there existed many varieties in full evolution that would later have given birth to the modern breeds. The Barbet, a typically French breed, and ancestor of the Poodle, was then quite common and frequently used for hunting ducks. A great swimmer and very able at bringing back the hunted prey, this breed was often kept on board ships. He was described as an animal with a wide and rounded cranium, a strongly developed forehead and a woolly coat.

Also French, but probably originally from Spain, was the Epagneul, a descendent of the pointer used for quail hunting and also very able at hunting in marshlands.

On the Iberian Peninsula there were various species of Spanish and Portuguese hunting dogs, probable ancestors of the Pointer and of the Perdiguero. At the same time in England there were the spaniels and the bird-dogs, crosses between the Epagneul and hunting dogs, ancestors of the setters.

Hauling timber in the Yukon.

Along with these breeds of hunting dogs, there existed a vast number of molossus, used mostly as guard dogs and sometimes as hunting dogs for large prey.

The ancestors of the French Pyrenees Mountain Dog and the Spanish Pyrenean Mastiff were at the time a single breed. A very diffused breed at the time was the English Mastiff, then mainly black. In some regions there were dogs similar to the Scottish Sheepdog, only more massive and squared than those of the present day, who became more fragile looking through the Borzoi. There also existed a whole category of "butcher dogs," ancestors of the Dogue de Bordeaux in France and called butcher or estate dogs in England.

Most certainly those who went to the New World brought some of these animals along, some of which clearly bred with indigenous animals. This is proved by Sir Joseph Bank, member of the Royal Geographic Society, who upon returning from his trip to the island of Newfoundland, stated that there were dogs, mainly mixes with Mastiff blood, some able to swim and others who could not. The span of a little more than a century is certainly too short for the specific characteristics of a breed to be strongly implanted.

According to Dr. Heim, the crosses with the Pyrenean dogs and the estate dogs probably led to the Landseer. The opponents of this theory claim that one of the characteristics of the Pyrenean dogs is the polydactyly, or the presence of the double spur, or dewclaw, on the hindquarters. They also claim that the Newfoundland has never had problems with spurs. However, the presence of a single dewclaw is not common enough in young Newfoundlands that the standard states that "The dewclaw, if present, must be removed."

I have been struck by a particular characteristic quite common in the Montagna and the Pyrenean Mastiffs, and not infrequent in the Landseer: the noticeable development of the third eyelid of one or both eyes. Furthermore, the fact that the Continental Landseer, bred purely, tends to be different from the white and black Newfoundland would suggest the introduction of a different bloodline in the white and black variety.

Once all of these theories have been taken into consideration, there remains only one honest conclusion to make: it is not certain what the first explorers found on the coasts of Labrador and Newfoundland. Maybe among so much that was new, the dog remained unobserved, or maybe it was taken for granted that where there was man there would also be his faithful companion. However, those early navigators were not necessarily canine lovers or naturalists, but only explorers, fishermen or adventurers. Probably their first contacts with the indigenous populations gave them a chance to appreciate those indigenous dogs, so obedient and able, so useful and intelligent, so in love with water and hunting, and all of these characteristics must have impressed those strong men. This must be true because they began taking them home.

And here begins the story of the Newfoundland.

History

In 1497, John Cabot stated that he had not noticed the existence of domesticated animals on the island. The same was stated by Captain Whitbourn of Exmouth in his tales of his visit to Newfoundland. Five years later though, after another stay, he told of witnessing, with his companions, various encounters between their Mastiffs and the wolves and other animals of the island. These dogs played and barked loudly, and while the men were intent on curing and smoking their fish, the dogs would disappear only to return after quite long periods of time and showing no signs of hostility. These animals, not well identified, could very well have been the indigenous dogs of Newfoundland, perhaps undomesticated, but with whom in all probability the large Mastiff would have bred.

In the following years, trips between Europe and America increased, along with the colonization of the New World. In 1696, approximately 400 Frenchmen and 2300 Englishmen lived in Newfoundland. They were primarily fishermen, hunters and lumberjacks. For these activities, they often used dogs as aids; thus, they needed at their service strong, balanced and multipurpose animals. Obviously these

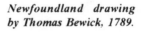

Newfoundland drawing by Thomas Bewick, 1789.

7

1843: Newfoundland by Ash.

dogs were not chosen for the color of their coats or the shape of their tails, but rather for the strength of their bone structure, their docility and their intelligence. They probably chose the sons of those dogs for their ability to drag heavy loads, to bring back the hunted prey, and to not be frightened by a stormy sea. It is likely that either they found all of these characteristics in an existing breed or that they tried to make these animals better by crossbreeding them. Clearly though, function and utility were the principal factors in choosing an animal, and this creative principal brought a group of genes together to make the foundation of what would become our present breed. Indigenous or not, word

Saved. *Painting by Sir Edwin Landseer.*

spread, and the fame of this new breed of dog that was superbly adapted to work, swimming and retrieving, traveled as fast as the ships that sailed the Atlantic.

In 1732, the "bear dog" was described in the following manner: "The bear dog is usually a very large dog, with docile movements, but very alert. He comes from Newfoundland where he is used to guard houses; he possesses a thundering voice, and is able to turn a water wheel." It was this description that pushed Sir Joseph Bank to go and seek the new breed. In his *Journal of a Voyage to Newfoundland*, he wrote of having been very surprised at finding that there was not a specific breed of dog on the island. The various crossbreeds that he encountered were able swimmers, but were mainly appreciated for the ability and strength that allowed them to be used during the winter to pull sleds and lumber. He later learned that in Trepassey County, there was a man who bred specific dogs called the Newfoundland.

He did not have the chance to meet this man during that voyage, but on later excursions he acquired the desired animal specimens and brought them back to Europe. Thanks to him, many important persons of the time came to know the breed and its virtues.

Napoleon (1769-1821), Cook (1728-1779), Scott (1772-1832), Byron (1788-1824), George the third (1738-1820), Landseer (1802-1873) and Wagner (1813-1883) all wanted these animals as companions.

While the breed was spreading throughout Europe, however, it was undergoing severe threats in its native land. The animals were used to exhaustion during the winter months when needed, and then abandoned to fend for themselves in summer.

As always, the thoughtlessness and greed of man had negative effects. These animals, forced to find food for themselves, at times formed packs and attacked herds of domesticated animals. This enraged the shepherds to such a degree that in 1780 the governor of the island, Edward, to increase the bovine production, prohibited inhabitants of the island from owning more than one dog per family. Probably more than one man disobeyed, considering the utility of these animals, but in any case the canine population was greatly decreased.

As if this were not enough, a decree in 1815 further diminished the number of animals. The Grand Jury of St. John, with the excuse of wanting to stop an epidemic of rabies, ordered that all dogs found free in the city, with an exception made for those carrying lumber, were to be immediately exterminated. To encourage this initiative, a bounty of five shillings was offered for every animal killed.

Such a harsh procedure should not be of surprise, considering that even today, in the twentieth century and in so-called civilized countries, the superficiality of those who abandon dogs causes the formation of packs of wild dogs which in turn provoke cruel reactions.

1872: Leo.

1878: Ch. Black Prince.

However, perhaps this sad decree pushed men to keep with them the best, the strongest and the most capable dogs.

In 1882, the Scottish explorer Cornack wrote of having met an Indian family on the island that owned only one dog: a large Newfoundland. During this time, a new interest for the dog in its various forms was taking place.

In 1775, the French naturalist, Buffon described more than thirty canine breeds, classifying them on the basis of their origins and some exterior characteristics. In 1800, the authoritative book on dogs of its day, the *Cinographia Britannica* was published. Naturally, the Newfoundland became more known along with the others. After he had been given an official name for the first time by Cartwright, numerous descriptions of the breed began appearing in various publications of the time.

The History of Quadrupeds of 1790 by Buffon described a beautiful specimen of a Newfoundland in the following manner:

-length of the body from the nose to the attachment of the tail: 6 feet 2 inches
-distance between the anterior limbs, passing above the shoulder: 5 feet 7 inches
-circumference behind the shoulder: 3 feet. inches
-circumference of the head above the ears: 2 feet
-superior circumference of the anterior limb: 9.5 inches

It also mentioned webbed feet, swimming ability and a passion for trout fishing.

At the same time a drawing by Thomas Bewick, the illustrator of Buffon's *The History of Quadrupeds* showed a strong animal, quite tall on its limbs, with a coat shorter than the present one, and a high, curved tail. The head, somewhat longer, had a slightly accentuated stop, but the muzzle already presented some squareness. The coat was white with small black patches. Other illustrations of the time also show multicolored animals. This is not at all surprising because between 1690 and 1798 it was mainly the patched specimens that were brought to Europe. Evidently these corresponded to what the English buyers wanted: height and presence.

The demand for tall specimens was such that dogs were exported to Nova Scotia where they were bred to create height. From Halifax these animals were then sent to Poole, in the county of Dorset, which was the principal commerce point with the colonies. Consequently, the dogs that arrived in England at the time presented various colorations: black, brown, bronze, black and white, brown and white, and black with reddish hues and highlights.

In the beginning of the 1800s, though, this tendency changed and preference was given to the black type. In 1810, Robert Steel rose to defend the original breed, saying that it had been made impure by the introduction of European dogs.

In those years, various mixed breedings of the past generated some confusion. The plurality of types tended toward a new breed, but as it was not yet clearly differentiated, names and descriptions caused confusion.

There was in the beginning a non-clearly identified breed, perhaps subdivided in two groups of different sizes. The common description of these animals though was their great passion for swimming and retrieving. It is from this primitive group that the category of retrievers originates.

The geographic area that birthed this category was not only Newfoundland, but included all of the territories of the continent around the Gulf of St. Lawrence and down to Maryland.

Thus, while in Nova Scotia, the small Newfoundland of St. John was bred with the pointer generating the Long Coated Retriever, and from this the short coated Labrador. On the island of Anticosti the same dog was bred with the Poodle and the Irish Water Spaniel to produce the Curly Coated Retriever.

Meanwhile, on the American coasts, the original dog was mixed with the setter and the Epagneul to produce the Flat Coated Retriever from which, through more crossings with the Setter and the Bloodhound, came the Golden Retriever.

Simultaneously, on the eastern and western coasts of Chesapeake Bay, Sailor and Canton, male and female Newfoundlands who had survived the shipwreck of an English frigate in 1807, were continually bred with Water Spaniels, Coon dogs and Hounds, giving origin to the Chesapeake Bay Retrievers.

Along with these new breeds, there remained the original type, contrasted to the taller and more heavyset European type.

In 1840, Hamilton Smith, after having visited Newfoundland, wrote in the *Naturalist Library* that the original dog was black and bronze. He preferred the heads of the English dogs that were better shaped than those of the dogs of the American colonies; he thought that the English dogs had more rounded craniums and less pointed muzzles.

A unsigned picture of an original Newfoundland, taken from the 1843 treatise by Ash, shows an opaque black animal with a receding profile. In the subsequent European type, the addition of Mastiff blood contributed to the formation of a more powerful cranium and depth of muzzle along with heavier bone structure.

Crosses with the St. Bernard are also known to have occurred. In 1830 and 1856, the St. Bernard breed risked extinction following calamities and a genetic overuse, probably caused by inbreeding. The monks of the Hospice thus used the Newfoundland to give the St. Bernard new bone, strength and vitality.

It is obvious that among these crosses, not all looked like the St. Bernard; in fact, some may have looked like black or patched Newfoundlands.

In 1887, in *British Dogs*, Dabziel wrote: "Though it seems obvious that the statement "imported" referred to the Newfoundland, in the text of Origins of the British Kennel Club, it means coming from Newfoundland; it is not certain...many great Newfoundlands come from other areas and some, it is said, were even imported from St. Bernard kennels."

Nevertheless, in England, the passion for the purebred dog was growing. Between 1840 and 1860, even the bronze patches disappeared, and black became the dominant color. We must be grateful for the passion and the art of the great animalist painter Edwin Landseer that the white and black type, which was named after him, was saved. Preferring the effect that those colors created in his paintings, he generally depicted patched subjects, though some were actually entirely black, and thus generated among the public a fashion and taste for the white and black coat.

Definition of the Breed in England and its Diffusion

In the second half of the 1800s, a certain number of dog lovers in England became interested in the breed. These were usually wealthy people who dedicated time and money to breeding programs, aided by a staff of helpers who cared for the dogs.

Among the most important was Henry Farquharson. His first Newfoundland had reached Poole from the namesake island in 1830. Following this, he imported other dogs and many of his subjects became successful. One of the last was Scamp, father of Joe Saddler, who in the coupling with Lady in Waiting generated Ch. Alderman, one of the first Newfoundlands registered in the Netherlands.

The imports from the island of Newfoundland were common at that time. In 1860, at the Birmingham Exposition, the winner of the six dogs shown was a female imported from St. John. Mr. Milvan, an important breeder, also resorted to importing dogs. His dog Leo, the first registered in 1875, came from Newfoundland. He was black with rust shadings, 30 inches tall and weighed about 127 pounds. Also imported were Derby and Old Gipsy, the parents of Heenan , the first dog produced by this breeder, and father of an exceptional number of descendants. His son Cato, owned by Rev. Atkinson, was black with a white blaze, and was described as an exceptional subject, and became famous for having saved both a drowning woman and his owner who had gone to her rescue.

One of the better known personalities of the time was Gordon Stables, an author of children's books and an enthusiastic Newfoundland breeder. He wrote many articles about the breed and imported, among others, Ch. Theodore Nero, a subject described as a typical Newfoundland of St. John.

Another important breeder was Mr. Nichol, owner of Ch. Nelson I. From this subject, he generated many other important dogs such as Lady Mayoress, Lady in Waiting, Ch. Courtier and Ch. Black Prince (Nelson + Jennie, 1883). Black Prince was one of the most famous dogs of the breed. As the caption to a drawing that depicted this dog of modern type, there was written: "His large head, small ears, sweet expression, and his well proportioned and powerful body are reproduced in this live portrait by R. H. Moore. Though he is quite heavy set, he is very agile, and moves with great freedom."

Black Prince, along with Lady Mayoress, Ch. Gunville and Ch. Courtier, was bought by Mr. Mansfield who had become an important breeder by 1878. He always had thirty to forty dogs of famous pedigrees, and he later became a judge of some importance. He opposed the race that was taking place in order to achieve taller dogs. He believed that this would make the breed more delicate, taking away its massive substance and proportion. With Mansfield, Black Prince furthered his brilliant career as a stud dog and influenced European bloodlines through some of his offspring including Lady Ramp, imported by Hartstein to Germany, and Black Princess, exported to the Netherlands.

Thanks to the enthusiasm of lovers of this breed, the number of purebred dogs raised with a proper selection criteria grew. In 1862, the registered subjects at the Agricultural Hall reached forty-one. It was during this time that the shape of modern canine science was being born. People wanted more than dogs bred haphazardly, evaluated solely for their exterior appearance. They wanted to be certain of their genealogy and utilize more precise evaluation criteria. If the breed had suffered in the past from cross breeding, it was necessary to rid it of the unwanted traits, focusing on the concept of functional morphology. The size, color and carriage of the tail were all discussed, and many interesting articles were written.

In 1875, free pedigree registrations began in England. In 1886, the English Newfoundland Club was born giving this breed its first standard. This standard was very similar to the one existing today and finally made the breed official.

This led to a surprising development. In 1892, a record-breaking 128 Newfoundlands registered for the Preston Exhibition, an exceptional number if one thinks of the complexities of transportation existing at that time.

In the following years, many important breeding kennels were born, as Mr. Cooper, breeder, judge and author of interesting articles, involved more people. Mr. and Mrs. Wetman founded the Shelton Kennel where, in 1903, Ch. Shelton Viking would be born, the only Newfoundland to win Best in Breed at Crufts in 1906. Shortly after, Mrs. Goodall established the kennel that would become famous with the prefix "Gipsy." The most famous of her champions was Gipsy Duke, son of Shelton Viking, and father of Zingari Chief. The mixture of these two famous kennels would generate a few years later one of the most famous Newfoundland stud dogs, "Siki."

Meanwhile, the interest in the breed was also growing on the continent. While in the first half of the 1800s, all dogs in Europe with long black, white and black, brown and white, or black with reddish hued and highlighted coating went under the name of Newfoundland; however, with the first imports from England and publication of the standard it was noticed that many of the subjects did not match the description of the Newfoundland.

In 1883 in Germany, Max Hartenstein, with his English dogs Gumo, Tello, Nero and Guida, had established the "Plavia" Kennel in Alsace. He later enthusiastically dedicated himself to this breed, importing dogs for other breeders as well. The results he achieved were evident at the Berlin Exhibition where he brought sixteen Newfoundlands of very high quality. Also among the dogs he imported from England was Lady Ramp, a daughter of Black Prince, born in 1885 in the Mansfield kennels. She was described as a subject with a great temperament, black with a white blaze, 25 inches tall, intelligent, a good swimmer, diver and retriever. This interesting information appears in the German kennel book, *Neufundlander Stammbuch*.

In 1893, Doctor Herting of Augsburg founded the Neufundlander Klub fur den Kontinent with a group of amateurs of different nationalities. In 1868, the club members numbered sixty-nine, and the

Ch. Westerland Sieger of the Honorable Harold MacPherson,
immortalized on an Island's postage stamp.

first publication of the *Neufundlander Stammbuch*, edited by Dr. Waszily, appeared. This important work covers the years between 1898 and 1902, for a total of 144 registered dogs. In addition, it also describes the origins, the prizes, the measurements, and some characteristics of the breed. It contains photographs, over eighty illustrations and a comment about the particular standard that the German club had taken from England.

The Neufundlander Klub fur den Kontinent with its publications became a reference and meeting point for all of those throughout Europe interested in this breed. One of the first members was Dr. Albert Heim (1849-1937), an eminent Swiss researcher. He increased his knowledge about the breed and worked toward achieving good standards of robustness and type for his country.

In 1886, other dogs were imported into Switzerland from the island of St. Pierre: dogs such as Fox, Melanie and Turk. In 1887, Heim bought Pluto in Germany and the following year Thetis of the "Plavia" Kennel. From England he imported Pirate King, son of Ch. Courtier. The Newfoundland spread rapidly; this is clear when looking at the Zurich Exposition where out of 200 registered dogs in 1881, only two Newfoundlands participated, whereas in 1900, the number of those registered rose to fifty-one. Prof. Herting, president of the Neufundlander Klub, who was the judge on that occasion, stated that he was surprised and pleased by the number of dogs present and by their quality. The import of dogs from the island of Newfoundland had been a good idea. The imported specimens were smaller than the English ones and at times the coat was wavy but, when bred with the English dogs, they produced good sized dogs and spread good characteristics and temperament. One of the most important Swiss dogs was Wodan, owned by Prof. Heim, and son of Turk and Sasha II. Wodan fathered more than 200 puppies. In 1900, he won the water trials in Zurich, and Heim wrote that at nine years of age he still chased street cars and jumped from a still position. Very intelligent and able, he could deal with any and all situations.

With the publication of books on the origin and pedigrees of the breed, the passion of Newfoundland breeding began spreading to other countries, which watched with interest the results achieved in other countries such as England, Germany and Switzerland. In the Netherlands, dogs such as Ch. Alderman and Black Princess, a daughter of Black Prince, were imported from England. Later, Mrs. Cate-Roorda imported Moro and Norma from Germany; these two were followed by Ch. Herta v. Warrin. The Scandinavian countries maintained contacts mainly with German breeders; in Sweden, Eric Lundin imported the German Champion Tedesco Harras who, through his son Vild, would influence the bloodlines of the time. Italy also imported from Germany and Switzerland.

In France, on the other hand, the breed was represented by dogs brought back by seamen from trips to the islands of St. Pierre and Miquelon. These abundant and appreciated dogs aided men by pulling milk and fish carts. In the past, the seamen mainly had imported males, so as not to ruin a potential market. Those had been then bred with local breeds, not allowing for the creation of a true breed. In the beginning of the 1900s, the imports ceased and the Newfoundland became nonexistent on the French coasts. This was caused by the fact that even on the island of Newfoundland it was hard to find acceptable specimens. The hostile politics and indiscriminate exportations had diminished the number and ruined the quality of the breed. This was noticed in 1901 by the Hon. Harold MacPherson, after his difficulties in finding proper dogs for the Duke and Duchess of Cornwall and York. Having had a passion for the breed since childhood, he realized that it was becoming extinct in its land of origin. With some local subjects and some other subjects imported from various European countries, including Gannel Echo, an uncle of Siki, Harlingen Peg, and others, MacPherson established the Westerland Kennels in St. John. This kennel would later become famous throughout the world and would produce champions such as Westerland Sieger, immortalized on the postage stamps of the island of Newfoundland, and Am. Ber. Ba. Ca. Ch. Newton, one of the most famous show dogs of its time.

The Twenties and Thirties

World War I was a harsh blow for the breed. Not only was there a drop in the number of dogs born, but the ones alive were also greatly diminished: some were taken for military service, others starved to death. The comeback was slow and difficult, but in various countries, Newfoundland lovers were able to save precious specimens for new growth.

In Switzerland only the kennel "V. Toggenburg," owned by U. Mejer-Bosch, continued without interruption and was able to save those fantastic subjects that in the postwar years became the basis of many new kennels. Through Miggi v. Leutberg, exported to England, the "Bloodline of the Toggenburg" eventually reached Canadian and American pedigrees.

In Germany, the number of dogs that survived was also quite small and the risk of inbreeding was a menace to the survivors. Some breeders tried, as in the past, to import from the islands of St. Pierre and Miquelon or from the northern French coasts, but these efforts were in vain.

It was in this climate of desperation that Ch. Satan arrived in Europe. Satan was born in 1921 in a St. John kennel. The son of the owner had chosen to take him along on one of his trips to Europe. Upon returning home, because of legal complications, it was not possible to bring Satan back to St. John and he was obliged to sell him. After Satan was purchased by a dog expert and judge, Satan repeatedly won at the Antwerp Expositions. The American judge, Thomas wrote: "I have never seen such a perfect dog, and I cannot understand why he was allowed to leave America." Satan was also noticed by the German breeders, and after much negotiation the German club president, Buchner, was able to acquire him for his Mannheim Kennel. Heim judged him in 1923, and wrote with such praise about him that he is kept alive in the history of the breed:

Left: Ch. Sieger Satan, Winterthur, 1927. Right: (from left) Dr. Rickli with Attila v. Wolfbach; Feer with Tom v. Togenburg; Professor Heim with Balu v. Wolfbach.

Ch. Siki, father of Champions.

"Satan ranks above all of the subjects present at this exhibition, as well as all of those seen in the past in Europe. It is a pleasure to the eye to watch this dog in his every pose and movement. As with all of the foreign Newfoundland dogs, he too is a bit smaller than how we would want him; he is 25 inches tall, but we know that by breeding indigenous dogs with some of our own we will be able to get good sized dogs. He is of a magnificent quality in every detail and deserves an excellent rating in everything. The coating is long, luminous, very black, without marks, and very dense. The eye is dark brown. He is all together larger than the other St. Pierre and Miquelon dogs. The tail is voluminous and well carried. The shape of the head is that which we seek, but have difficulty creating with such perfection. The most important thing though is the absence of any defect and the beautifully typical and harmonious figure that denotes both power and elegance. In this subject there is not the slightest disproportion. He is the true ideal Newfoundland that we have only been able to approximate."

Naturally, with his influence and the passion he had for the breed, Heim was able to have this dog acquired by Emile Buckhard, the Swiss owner of the Waldstatte Kennel. In 1925, Heim, Buckhard and twenty other lovers of the breed founded the Schweizer Neufundlander Club in Basil. The exchanges among countries increased at great pace. In Germany, various kennels were founded, among them v. Radegast, Charlottenhof, v. Neiderhein, v. Peck-Bergen and so forth.

In the Netherlands, this breed found an enthusiast in Johan Pieterse, who in 1916 acquired Tom, son of Moro and Norma. In 1917, eleven breeders founded the Nederlandse Newfoundlander Club in Haarlem, of which Pieterse became secretary; he would later vacate this position in 1932 to become president. He continued with the club until his death in 1958, aided by his wife who had become secretary.

The v. Negerhut Kennel, founded by him, produced many important dogs including Ch. Henk v. Negerhut, father of Kentucky Home's Boy and Ch. Tom v. Negerhut. With the collaboration with other Netherlands kennels (v.d. Ouge Plantage, v.d. Onderneming, Kentucky Home's and St. John) interesting bloodlines were born, bloodlines that would later spread to other countries such as Germany, Switzerland, England and Italy.

In the beginning of the twenties, the number of Newfoundlands in England had also greatly diminished. In 1927, registered subjects numbered only twenty-two, but by 1928 the number had risen to seventy-five. Miss Goodal, who had dedicated her life to this breed, died soon after the war, but she left many great bloodlines. In 1922, from a line that repeatedly included Ch. Shelton Viking and his descendants Gipsy Duke, Zingari Chief, Gipsy Viscount and Shelton King, the famous Ch. Siki was produced, owned by George Bland. He was not the only champion produced by this breeder, but he is without any doubt the most famous. The large and heavy set head, with small and expressive eyes, the squared muzzle, the size and the massiveness of Siki made him an excellent subject, but what made him famous was his capacity for reproducing the best of his traits with different females. This is certainly due to the homogeneity of his pedigree. He was called "father of champions" and owning one of Siki's offspring became the ambition of all breed lovers of the time. Among his most famous offspring were Brave Michael, Ganel Echo, Help, Black Bess, Seagrave Blackberry, Seafarer, Harlingen Neptune, Shelton Baron, Shelton Cabin Boy and Monna Vanna.

May Van Oppen, born in Britain and whose father William Van Oppen was one of the founding members of the Newfoundland Club in 1886, took out the prefix "Harlingen" before she married her husband, Col. Charles Roberts in 1931. She bred Newfoundlands from the 1920s to the time of her death in 1977. In 1924, Mrs. Roberts bought Judith v. Negeruth from Johan Pieterse. Judith produced no offspring for the Harlingen Kennels, but once given to the breeder Miss Deane, she produced excellent subjects, first with Captain Courageous, and then with Siki's son Brave Michael. Among the latter were Water Rat and Uncle Tom, also known as Maso, who was imported to Italy by Eduino Colnaghi, and, there, became famous.

These were glorious days for English dogs who, in addition to winning all over the world, were spreading English bloodlines. The importation of English dogs was of great importance in the United States of America because it modified the type of subjects bred in a short time. These modifications included more massive subjects with larger heads and denser, softer coats. These imported dogs were mostly Siki's offspring.

In 1929, the Waseeka Kennel in the United States was the first to import Newfoundlands beginning with Ch. Seafarer, immediately followed by Seagrave Blackberry, Harlingen Neptune of Waseeka and Harlingen Jess of Waseeka. The breed grew quickly in those years; water trials were started and, in 1930, the Newfoundland Club of America, affiliated with the A.K.C., was founded. In Canada Ch. Shelton Baron was imported by Mr. Oliver, who would keep the Shelton Kennel alive, acquiring it from Mr. and Mrs. Wetwan. He also imported Ch. Shelton Cabin Boy, who would later go to the Drumnod Kennel owned by Montague Wallace. The English bloodlines also spread throughout Europe as Harlingen Black Pete was acquired by the Helluland Kennel in Sweden, owned by Betty Berg, whose products would become the foundation for the Danish, Norwegian and Finnish kennels.

This diffusion of dogs was important and would be useful in the difficult years ahead. Once again war would hit the world and with its arrival activities that had flourished during periods of peace, such as dog breeding, would cease.

The Forties and Fifties

During the Second World War, only one litter was born in England; it was that of Brave Michael and his daughter, an offspring of Harlingen Waseeka Ocean Spray, imported just before the war. The litter was produced by Mr. and Mrs. Handley of the Fairwater Kennel who had various Newfoundlands and had vowed to have them survive through the conflict. At night after work, Mr. Hadley rode several miles on his bicycle under a shower of bombs to procure food for his dogs. Of this litter, they kept Brave Serestus, who became the father of four champions and who appears in many postwar pedigrees.

In the Netherlands, the Newfoundland fared better, and various litters were born. In 1943, there was born, among others, Ch. Alex v. Froonacher, father of the famous The Baribals Anca. In 1944, also from the v. Negeruth, v. Oude Plantage, and v. Onderneming lines, Cerberus v. Vriedshap was born who with The Baribals Anca would form the foundation for the kennels v.d. Drie Ajers and Vant' Zeepardje.

At the same time, the imported English dogs spread their bloodlines through the Waseeka, Seaward, Oquaga, Coastwise, Dryad, Midway and Little Bear kennels in America. At the end of the war, these lines returned to Europe and aided in the reconstruction of the breed in many countries.

In 1949, Harlingen Waseeka Black Gold, who was expecting a litter from Waseeka Dauntless, was sent to England by Mrs. Power to the Harlingen Kennel, owned by the Roberts, as gift of the American Newfoundland club. From this litter, three champions were born: Harlingen Coastguard Harlingen Pirate and Harlingen Brigantine. Brigantine with Brave Serestus produced Harlingen Black Cherry, who was then bred with Harlingen Coastguard to produce Patriot of Witchazel. In 1955, the Harlingen Kennel also imported Midian Dryad's Sea Anchor of the Dryad Kennel of M. and K. Drury.

Meanwhile Mona Bennet, owner of Perryhow, a well-known kennel in the 1950s and 1960s, imported from the Netherlands The Baribals Anca of Perryhow, a female that had already bred for the v. Drie Anjers Kennel, and that became famous for being present in pedigrees throughout the world in the postwar period. Anca was first bred with Brave Serestus and then with Midway Gipsy Seaolar of Perryhow, whom Mona Bennet had imported in 1951 from the United States. Gipsy Seaolar was a

Pit v. Margarethe.

Janko von Peck-Bergen.

Ch. Barry v. Grenzberg.

Cdn. Ch. Romy v. d. Schurz.

child of the champions Shelton Mermaid Queen Gipsy and Mill Creek Seafarer of Manitou, both of Canadian origin, and Gipsy Seaolar brought to the Midway Kennel the blood of Siki's offspring Shelton Baron and Shelton Cabin Boy, and from whose lines came also the Am. Can. Ch. Midway Blackledge Sea Raider.

Gipsy Seaolar and Anca generated many champions including Neptune of Perryhow, one of the foundations of the Italian kennels of the 1950s. Anca's line in the Netherlands was also greatly diffused. Sjoerd v. Drie Anjer, born from Anca and Cerberus v. Vriedshap, when bred with Annie v. Oldersheim, would give birth to an important litter for the v.t. Zeepardje Kennel. From this litter, Beatris v.t. Zeepardje was imported to the United States by the Dryad Kennel; her daughter, Ch. Dryad Christine of Glenora, mothered the famous Edenglen Banner, winner of the Lenox Specialty of 1967.

Baldur v. Zeepardje became an international champion, and fathered one of the most important Swiss and German dogs: Barry v. Grenzberg. Brigitte v. Zeepardje produced Ch. Duke v. Zeepardje, a famous brown that is still present in modern lines.

The bloodlines from the Netherlands were successful in Finland as well. In the fifties, the breeding of the Newfoundland became quite important in this country thanks to Gerold Blomberg. He imported two important subjects from the Netherlands: Père Noble v. Nordwige (Rena v. Drie Anjer + Goliath v. Froonacher) and Theresja v. Drie Anjers (Ria v. Drie Anjers + Ivan v. Froonacher) and planned some breeding programs, intensifying contacts with foreign countries. This work made Finland an important source of dogs that were later exported to other countries. Some of the kennels born in the following years were Taran, Trappers, Marun, Merikarhun, Gerogest, Nattanin, Biorntorph, Alderbay and Harmonattan.

Germany and Switzerland, on the other hand, brought forth the lines of the following kennels in the postwar period: v. Charlotteenhof, v. Tannenburg, v. Biebertal and v. Peck-Bergen who came from the foundations of v. Radegast with the insertion of bloodlines from the Netherlands (v. Oude Plantage, St. John and Posseidons). From these foundations, new kennels were established in the 1950s. In Germany, among the most well-known were v. Wilhelmsohe, who produced Int. Ch. Bundessieger; Susi v. Wilhelmsohe, mother of Barry v. Grenzberg; St. Florian, v. Giskadi; v. Nordlingen; and v. Zchimmeroth.

Cito v. Zchimmeroth became an international champion and Bundessieger, in 1958, gave his imprint to generate important bloodlines: with Candra v. Giskadi he produced Ch. Anuk v. St. Florian and Int. Ch. Ara v. St. Florian, mother of Barry v. Grenzberg from Int. Ch. Cherry v. St. Florian; with Eileen v. Giskadi he produced Halef v. Giskadi, Bundessieger and Club Sieger in 1961. From the breeding of the two offspring of Cito v. Zchimmeroth in 1959, Ria v. Nordlingen was born. Ria and Cherry v. St. Florian produced what is said to be one of the most well-known dogs of the next decade: Int. Ch. Felix v. Nordlingen.

In Switzerland, the lines of the v. Peck Bergen, through Int. Ch. Bob v.d. Warte were fused with those coming from v. Waldstatte, owned by Emile Buckhard. Buckhard maintained his kennel throughout the war years, importing from the Netherlands Ottoline v.d. Oude Plantage, and Siegerin in 1942. From this fusion, the kennel produced various champions including Gido v.d. Schurz, Pan v.d. Schurz, Hexe v.d. Schurz and Romy v.d. Schurz, which were exported to Canada.

Another famous dog in those years was Schw. SG59 Barree v. von Grenzberg, whose call name became Sieger (or Champion) in 1959, and who had quite an influence on the Swiss bloodlines. From Dina v. Hussenstein, daughter of Gido v.d. Schurz, he produced Amor v. Grundhof, father of two great stud dogs, Int. Ch. Rik v. Blattenhof and Int. Ch. Simbo v. Schwarzen Mutz. One of Amor's daughters, Int. Ch. Zara de Novai, was imported into Sweden by the Klovagardens Kennel.

The Last Thirty Years
The 1960s saw a great expansion of the breed that became even more evident in the 1970s and 1980s.

Ch. Stormsail Matterhorn and Ch. Stormsail Wetterhorn, owned by Oriani.

Stormsail Sacred Spirit, owned by Oriani.

Ch. Wellfont Admiral, owned by Birch.

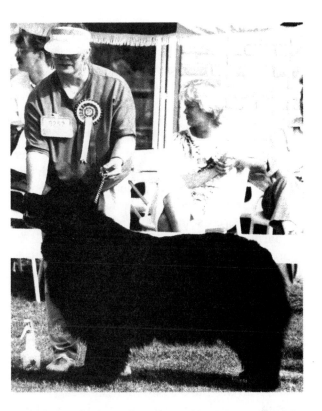

Ch. Stormsail Black Walnut, owned by Oriani. (Photo by Dave Freeman)

Ch. Kelligrews Terre Neuve with Seaquaybear, owned by Schothern. (Photo by Ernest T. Gascoigne)

The growing number of lovers of the breed led to an increase both in the number of kennels and to the number of international exchanges made to renew the bloodlines. Many Newfoundland clubs were also founded in countries where they had not previously existed.

England

England, despite the obstacle of quarantine, imported various subjects from the United States, Finland, Holland and later Denmark. From Germany the imports consisted mostly of Landseers. These lines united with the ones already present: Perryhow, Sparry, Fairwater, Little Creek, Verduron, Bonnybay, Storytime and Esmeduna, supplying new material for the developing kennels.

From Finland, the Harlingen Kennel imported a white and black female, Taaran Taru. Mr. Morgan imported Harmonattan Hokay and Marun Kiva, from whom Ch. Lord Hercules of Fairwater was born. He sired some of Esther Denham's Attimore Kennel champions including Ch. Attimore Aquarius. Also in the 1960s, Mr. and Mrs. Warren of the Littlegrange Kennel imported Avalon's Ikaros of Littlegrange (Nattanin Ralli + Avalon's Castalia) from Holland who had a number of very high quality descendants including six champions. From Ch. Attimore Aquarius, Ikaros produced Ch. Attimore Royal Sovereign. He was used as stud dog by the Stormsail Kennel, founded in 1972, and owned by Mr. and Mrs. Oriani. From Ch. Bachalaos Bright Water of Stormsail, he produced five champions in only one litter, among which were Stormsail Matterhorn and Wetterhorn. Even the Sigroc Kennel, owned by Miss Davies, secretary of the British club for many years, used Finnish bloodlines. In 1966, she imported Merikarhun Fay of Sigroc, who was later bred with Ch. Sigroc King Neptune, son of Harmonattan Hokay and Marun Kiva. A product of this line was Ch. Sigroc Sail by the Stars, who was the top Newfoundland in 1979 and who was one of the top prize winning dogs in Great Britain. From the United States the imported dogs were: Dory O's Harbour Grace, who produced Ch. Gentle Giant for the Wanitoba Kennel, Seawards Sea Billow from the Suleskerry Kennel, and other subjects for the Little Bear and Nashau-Auke kennels for Mr. Cassidy's Little Creek Kennel.

Mr. Frost, owner of Harratons Kennel, who was very interested in the white and black variety, imported American dogs from the Morycis and Seaward Kennels; in addition he purchased some Continental Landseers from the following kennels: v. Heidenberg, v. Weilerhoe, v. Petersberg and v. Bellandseer. The Shermead Kennel, owned by Mr. and Mrs. Adey, imported Lancelot of Shermead from Finland and Shermead Bijou of The Thatch Roof from Holland.

At the end of the 1970s, the attention of some new breeders was turned to Denmark. The Wellfont Kennel of Mr. and Mrs. Birch first imported La Bellas Ibrahim of Wellfont bred by Moller-Hansen and later Ch. Ursula's Figaro of Wellfont and Ch. Ursula's Brigitte of Wellfont bred by Gothen Christensen. La Bellas Ibrahim of Wellfont, bred with Mapleopal's Who Loves Ya Baby, once owned by the Ludlows who had bred an Esmeduna line with success. (The Ludlows own the Mapleopal prefix; this line was based on the Esmeduna line.) This litter produced four champions: Ambassador, who became Australian and New Zealand champion, Amanda, Angie and Admiral, who won a great number of prizes beating the record held since 1910 by Gipsy Duke. Wellfont Admiral was also used by the Karazan Kennels of Mr. And Mrs. Colgan to generate many winners with Ch. Shermead Fragrant Cloud including Ch. Karazan Goldigger and Ch. Karazan Golddust. Mr. And Mrs. Birch imported Ch. Ursula's White Sails from Denmark, and Mr. and Mrs. Colgan also imported a brown female, La Bellas Abba, which would then produce two other brown champions: Karazan Hot Chocolate and Karazan Sweet Charity.

In the last decade, some dogs were imported from the German kennel v. Soven, owned by Karl Schmitz: Ch. Quay and Quanda v. Soven, offspring of Ch. Ferro v. Soven of Swanpool and Ch. Samson v. Soven of Swanpool, offspring of Black Bear Caesar, who won numerous prizes and fathered Ch. Stormsail Black Walnut. Another import that gave great results was La Bellas Winston, owned by the Baggaleys, who reproduced for several kennels including Nut Brook and Wellfont. Also in these

Ch. Pouch Cove's Favorite Son.

same years, some American subjects were imported from the kennels of Brunhaus, Lifebuoy, Grers, and in particular, Ch. Kelligrews Terre Neuve for the Seaquaybear Kennel owned by the Scotherns.

The United States

In the 1960s and 1970s, the breed grew quite rapidly in the United States as well; many new kennels were established and those already in existence grew. Particularly of note are the Dryad and Little Bear Kennels. The Dryad Kennels of Kitty and Maynard Drury had brought forth the Waseeka lines, including Oquaga, Coastwise and Topsail, producing many champions. Among these were two stud dogs that would be present in many future pedigrees: Dryad's Sea Rover and Dryad's Goliath of Gath. In the beginning of the 1960s, Ch. Dryad's Sea Rover was bred with Ch. Dryad's Christine of Glenora, carrying the Netherlands line of Beatris v. Zeepardje and generating for the Edenglen Kennels the previously mentioned Edenglen Banner.

The Little Bear Kennel, owned by Margaret and Vadim Chern had as a "founder" Am. Can. Ch. Midway Black Ledge Sea Raider, father of Am. Can. Ch. Little Bear James Thurber. This kennel produced many successful dogs: Thunder, Canicula Campio, John Paul Jones, Bonnavista, Black Sambo and Royal Top Gallant. In the 1950s, the Little Bear Kennel imported English blood from Perryhow; later, the Newton line was also brought in through Ch. Dryad's Christine of Glenora. Newton was a famous Newfoundland of the 1960s, achieving great success in shows. He was raised by the Hon. Harold MacPherson from 1958, and was son of Topsail's Captain Bob Bartlett and of Merry of Sparry.

Owned by Melvin Sokolsky, and handled by Alan Levine, Newton won many times, becoming an American champion, as well as a champion in Canada, Bermuda and the Bahamas. These results contributed to augmenting the interest in the breed, and the number of kennels grew. The list of breeders published in 1971 by the Newfoundland Club of America (NCA) included fifty-three breeders; in 1986 this number rose to about ninety, and by 1990 the number was 115.

Most pedigrees included subjects from Dryad and Little Bear and their descendants. The Dryad Kennel had quite an influence on the Shipshape, Edenglen, Indigo, Harobed, Kilyka, Halirock and Pooh Bear kennels. Little Bear was instead important to the Irwindyl, Black Mischief, Nashau-Auke, Kwasind and Shipchandler kennels. Both of these lines were then fused together. Other kennels included Tranquillus, Ebonewf, Britannia, Peppertree, Hilvig and Barbara Allen. The Seaward Kennel imported a certain number of white and black subjects from Europe, including Eaglebay Domino and Domino of Sparry who, when bred with Dryad's Blanca Sultana, produced a group of greatly homogeneous champions, several time winners of the "Team Class." Other imports worth mentioning are: from Finland, Marun Kille for Mischief Kennel; from Holland, Avalon's Galatheia for Edenglen; from Denmark, Birkegarden Brave Boatswain for Barbara-Allen. The Dryad Kennel also used the Swiss line of Romy v.d. Schurz, imported to Canada by Harbour beem Kennel. His daughter, Dryad's Christmas Cheer, won Best of Opposite Sex at Lennox in 1967.

In the beginning of the 1970s, other new kennels were begun: Newton-Ark of J. and A. Levine, Brunhaus in Alaska, Pouch-Cove of D. and M. Helming, Tuckamore of G. and B. Finch, Shadybrook of R. and J. Krokum, and others that would go on to produce winning lines in the 1980s.

Canada

New lines were brought from the established Canadian kennels of Laurel Brae, Shelton, Perivale, Millcreek, Drumnod, Topsail and Black Ledge. In 1963, Mrs. Navin, owner of the Shipmate's Kennel, founded, along with forty other lovers of the breed, the Canadian Newfoundland Club. The first president, Douglas Irvin, contributed to the diffusion of the white and black variety by importing from Switzerland, in 1966, the Landseer Fjord v. Arx. In the following years, many new kennels were born,

*Ch. Caniz Major Skipper,
owned by Kumler.*

Ch. La Bellas Dolittle, owned by
Møller Hansen.

Ch. Bellas Winston, owned by
Baggaleys.

Ch. Ursula's Captain Cook,
owned by Gothen Christensen.

including Topmast of M. Willmott in Saskatchewan, Kimtale of Mackensie in Ontario, Littlecreek in Ontario, Dulrick and Bearbrook in Quebec, in addition to Spokinewf, Greer, Marcarpents, Nordstrand and others

On the island of Newfoundland, two kennels kept the Westerland lines alive: Glenmire of Mrs. Baird and Harbour beem of Mr. and Mrs. Nutbeem.

Scandinavia

Like other countries in the early 1960s, Scandinavian countries sought dogs from Finland for their kennels. In Sweden, the old Dutch lines had been crossed with Finnish lines. The Auricco Kennel of Sandra Larson had produced Auricco Black Archibald, a stud dog, father of Chicka, the foundation dog of the Klam Kennel. The Bambella Kennel of Karin Fern had imported from Finland Marinelle de Ros Lodge and Ch. Alderbay Bamse. Ulla Anderson of the Klam Kennels introduced other notable stock: Nattanin Rita and Nattanin Jyry, Biorntorp Una, Biorntorp Ulrica and Int. Ch. Finbear Ikaros (Avalon's Daphne + Ch. Punnillah Turja) who, with different bitches, produced fifteen champions. Later imports included the Netherland's Avalon's Illione, the German Dick. v. Hedelweissgrotte, and later Dulricks Canadian Ambassadeur from Canada. This intense activity led to the foundation in 1967 of the Svenska Newfoundlandhund Klubben of which Ulla Anderson became president. In the following years new kennels were begun: the Klovagarden Kennel of the Johansons, which imported Zara de Novai from Switzerland; Biorntorp Taifun from Finland; Caniz Major Newton from Denmark; the Kariland Kennel of the Thoranders; the Gas-Cohns Kennel, which imported Ursula Mac Mortensen; Ominmac, which imported La Bellas Goliath; and among the most recent, the West Side Kennel, which dedicates itself primarily to the white and black variety.

In those same years, the breed expanded greatly in Denmark. The Swedish lines, kept alive by the Biornegard and Store Bjorn kennels, were invigorated by the introducing lines that allowed strengthening of characteristics. In 1967, the Newfoundland Klubben in Denmark was founded with Fleming Uziel, owner of the Caniz Major Kennel, as president. He introduced quite a number of subjects particularly Storytime Cachalot from England, father of many champions among which was Ch. Nero and Ch. Sparry's Treasure of Littlegrange was bred with Ch. Black Alexandrov of Swedish-Finnish origin. Uziel produced a great number of excellent subjects including Caniz Major Skipper, son of Little Bear Royal Top Gallant who was imported from the United States. Caniz Major Skipper became quite a famous dog; he was an International Champion and produced many notable descendants of which Ch. Tedesco Ferro v. Int. Dk. Ch. Vdhch. Klub Sg. Ferro Von Soven, whose name appears on many of today's pedigrees, must be remembered.

In 1973, Ch. Little Bear Two If By Sea, father of Int. Ch. Biergegards Wilma, was imported from the United States. Another kennel, Birkegardens, imported Klovagarden Ea from Sweden, who possessed a Swiss line, and Swe Danes Black Cukardo. The two generated excellent offspring among which were Birkegardens Tina and Birkegardens Don Camillo who became an Int. Ch. and was internationally used as stud.

The Ursulas Kennel, owned by Brigitte Gothen Christensen, merged the German line of Cita v. Gramshatzerwald and the American line of Edenglen's Koks producing, among others, Ursulas Castor, who went to the German kennel v. Schwabenland where he fathered many litters. In 1971, Christensen imported Int. Ch. Cora v. Ostseestrand from West Germany who had an excellent career as a show dog. In the 1970s, the Ursulas Kennels imported Halirock Rambling Rose from the United States and some white and black subjects from England: Harraton's Sea Cloud, Roydsrook Sea Shanty and Roydsrook Star Maiden. Ch. Star Maiden was successfully bred with Ch. Topmast's Hannibal who had been imported from Canada by Danish breeders. Among the most important offspring were Ch. Ursula's Alexandra and Ch. Ursula's Captain Cook. Topmast's Hannibal was bred with numerous other bitches and was father of Black Dome's Sir Coxwain, Ch. Ursula's Admiral Ascot and Ch. Ursula's Goldigger.

Ch. Mond. Dag, owned by V. Doremalen.

Ch. Dennis v. Orfeu Negro, owned by V. Doremalen.

Ch. Aaron v. Hoogven, owned by Mulderij.

Ch. Basco v. Zonegge, owned by V. Dijks.

The La Bella Kennel, owned by Palle Moller Hansen, instead used lines from Germany and Holland. From Germany, he imported Jan v. St. Florian and Leonie v. Niederburg; from Holland, Black Beauty v. Papenhof, carrier of the Duke v. Zeepardje bloodline. From these subjects he raised a great number of specimens, with particular interest in the browns. He also exported to many countries: La Bella's Goliath went to Sweden, La Bella's Funny Girl to Holland, La Bella's Ibrahim, La Bella's Abba and La Bella's Winston to England, La Bella's Gazelle and La Bella's Favorite to Switzerland. Another subject that must also be mentioned is Int. Ch. La Bella's Faust.

In the last few years, many new kennels were begun in Denmark: Borghois, Black Bear, Fjordblinks, Topsail, Mira Nobilis, Bjornebandens and others; these and existing kennels have increased the number of attendees at the breed meetings to 200.

Holland

Holland was among the countries that exchanged the most bloodlines, uniting their own bloodlines of the past with modern English, German, Swiss, Danish and Finnish ones. In the 1960s the v. Papenhof Kennel had quite a success, and these dogs were subsequently used by other kennels. From the line of Duke v. Zeepardje and Avalon's Aphrodite the following specimens were born: Achilles v. Papenhof, winner for four continuous years of the Amsterdam Special, Anka and Astrid, winners as well, and Int. Ch. Brigitte v. Papenhof. Astrid v. Papenhof, bred with the German Ch. Cherry v. St. Florian, was mother of Ch. Chico v. Papenhof which, when bred with Ch. Brigitte, produced Ch. Isodorus Christian v. Hertogsven. Bouncer v. Papenhof and Cerafine v. Papenhof went to the Marskwa Kennel where they produced Marskwa Amand. Black Beauty v. Papenhof was sent to the Danish kennel La Bella.

Ch. Karel v. Niederburg, owned by Jeannot.

Left: Ch. Felix v. Nordlingen, owned by Ziegler. Right: Ch. Ferro v. Sovën, owned by K. Smitz, with his little masters.

Emilia Biemond's v. Porte Amarre Kennel used Douglas v. Papenhof with Trappers Black Suomi, imported from Finland, generating Shalom v. Porte Amarre which, with the Swiss Karlel v. Niederburg, produced Joungster v. Porte Amarre, father of the world champion, Dag. The Thatch Roof Kennel, with Anton v. Doremalens, initially put together Dutch lines from Papenhof and Blauwof with the British line of Shermead Lively Lad, and to these, the German, Danish and Finnish ones. He also imported the line of Caniz Major Skipper through Ch. Dag, son of Youngster v. Porte Amarre and Josephine, sister of Maximo and Ultima, Danish winners.

The v.h. Hoogveen Kennel, begun in the 1970s and owned by S. Mulderij, imported quite a bit of the Papenhof lines through Marskwa Amand, sire of Int. Ch. Fleur v.h. Hoogveen, and Ch. Isodorus Christian v. Hertogsveen which, bred with Fleur, produced Ch. Aaron v.h. Hoogveen and Ch. Rimmo and Royo v.h. Hoogveen. From the inbreeding of Fleur and Aaron were born Ch. Lin and Ch. Lars and Loko v.h. Hoogveen.

The Avalon Kennel of the Van Zijls merged the lineage from Holland with some from the United States and Finland. From Finland they acquired Avalon's Daphne, mother of Finbear Ikaros, and in 1963 they imported Nattanin Ralli, father of numerous litters, and Biorntorp Zenita. From the United States, they imported Edenglens Galateia, coming from the Newton and Beatris v. Zeepardje lines, and Dryad's Avalon. Later, they also used the German lines of the v. Brungerst kennels.

In the 1970s, Holland also introduced the Swiss line of Ch. Marco v. Neufundlanderheim, which was joined to that of Fleur v. Papenhof. From this bloodline, united with that of Aaron v.h. Hoogveen, Ch. Basco v. Zonegge was produced, owned by the Dijks-v. Wolven, owners of the v. Zonegge Kennels.

The latest imports include the white and black Ursula's Ocean Pirate and Brunhaus Liberty Belle of G.M. Broekkamp-Brouwer and the black Fjordblink's Hakon. In the last decade the number of kennels has risen considerably as well; among the newcomers are v. Amelterbos, v. Tafelronde, Of The Dark Blossom, Dukeroy's, El Corsario, Zilimondus and others.

At the Nederlandse Newfoundlander Club's meeting in 1991, registrations reached 348.

Switzerland and Germany

In the 1960s and 1970s, Switzerland and Germany operated mainly with older bloodlines. In Germany one of the most well-known kennels was V. Niederburg owned by Erika Toppius of Costanza,

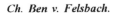

Ch. Ben v. Felsbach.

Blacky v. Murgwai, owned by Sieder.

Aura, Arina and Amor v. Murgwai, owned by G. Kollbrunner.

Bolette, Lord Byron's Argus, Ursula and Aldemarin, owned by C. Buttner.

who used stud dogs such as Halef v. Giskadi, Felix v. Nordlingen and Rik v. Blattenhof, obtaining homogeneous and very typical subjects who would influence various countries including Switzerland, Italy and France, in particular. Among the most well-known subjects of this kennel are Ch. Marke, Karel, Fafner, Ingrabam, Illo, Elodie, Ombra and Galathee v. Niederburg.

The St. Florian Kennel in Monaco continued the lines of Ch. Cherry and Larry v. St. Florian and of Int. Ch. Olly v. St. Florian, crossing them with the Meggenhorn and v. Gollorina Kennel of Switzerland to produce quite a number of great browns. The v. Nordlingen Kennel produced from Ch. Cherry v. St. Florian some excellent subjects, the most famous of which was Int. Ch. Felix v. Nordlingen owned by the Zeiglers. Felix v. Nordlingen had a great career as a stud dog and appears in many pedigrees. The v. Brungerst Kennel of Heinrich Ippen used the lines of Halef v. Giskadi, Bauschan v. Fichteberg and Mara v. St. Fridolin, parents of Quax and Quintos v. Brungerst, and of Meggenhorn, Uckermark and Schwabenland. The v.d. Uckermark Kennel of Herbert Kretschmer melted the St. Florian, Hurbestrand and Schwabenland lines to produce, among others, Int. Ch. Froni v. Uckermark and Siegerin Laila v.d. Uckermark. The Schwabenland Kennel produced various litters in the 1970s, mostly daughters of Ursula's Castor, imported from Denmark.

In the 1970s, new kennels were founded, among them: v. Soven, owned by K. Smitz, which would later produce Ferro v. Soven, father of interesting pedigrees such as that of Int. Ch. Erik v.

Ch. Vercors de La Pierre Aux Coqs, owned by Engrand.

Ch. Sirius des Coteaux Rouges.

Luxembourg; v. Broibachtal, which repeatedly used Cicero v. Galloway as stud dog; and v. Hurbestrand who produced the Int. Ch. Prince v. Hurbestrand. In the following years, the number of the breeders grew yet larger; among these were the kennels v. Sonnenberg of Mrachatz, v. Wassernach of M and P. Krotsch that produced a great number of litters using Int. Ch. Graf v. Luxembourg and v. Reisrand of Evi Grosshauser that produced using Ch. Black Domes Sir Coxwain and Gammel-Dansk v. Reisrand.

In Switzerland, the line that surely influenced the breeding most was that of the sons of Amor v. Grundhof, Rik v. Blattenhof and Simbo v. Schwarzen Mutz, both international champions. Simbo v. Schwarzen Mutz was used as a stud by many breeders, both Swiss and foreign. Rik v. Blattenhof was the sire of many excellent subjects that appear in various pedigrees: Ben v. Felsbach, Asso de la

Ch. Graf v. Luxemburg, owned by Krotsch.

Ch. Mond. Erasmus Graf v. Luxemburg, owned by Kilber.

30

Chassotte, Cicero v. Galloway and Karel v. Niederburg. These lines left their imprint on the following kennels: v. Newfoundlanderheim, v. Felsbach, v. St. Silvester, v. Salzweid, de Soremont and others. Karel v. Niederburg was also the foundation for the Lord Byron Kennel, owned by C. Buttner, through the son, Lord Byron Argus. The v. Murgwai Kennel of Mr. and Mrs. Kollbrunner blended the v. Schwarzen Mutz and the Rik v. Blattenhof lines, producing excellent subjects such as Ch. Aura v. Murgwai and Black v. Murgwai. From Aura and Karel v. Niederburg they produced Ch. Felissa v. Murgwai. Later they also introduced the Koko v. St. Fridolin line.

The v. St. Fridolin Kennel used both the Rik v. Blattenhof and the Danish La Bella's Favorite, father of Koko, lines. Koko v. St. Fridolin was bred for the v. St. Johanniswald Kennel, which is owned by V. Sterki who exported a number of subjects to Italy and France.

The v. Fuchsalden Kennel of Mr. and Mrs. Christen put together the St. Johanniswald, the German v. Brungerst, Meggenhorn and v. Luxembourg lines, also obtaining some browns.

Swiss breeding was quite influential in the diffusion of the Newfoundland in France.

France and Luxembourg

In France, the number of those interested in the breed grew rapidly in the 1960s. In 1963, the Club Français du Chien Terre-Neuve was founded. Among the kennels who used the Swiss bloodlines were Tiad Douar Nevez, De Men Ar Groas, De Terres Vieilles and De la Mare Bleu, who also imported from England. Another Swiss subject imported into France who had quite a bit of success was Asso v. Schnetzenschachen, owned by J. C. Brun, who went on to become an international and world champion.

In the 1970s, the De la Pierre aux Coqs kennel of the Engrands melted the old French lines, the Danish and Swedish ones of Ursula's Illione and Klovagarden's Rudolph, the German ones of Quax v. Brungerst, and the English ones of the Bachalaos Kennel. Among the stud dogs used were Ch. Enrik v. Luxembourg and Ch. Gammel-Dansk v. Riesrand. Among the most important dogs produced by the kennel were Ch. Jolie Belle de la Pierre aux Coqs, Ch. Roz Belle de la Pierre aux Coqs and Ch. Vercors de la Pierre aux Coqs.

In the south of France along the Riviera coast, the Coteaux Rouges Kennel of I. and M. Verrier produced, from Swiss and German lines of the Terres Vieilles, a great number of notable subjects including Ch. Sirius des Coteaux Rouges. In the last years, they imported Inuk v. Luxembourg, which was repeatedly used for stud.

Other kennels included La Caverne aux Fees of M. Tetart, du Pré de La Croix Verte of Durand-Picandet and the du Lac aux Genets.

In Luxembourg, the v. Luxembourg Kennel, founded in the 1970s by Christiane and Claus Brocker, produced quite a number of excellent subjects in a very few years. These subjects included Ch. Enrik v. Luxembourg, owned by the Rinders, and Ch. Mond Graf. v. Luxembourg; both were used as stud dogs in various countries. Some other well-known dogs are Gina, Gibson, Graf and Heroine v. Luxembourg.

It would be impossible to trace a history of all breeders and of all countries. It is exciting to know that the Newfoundland breed continues to spread throughout South Africa, Australia and New Zealand. New contacts may even spread the breed to eastern countries that have only recently opened their borders. However, that story is for the years to come.

The Newfoundland in Italy

The written history of the Newfoundland in Italy begins with the "Libri Origine," the pedigree books written in 1898 by the Italian Kennel Club, but the actual presence of the breed goes a great deal further into the past. In dictionaries and encyclopedias of the time, under the word "dog," one finds descriptions primarily of this particular breed. From the 1891 illustrated encyclopedia we read:

An historical photo in Florence, Italy, 1931. From left to right: Mr. Cesare Petri with Senor del Serchio, Mrs. Cipolla with Vera del Serchio, Mr. Eduino Colnaghi with Ch. Monna Vanna and Ilaria del Serchio, and Mr. Guidi with Uncle Tom.

"The Newfoundland dogs (Canis Terrae Novae) are the giants of the dog world. This large and magnificent animal is probably a cross breed of the large Poodle and of the French Butcher dog, which has maintained its purity on the island of Newfoundland. It is not certain when nor how this breed was born on the Newfoundland island. It is certain though that when the English first landed in Newfoundland in 1662, this dog was not yet existent, and it is supposed that the ancestors of these dogs were brought in later by the colonists. The Newfoundland carries, as do all cross breeds, all of the characteristics of his origin: the shape, the size, and the strength of the French butcher dog, who is a cross between a Greyhound and a hunting dog. In him one finds the coat and shape of ears which are characteristic of a large, silky-coated dog. The Newfoundland is a powerful dog, strong and robust, with a long and wide head, thick muzzle, medium length ears, adorned by sturdy hairs, a strong chest, powerful neck, with long and robust legs. The coating is thick, long, ruffled, soft, almost silk-like; the tail is quite long and curled, and between the toes there is a well developed membrane. His color is quite variable. Most are black, with vivid rusty-yellow patches on the eyes, at the throat, and at the foot joints. The black and white color is less frequent, as is the spotted brown and white or uniformly black-brown and white."

An entire page is dedicated to his personality, and the picture is completed by a large drawing portraying this dog with a lantern in its mouth.

A love for the breed runs in the family—the author's mother in 1918.

In the Melzi Italian dictionary, the breed appears alongside other guard dogs of various types. Near a St. Bernard and a Great Dane, there are a Mastiff and a sheep dog, not well identified. In the center, there are two dogs that appear to be somewhere between a bulldog and a boxer; these are called Mastiff and Great Dane. The Newfoundland, though, is depicted in a more precise manner and is described as follows: "Large Mastiff, native of Newfoundland Island, with a long and curly coat. He dives into the water to save people."

It is not difficult to imagine that in a country where there is a tradition of sailors, and in a period where sailing was quite common, some captains brought these famous island dogs along as mascots for the crews on long voyages, clearly aware of their utility in case of need. Certainly some of these dogs remained in families, and probably some also reproduced, but of these there is no trace. This is quite understandable, considering that at the beginning of the 1900s most Newfoundlands were not registered. The concept of the pedigree had yet to be born, and these dogs are now remembered only through depictions of the time.

The first registrations appear fragmentary and imprecise, and regard mainly German and Swiss subjects exhibited at dog shows. Among these one cannot help but notice a group of dogs of the Von Mollis kennel, presented in Milan in 1901, and the name of a certain "Ras," born in January of 1903 and raised by an unknown fisherman of the town of St. John on the island of Newfoundland.

The first kennel in Italy was founded in the 1920s by a lover of the breed, Eduino Colnaghi. He had gotten to know this breed in 1889 in Austria when, at the age of 14 and staying with friends, he was saved from the attack of a vicious Great Dane by a Newfoundland named Robur. He fell so deeply in love with the breed that as soon as he became adult and able to, he bought a dog of the breed and named him after the unforgettable Robur.

Robur v. Radegast was the father of the famous Canile del Serchio Kennel, which from 1920 to 1936 produced a number of excellent subjects, among which were Argo, Broba, Tom Mix, Siro, Ilaria, Maryelsa, Oretta—and Cape Race, depicted in a famous drawing by his owner, the painter Amos Nattini.

Ch. Christian and Ch. Ethel of the Angeli Neri Kennel.

In 1925, Colnaghi imported from England Monna Vanna, daughter of the famous Ch. Siki and of Southlands Pride.

Mr. Colnaghi's love of the breed, the intensity of his activity and his disposition toward other breeders soon bore fruit. At the Milan exposition in 1930, a great number of excellent subjects were present.

Meanwhile, in 1929 the SIT (Societá Italiana Terranova—Italian Newfoundland Society) was founded; Colnaghi became its president, and was later nominated by the ENCI (National Italian Kennel Club) as a specialized judge of the breed. Guided by Colnaghi, a very capable man with contacts in foreign countries, many interesting imports for the new kennels occurred.

In 1928, the Apuania Kennel of Umberto Catania in Viareggio imported Dewet v. Waldestatte, raised by E. Buckhard and son of Attila v. Wolfbach of Heim. Other dogs were also imported from

Germany: Ajax v. Eichwald and Nelly v. Biebertal for the Eliseo Kennel of Lionello Canali of Genova, and Barry v. Walterstein for the Berengo Garden Kennel in St. Margherita Ligure. Two important subjects, Uncle Tom and Duskje Dinah, offspring of Brave Michael and Judith v. Negeruth, were imported from England in 1930 from Daventry Boatman of the Harlingen Line for the Aliprandi Kennel in Milan. Uncle Tom, also known as Maso, became a champion, and went to the Agogna Kennel of Agnese and Silvio Cipolla who also imported Nori v. Walterstein and Anita v. Frachstein.

In 1931, the number of registered puppies had grown to thirty-seven, quite a number for those times. In 1934, there were forty-five, but the winds of war were beginning to be felt.

The SIT (Italian Newfoundland Society) newsletters, which today represents an important source of information, were forced to cease publication. Newsletter 6, year III of May 15, 1932, explained the reasons for this: The SIA (Societa' Italiana Alani—Italian Bulldog Society) was disbanding, and the SIT would follow them to await better times. These were the depression years felt throughout the world.

However, the number of registered puppies in 1935 and 1936 remained quite high. In 1934, Colnaghi was able to import Westerland Ramsay of the Newfoundland kennel of Harold MacPherson. From Ramsay and Brixia del Serchio, he produced on October 5, 1936, the last litter of this kennel, composed of only two females, Masa and Carmen.

A group from the La Venaria Reale Kennel.

Favola of the Venari Reale Kennels.

Athos of the Moicani Kennel, owned by P. Marenghi.

Geminorum Kennel: Ch. Aldebaran, Ch. Carina delle Acque Celesti, Ch. Alhena Geminorum and Ch. Alrai Cephei.

In the following years, the number of registered puppies diminished rapidly. In 1937, the Agogna Kennel exported Lidia dell' Agogna to Holland and imported Otto v.d. Oude Plantage.

In 1941, the last prewar litter was born from Otto v. Oude Plantage and Nivea; after this, registrations ceased completely. The next litter would not see light until 1950, from Aldo v. Friedbuhl and Flora v.d. Schurz of Armando Piaggio in Genoa.

Of the kennels of prewar years, only the Agogna Kennel continued activity in the postwar years. It was thus necessary to import new subjects. In 1950, an 11 month-old female arrived from Switzerland, Nyusa de la Pommeraie, along with Banco de la Maison Neuve. In 1951, their first litter was born: Nilo, Niso, Nike, Ninfa and Nivea. In 1951, there was another excellent import: Neptune of Perryhow, son of Sea Gipsy Seaolar of Perryhow and the famous The Baribals Anca, which became champion and produced from Nivea and Nyusa quite a number of litters.

Between 1950 and 1960, sixty-two puppies were registered, mostly from the Agogna Kennel, or off-spring of dogs from this kennel. In 1956, Serio of Agogna was born from Neptune of Perryhow and Nivea of Agogna. He went to Ing. Olper of Milan who imported Bounty of Sparry from England in 1959.

In the 1960s other imports occurred. The Agogna Kennel acquired Roderick of Sparry from England, Tania and Annette v. Schwabenland from Germany, Avalon's Itulos, which later became a champion, and Avalon's Olympia from Holland. From the island of Newfoundland, Claire Weener imported Harbour beem Killick (Romy v.d. Schurz + Glenmire Tam of Harbour beem) and Glenmire

World Champion Mond. Topmast's Blackberry Blossom, owned by Cayuga Kennel. (Photo by Søren Wesseltoft)

B'osum (Newton + Westerland Lady of Glenmire), from which It. Ch. Fogo was later born. Other subjects from the Swiss, French and English lines followed. In 1968, Avalon's Itulos and Tania v. Schwabenland would generate Ch. Gaio dell'Agogna, owned by Cesare Gallia.

In 1966, from Serio dell'Agogna and Bounty of Sparry, Cora was born, my first Newfoundland, who would later become Int. It. Ch. M.R. and the first dog of the kennel "degli Angeli Neri." Cora was bred with Int. Swiss Ch. Simbo v. Schwarzen Mutz in 1969; Amanda, Ambra Aar, Astro, Asthom, Ascot and Araq were the result; the two most important of this litter being Int. It. Ch. Rip. Aar and Int. It. Ch. R. Amanda.

Aar became the foundation dog of the Acque Celesti Kennel, belonging to M. Luisa Bruzzo, producing a great number of subjects. From Ch. Hilvig's Ondine, imported from the United States, she generated Int. Ch. Aldebaran and Ch. Baten delle Acque Celesti, owned by Giuseppe Rossi; from Ara v. St. Peter, Ch. Fjord was born, who would become the father of Kluna v. Kilombero, daughter of Karel v. Neiderburg, which went to the Moicani Kennel of Tina Justi Rabbogliatti. In France he reproduced for the Terres Vieilles and Belvezet kennels, producing Fr. Ch. Jupiter de Belvezet and It. Int. Ch. Jubal de Belvezet, owned by Bartolo Ruffinengo.

Amanda, also known as Uri, remained at the Angeli Neri Kennel and when bred with the Swiss Asso de la Chassotte, son of Rik. v. Blattenhof, produced two subjects who had great success in the

Ch. Berry The Perry, owned by Schiatti and Baronti.   *Bonavista Bop Drop, owned by Vertigo Kennel.*

1970s: It. Int. Ch. M.R. Christian degli Angeli Neri, and Int. It. Ch. Ethel degli Angeli Neri. In particular, Ch. Christian degli Angeli Neri left an important mark for the kennel, producing about twenty litters with different bitches: from Ch. Baia degli Angeli Neri (Ch. Cora + Pirat v. Juliana) he generated, among others, Ch Felix degli Angeli Neri, owned by Paolo Trevisi, and Ch. Mabel degli Angeli Neri, owned by Annalisa Pisaneschi.

Ch. Zeder of the Angeli Neri, owned by G. Pasini.

Lower left: Ch. Dulrick'n A Tail Spin, owned by Cayuga Kennel.

Lower right: Ch. Arnoux, owned by Rita Cadonna.

From a later breeding with Karel v. Niederburg, Amanda produced two more champions: Ch. Hans degli Angeli Neri, owned by Oreste Diazzi, and Ch. Harold degli Angeli Neri owned by Dina Laugeri Zaccone, who would become the foundation dog of the kennel La Venaria Reale, and who produced with Nuvola v. Neufundlanderheim an excellent number of subjects including Ch. Alone.

In the 1960s, eighty-five puppies were born in Italy, and twelve were imported; in the 1970s, the number quickly rose to 370 puppies born, and sixty-three imported subjects.

Among the imported subjects there was, from Switzerland, Sol v. St. Johanniswald (Koko v. St. Fridolin + Oron v. St. Johanniswald) who was bred with Aldebaran, and produced Ch Cygnus, Ch. Cassiopea and Griffa. Also imported was Flipper de Soremont, son of Int. Ch. Ben v. Felsbach, who went on to become an Italian International Champion, father of World Champion Malva and the basis of the Orsi di S. Michele Kennels, owned by Luciano Veronesi. Avalon's Boreas was imported for the Agogna Kennel as was Bluf, a Swedish male of the Klam Line, owned by Umberto Chiostri, and father of Ch. Chantal, who would later be bred for the Incise Kennel of Baldovino Incise di Camerana. Furthermore, French and English subjects were imported for the Gabanina Kennel of Francesco Rocca, for the Laghetto Kennel of M. Zerilli Marimò and for Daniela Cavalli Funiciello.

The breed kept growing, attracting an always greater number of dog lovers; the time had come to organize a club. In September, 1976, in Genova Nervi, forty-two founders put their signatures on the new constitution. The Club Italiano del Terranova was born. The future was filled with programs that would increase with the spread of the breed.

The 1980s saw huge growth: 58 puppies in 1980, 82 in 1981, 93 in 1982, 81 in 1983, 89 in 1984, 105 in 1985, 164 in 1986, 162 in 1987, 247 in 1988, and 369 in 1989.

In the first half of the decade, production was tied to activities of existing kennels and the introduction of some foreign bloodlines. Among the stud dogs used were Mirko v. Murgwai and Lord v. Murgwai, which produced respectively for the Venaria Reale and for the Moicani kennels, Int. Ch. Enrik v. Luxembourg (Ch. Ferro v. Soven + Blackie), which reproduced for the Angeli Neri and the Venaria Reale kennels, Ch. Ferro v. Soven, which produced It. Int. Ch. Sv. F. R. Alhenageminorum, It. Int. Ch Sv. A. Alraicephei and Int. Ch. Geminorun Corona, the Netherlands Ch. Basco v. Zonegge, It. Ch. Bartok, Lord Byron Billy Budd, and Int. Lux. World Ch. Erasmus Graf v. Luxemburg, which reproduced for the Angeli Neri and Venaria Reale kennels. With Suomi of the Angeli Neri, daughter of Ch. Christian degli Angeli Neri, he generated seven champions, five in the first litter: It. Int. Ch. R. SM. A. Zeder degli Angeli Neri, It. Ch. Zenith degli Angeli Neri, It. Ch. Zeus degli Angeli Neri, It. Ch. Zingarella degli Angeli Neri, It. Ch Zelda degli Angeli Neri, and in the second litter in 1987, It. Int. Ch. Dilys degli Angeli Neri and It. Ch. Debbie degli Angeli Neri.

In the second half of the 1980s, new kennels were begun, some of which worked mainly with the white and black variety. In 1985, the Cayuga Newf Kennel, of M. Massa and F. Vitale was born; this kennel chose to build the foundation of its line first on some Danish subjects of the Ursulas Kennels, importing It. Int. Ch. Ursulas Goldigger, Ursulas Lady Luna, Ursulas Near to my Heart and Ch. Ursulas Admiral Ascot. Later, they used Canadian lines from the Topmast and Bearbrook kennels importing Am. Can. Dk. Sm. It. Int. World Ch. Topmast's Blackberry Blossom, Topmast's Peg O My Heart, It. Int. Ch. Topmast's Applesauce, Can. Int. Am. Ch. Topmast's John Houston, Can. Am. R. Int. It. Ch. Bearbrook Barnacle Bill and It. R. Ch. Dulrick In A Tailspin, son of Ch. Bearbrook Domino de Dourga. Bearbrook Barnacle Bill produced, with Topmast's Blackberry Blossom, Can. It. Int. Ch. Cayuga I'm Juliet of Bonaventura and It. Int. A. Ch. Iron Man Tyson of Bonaventura; with Topmast's Applesauce he produced It. Int. Ch. Cayuga Fearnaught. The Vertigo Kennel of Beatrice Schiatti was also born from these same lines to produce, from Bearbrook Barnacle Bill, Int. Ch. Athletic Grizzly, and from Dulrick In A Tailspin, Int. Ch. Bear in Mind and Int. Ch. Berry the Perry.

Dulrick In A Tailspin also bred for the Geminorun Kennel producing, with Alhena Geminorun, Int. It. Ch. Geminorun Eridania and Int. Ch. Geminorun Electra.

Meanwhile, Venise des Coteaux Rouges was imported from France by her owner Fedorka Orebic Malfatti. With Ch. Zeder degli Angeli Neri, she produced some excellent subjects among which were Athos, Anouk and Int. Ch. Arnoux.

In the last years, some litters were bred privately and by club members for pet quality demand; these also contributed greatly to the breed's popularity. In 1990, Newfoundlands registered in the *Italian Book of Origins* reached 561. Such a quick increase in the number of dogs has both positive and negative results. Obtaining good dogs is not easy. The breeder who really cares about the breed is careful to have only the best subjects reproduce; this implies a numerically smaller production. If the supply grows too quickly, the end result is an abundance of animals that do not represent the necessary characteristics. In addition, because living creatures are hard to control, indiscriminate breeding not only increases the number of available dogs but also spreads unwanted traits.

Furthermore, fashion, which is synonymous with a temporary and mutating desire, could cause a cute two month-old puppy to become, a year later, a large burden for which one must care, feed and keep clean, thus generating the decision to have him change homes, a great trauma for any dog, and even more so for the Newfoundland, whose relationship with man is the motive for his existence.

As we end this discussion of history, let us look to the future, in hope that the breed continues to spread, but in an appropriate and responsible manner.

The pages that follow propose to introduce a better knowledge of the Newfoundland so that contact with him is not casual, but considered, thought about, and joyful both for dog and owner.

II. STANDARDS FOR THE NEWFOUNDLAND DOG

Based on the British Standard and the International Cinological Foundation:

The concept of breed is born when a group of subjects, belonging to the same species and considering factors such as the environment, history, geography and purpose, are able to reproduce and consistently produce the same traits.

Nevertheless, the mechanism of transmission of traits is such that there can be considerable variation from the norm. In order to avoid excessive deviations or even actual modifications of the breed, and in order to create more precise evaluation criteria, standards have been created.

Each standard is at the discretion of the country of origin. For the Newfoundland, this country is England; although today the island of Newfoundland is part of Canada, in 1886, when the breed was recognized, it was a British colony.

As a member nation of the Federation Cynologique International (FCI)-or the International Cinological Foundation, Italy recognizes the FCI standard that was revised and adopted on July 24, 1996. The United States, Canada and England have different standards.

New Federation Cynologique International (F.C.I.) Standard
(Date of publication: 7-24-1996)

Utilization: sledge dog for heavy loads, water dog.

Classification FCI: Group 2 C Pinscher and Schnauzer Type-Molossian and Swiss Mountain and Cattle Dogs

Section 2.2: molossian Type, Mountain Dogs without working trial.

Short Historical Survey: the breed originated in the island of Newfoundland from dogs indigenous and the big black bear dog introduced by the Vikings after the year 1100. With the advent of European fishermen a variety of new breeds helped to shape and reinvigorate the breed, but the essential characteristics remained. When the colonization of the island began in 1610, the Newfoundland Dog was already largely in possession of his proper morphology and natural behaviour. These features allowed him to withstand the rigours of the extreme climate and sea's adversity while pulling heavy loads on land or serving as water and lifeguard dog.

General Appearance: the Newfoundland is massive, with powerful body, wel muscled and well coordinated in his movements.

Important Proportions: the length of the body from the withers to the root of the tail is equal to the distance from the withers to the ground. The body is compact. The body of the bitch may be slightly longer and is less massive than that of the dog. The distance from the withers to the underside of the chest is greater than the distance form the underside of the chest to the ground.

Behaviour and Temperament: the Newfoundland expression reflects benevolence and softness. Dignified, joyful and creative, he is known for his sterling gentleness and serenity.

Head: massive. The head of the bitch follows the same general conformation as the male's, but is less massive.

Cranial Region:
Skull: broad, with slightly arched crown and strongly developed occipital bone;
Stop: evident, but never abrupt;

Facial Region:

Nose: large, well pigmented, nostrils well developed. Color: Black on bland and white and black dogs, brown on brown dogs;

Muzzle: definitely square, deep and moderately short, covered with short fine hair and free from wrinkles. The corners of the mouth are evident, but not excessively pronounced;

Cheeks: soft;

Bite: scissors or level bite;

Eyes: relatively small, deep set; they are wide apart and show no haw. Color: Dark brown in black and white dogs, lighter shades permitted in brown dogs;

Ears: relatively small, triangular with rounded tips, well set back on the side of the head and close lying. When the ear of the adult dog is brought forward, it reaches to the inner corner of the eye on the same side.

Neck: strong, muscular, well set in the shoulders, long enough to permit dignified head carriage. The neck should not show excessive dewlapxe "dewlap".

Body: bone structure is massive thoughout. Viewed from the side, the body is deep and vigorous:

Top line: level and firm from the withers to the rump;

Back: broad;

Loin: strong and well muscled;

Rump: broad, sloping at an angle of about 30 degrees;

Chest: broad, full and deep, with good spread of ribs;

Abdomen and underline: almost level and never tucked up.

Forequarters: the forelegs are straight and parallel also when the dog is walking or slowly trotting:

Shoulders: very well muscled, well laid back at an angle approaching 45 degrees to the horizontal line;

Elbows: close to the chest;

Pastern: slightly sloping;

Forefeet: large and proportionate to the body, well rounded and tight, with firm and compact toes. Webbing of toes is present. Nails black in white and black dogs, horn coloured in brown dogs. In case of white toes, the nails should not be black.

Hindquarters: because driving power for pulling loads, swimming or covering ground efficiently is largely dependent upon the hindquarters, the rear structure of the Newfoundland is of prime importance. The pelvis has to be strong, broad and long:

Upper thighs: wide and muscular;

Stifle: well bent, but not so as to give a crouching appearance;

Lower thighs: strong and fairly long;

Hocks: relatively short, well let down and well apart; parallel to each other, they turn neither in nor out;

Hindfeet: firm and tight. Nail color as in forefeet. Dewclaws, if present, should have been removed.

Tail: the tail acts as a rudder when the Newfoundland is swimming; therefore, it is strong and broad at the base. When the dog is standing, the tail hangs down with, possibly, a little curve at the tip; reaching to or slightly below the hocks. When the dog is in motion or excited, the tail is carried straight out with a slight upward curve, but never curled over the back or curved inward between the legs.

Gait/Movement: the Newfoundland moves with good reach of the forelegs and strong drive of the hindquarters, giving the impression of effortless power. A slight roll of the back is natural. As the dog's speed increases, the dog tends to single track with the topline remaining level.

Coat:

Hair: the Newfoundland has a water resistant double coat. The outer coat is moderately long and straight with no curl. A slight wave is permissible. The undercoat is soft and dense, more dense in winter than in summer, but always found to some extent on the rump and chest. The hair on the head, muzzle and ears is short and fine. The front and rear legs are feathered. The tail is completely covered with long dense hair, but does not form a flag;

Color: black, white and black, and brown:
black: the traditional colour is black. The color has to be even as much as possible, but a slight tinge of sunburn is permissible. White markings on the chest, toes and/or tip of tail are permissible;
white and black: this variety is of historical significance to the breed. The preferred pattern of markings is black head with, preferably, a white blaze extending onto the muzzle, black saddle with even markings and black rump and upper tail. The remaining parts are to be white and can show a minimum or ticking;
brown: the brown color goes from chocolate to bronze. White markings on chest, toes, or tip of tail or a combination of these are permissible.
White and black dogs and brown dogs are to be shown in the same class as blacks.

Size and Weight: the average height at the withers is:

for adult males 71 centimeters (28 inches);
for adult bitches 66 centimeters (26 inches).

The average weight is:
approximately 60 kilograms (132.45 pounds) for males;
approximately 54 kilograms (119.20 pounds) for bitches.

Large size is desirable, but is not to be favored over symmetry, general soundness, power of the structure and correct gait.

Faults: any departure from the foregoing points should be considered a fault and seriousness with which the fault should be regarded should be in exact proportion to its degree:

-general appearance: Legginess, lack or substance;
-general bone structure: Sluggish appearance, fine bone;
-character: Aggresiveness, shyness;
-head: Narrow;
-muzzle: Snipey or long;
-flews: Pronounced;
-eyes: Round, protruding, yellow eyes, showing pronounced haw;
-back: Roached, slack or swayed back;
-forequarters: Down in pastern, splayed toes, toeing in or out, lack or webbing between toes;
-hindquarters: Straight stifles, cowhocks, barrel legs, pigeon toes;
-tails: Short, long, kink tail, curled tip;
-gait/movement: Mincing, shuffling, crabbing, too close moving, weaving, crossing over in
front, toeing-out or distinctly toeing-in in front, hackney action, pacing;
-hair: Completely open coat.

Eliminating Faults:
-bad temperament
-overshot or undershot bite, wry mouth;
-short and flat coat;
-markings of any other color than white on a black or brown dog;
-any other color than black or white and black or brown.

Note: male animals should have two apparently normal testicles fully descended into the scrotum.

British Standard
(n.50 of 9-20-1988)

General Appearance
Well proportioned dog, noticed for its strength and activity. The entire bone structure is massive, but does not give the impression of heaviness or inactivity, rather noble, majestic and powerful.

Characteristics

Large dog used for draft work and in water, possesses the instinct of life-saving and is a devoted companion.

Personality

Extraordinarily sweet and docile.

Head and Cranium

Large and massive head, with well-developed occipital protuberances; the stop (or the depression in the face at the junction of the forehead and foreface) is not too emphasized. The muzzle is short, with a clean cut and quite squared, covered by a fine and short coat.

Eyes

Small, dark brown, deep set, without a visible conjunctivas (or the mucous membrane that covers the forepart of the eyeball), rather distant one from the other.

Ears

Small, attached quite far back, parallel to the cranium, adherent to the head, covered by a short, fringeless coat.

Mouth

Soft and well outlined by the lips. The scissors bite is preferred, this meaning that the top teeth are superposed and adherent to the lower ones and well squared with the jaw, the level bite closure is tolerated.

Neck

Strong, well inserted on the shoulders.

Front Legs

Perfectly straight, well muscled, with elbows adherent to trunk, and well sloped.

Body

Well rounded thorax, wide back, with straight

Ch. Amanda, Angeli Neri Kennel.

superior line. Strong and well muscled loins, deep and wide chest.

Hind Legs
Well constructed and strong. A weak loin and closed hocks are considered defects.

Feet
Wide, webbed and well formed. Flat or out turned feet are considered large defects.

Gait-Movement
Free, with a slight rolling motion. In movement a slight inward torsion of the tip of the front feet is admissible.

Tail
Of moderate length, reaching a bit lower than the hock, quite thick, well covered by hair that does not form a flag. When the dog is still, the tail hangs straight down with a slight curve at the extremity; when in movement the tail is held slightly higher, and when excited it is held straight up, with a slight curve at the extremity. Tails with bumps or curvatures toward the back are a serious defect.

Coat
Double, soft and dense, roughly wed and naturally oily and water resistant. When brushed in the opposite direction, it returns to its natural position. The front legs are well fringed. The body is well covered with hair, and does not produce fringes on the chest.

Color
The only colors permitted are the following: Black, somewhat opaque, eventually showing bronze shadings. A white patch on the chest, the toes, or the tip of the tail is permitted.

Brown, could be chocolate or bronze. Aside

Ch. Molly Mill's Bepo, owned by J. Bombe.

from their color, the brown dogs are identical to the others. A white patch on the chest, the toes, or the tip of the tail is permitted.

Landseer, or white with only black patches. The head is preferably black, with a narrow white line along the forehead; the saddle is well designed and the croup is black and extends to the tail. The beauty of the patches must be taken highly into consideration. Black dots (ticking) are a defect.

Size and Weight
The medium height to the withers is 29 inches in the male and 26 1/2 inches in the female. The medium weight for males is of 130 to 142 pounds.; that of the females is of 110 to 118 pounds.

Defects
Any and all deviations from the above mentioned standards are considered defects and should be judged in proportion of their seriousness.

Notes
The males must have two testicles of normal aspect, completely descended into the scrotum.

American Standard
(June 28, 1990)

General Appearance
The Newfoundland is a sweet-dispositioned dog that acts neither dull nor ill-tempered. He is a devoted companion. A multipurpose dog, at home on land and in water, the Newfoundland is capable of draft work and possesses natural lifesaving abilities.

The Newfoundland is a large, heavily coated, well balanced dog that is deep-bodied, heavily boned, muscular and strong. A good specimen of the breed has dignity and proud head carriage.

The following description is that of an ideal Newfoundland. Any deviation from this ideal is to be penalized to the extent of the deviation. Structural and movement faults common to all working dogs are as undesirable in the Newfoundland as in any other breed, even though they are not specifically mentioned here.

Size-Proportion-Substance
The average height for adult dogs is of 28 inches, for adult bitches, 26 inches. Approximate weight of adult dogs ranges from 130-150 pounds, adult bitches from 100-120 pounds. The dog's appearance is more massive throughout than the bitch's. Large size is desirable, but never at the expense of balance, structure and correct gait. The Newfoundland slightly longer than tall when measured from the point of shoulder to the point of buttocks and from withers to ground. He is a dog of considerable substance which is determined by rib spring, strong muscle and heavy bone.

Head
The head is massive, with a broad skull, slightly arched crown and strongly developed occipital bone. The cheeks are well developed. The eyes are dark brown. (Browns and Grays may have lighter eyes and should be penalized only to the extent that color affects expression). They are relatively small, deep-set and spaced wide apart. Eyelids fit closely with no inversion. The ears are relatively small and triangular with rounded tips. They are set on the skull level with or slightly above the brow and lie close to the head. When the ear is brought forward, it reaches to the inner corner of the eye on the same side. The expression is soft and reflects the characteristics of the breed: benevolence, intelligence and dignity.

Forehead and face are smooth and free of wrinkles. Slope of the stop is moderate but, because of the well developed brow, it may appear abrupt in profile. The muzzle is clean-cut, broad throughout its length and deep. Depth and length are approximately equal, the length from tip of nose to stop being less than that from the stop to the occiput, or the back part of the head. The top of the muzzle is rounded and the bridge, in profile, is straight or only slightly arched. Teeth meet in a scissors or level bite. Dropped lower incisors, in a otherwise normal bite, are not indicative of a skeletal malocclusion and should be considered only a minor deviation.

Neck-Topline-Body

The neck is strong and well set on the shoulders and is long enough for proud head carriage. The back is strong, broad and muscular and is level from just behind the withers to the croup. The chest is full and deep with the brisket reaching at least down to the elbows. Ribs are well sprung, with the anterior third of the rib cage tapered to allow elbow clearance. The flank is deep. The croup is broad and slopes slightly.

Tail

The tail follows the natural line of the croup. The tail is broad at the base and strong. It has no kinks and the distal bone reaches to the hock. When the dog is standing relaxed, its tail hangs straight or with a slight curve at the end. When the dog is in motion or excited, the tail is carried out, but it does not curl over the back.

Frontquarters

Shoulders are muscular and well laid back. The elbows lie directly below the highest point of the withers. Forelegs are muscular, heavily boned, straight and parallel to each other, and the elbows point directly to the rear. The distance from the elbow to the ground is about half of the dog's height. Pasterns are strong and slightly sloping. Feet are proportionate to the body in size, webbed and cat foot in type. Dewclaws should be removed.

Hindquarters

The rear assembly is powerful, muscular and heavily boned. Viewed from the rear the legs are straight and parallel. Viewed from the side, the thighs are broad and fairly long. Stifles and hocks are well bent and the line from the hock to the ground is perpendicular. The hocks are well let down. The hind feet are similar to the front feet. Dewclaws should be removed.

Coat

The adult Newfoundland has a flat, water resistant, double coat that tends to fall back into place when rubbed against the nap. The outer coat is coarse, moderately long and full, either straight or with a wave. The undercoat is soft and dense, although it is often less dense during the summer months or in warmer climates. Hair on the face and muzzle is short and fine. The backs of the legs are feathered all the way down. The tail is covered with long, dense hair. Excess hair may be trimmed for neatness. Whiskers need not be trimmed.

Color

Color is secondary to type, structure and soundness. Recognized Newfoundland colors are black, brown, gray, and white and black, or the Landseer.

Solid Colors

Blacks, Browns and Grays may appear as solid colors or solid colors with white at any, some or all of the following locations: chin, chest, toes and tip of tail. Any amount of white found at these locations is typical and is not penalized. Also typical are a tinge of bronze on a black or gray coat and lighter furnishings on a brown or gray coat.

Landseer

White base coat with black markings. Typically, the head is solid black, or black with white on the muzzle, with or without a blaze. There is a separate black saddle and black marking on the rump extending onto a white tail.

Markings, on either solid colors or Landseers, might deviate considerably from those described and should be penalized only to the extent of the deviation. Clear white markings or white with minimal ticking is preferred.

Beauty of markings should be considered only when comparing dogs of otherwise comparable quality and never at the expense of type, structure and soundness.

Disqualifications
Any color or combination of colors not specifically described disqualifies the subject.

Gait
The Newfoundland in motion has good reach, strong drive and gives the impression of effortless power. His gait is smooth and rhythmic, covering the maximum amount of ground with the minimum number of steps. Forelegs and hind legs travel straight forward. As the dog's speed increases, the legs tend toward single tracking. When moving, a slight roll of the skin is characteristic of the breed. Essential for good movement is the balance of front and rear assemblies.

Temperament
Sweetness of temperament is the hallmark of the Newfoundland; this is the most important single characteristic of the breed.

Disqualifications
Any color or combination of colors not specifically described are disqualified.

Canadian Standard (1-1-1979)

Origin and Purpose
The breed originated in Newfoundland from dogs indigenous to the island and from the big black bear dogs introduced by the Vikings in 1001 A.D. With the advent of European fishermen, a variety of new breeds helped to shape and reinvigorate the breed, but the essential characteristics of the Newfoundland dog remained. By the time colonization of the island was permitted in 1610, distinct physical characteristics and mental attributes had been established.

The large size, heavy coat and webbed feet permit the Newfoundland dog to withstand the rigors of the extreme climate and sea while serving both as draught animal and as lifeguard.

General Appearance
The Newfoundland is massive, deep bodied, well muscled and coordinated, projecting dignity in stance and head carriage. The appearance is square in that the length of the dog, from the top of the withers to the base of the tail is equal to the distance from the top of the withers to the ground. The distance from the top of the withers to the underside of the chest is greater than from the underside of the withers to the ground. The body of the bitch may be slightly longer and less massive than that of the dog. A mature dog must never appear leggy or lacking substance. The Newfoundland is a free moving dog with a slightly perceptible roll. Substantial webbing between the toes is always present. Large size is desirable but never at the expense of gait symmetry and balance. Fine bone structure is to be faulted.

Temperament
The Newfoundland's expression is soft and reflects the character of the breed: benevolent, intelligent, dignified but capable of fun. He is known for his sterling gentleness and serenity. Any show of ill temper or timidity is to be severely faulted. Bad temperament is a disqualification.

Size
The average height for adult dogs is 28 inches, for adult bitches, 26 inches. The average weight for adult dogs is 150 pounds, for adult bitches 120 pounds. Large size is desirable but it is not to be favored over correct gait, symmetry, soundness and structure.

Coat and Color
The Newfoundland has a water resistant double coat. The outer coat is moderately long and straight with no curl. A slight waviness is permissible. When rubbed the wrong way, the

coat tends to fall back into place. The undercoat is soft and dense, though less dense during summer months, but always found to some extent on the rump and chest. A completely open coat is to be faulted. The hair on the head, muzzle and ears is short and fine. The front and rear legs are feathered. The tail is completely covered with long dense hair, but does not form a flag. A short, flat, smooth coat, (Labrador Retriever type) is a disqualification. The traditional color is black. A sunburned black is permissible. White markings on the chest, toes or tip of the tail are permissible. Markings of any color other than white are most objectionable, and the dog is to be disqualified. The Landseer Newfoundland is white with black markings and is of historical significance to the breed. The preferred pattern of markings for the Landseer is a black head with a white blaze extending onto the muzzle, black saddle, black rump and upper tail. All remaining parts are to be white with a minimum of ticking. The symmetry of markings and the beauty of pattern characterize the best marked Landseers. Landseers are to be shown in the same classes as blacks unless special classes are provided for them.

Head

The head is massive with a broad skull, slightly arched crown and strongly developed occipital bone. The forehead and face are smooth and free of wrinkles. The stop is not abrupt. The muzzle is clean cut and covered with short fine hair. It is rather square, deep and moderately short. The nostrils are well developed. The bitch's head follows the same general conformation, but is feminine and less massive. A narrow head, or a snipey or long muzzle is to be faulted. Pronounced flews, or the pendulous outside part of the upper lip, are not desirable. The eyes are dark brown, relatively small and deep set. They are spaced wide apart and show no haw, or inflammation of the membrane at inner angle or the lower lid of the eye. Round, yellow, or protruding eyes are objectionable. The ears are relatively small and triangular

with rounded tips. They are set well back on the side of the head and lie close. When the ear of the adult dog is brought forward, it reaches to the inner corner of the eye on the same side. The teeth meet in a scissors or level bite.

Neck

The neck is strong, muscular and set on the shoulders. It is long enough to permit dignified head carriage and should not show surplus dewlap.

Forequarters

When the dog is not in motion, the forelegs are straight and parallel, with the elbows close to the chest. The shoulders are well muscled and well laid back at an angle approaching 45 degrees. The pasterns are slightly sloping. Down in the pasterns is to be faulted. The feet are proportionate to the body, well rounded and tight with firm compact toes (cat foot type). Splayed toes are a fault. Toeing in or out is undesirable.

Body

The Newfoundland's chest is broad, full and deep, with the brisket reaching to the elbows. The back is broad with good spread of rib, and the topline is level from the withers to the croup, never roached, slack or swayed. The loins are strong and well muscled, and the croup is broad. The pelvis slopes at an angle of about 30 degrees. Viewed from the side, the body is deep and shows no discernible tuck-up. Bone structure is massive throughout but does not give a sluggish appearance.

Hindquarters

Because driving power for swimming, pulling loads, or covering ground efficiently is largely dependent on the hindquarters, the rear structure of the Newfoundland is of prime importance. The hip assembly is broad, strong and well developed. The upper thighs are wide and muscular. The lower thighs are strong and fairly long. The stifles are well bent, but not so as to give a crouching appearance. The hocks are well let down, well apart and parallel to each other. They turn neither in nor out. The feet are firm and tight. Dewclaws, if present, should have been removed. Straight stifles, cow hocks, barrel legs or pigeon toes are to be faulted.

Tail

The tail acts as a rudder when the Newfoundland is swimming, therefore it is strong and broad at the base. When the dog is standing, the tail hangs straight down, possibly a little curved at the tip, reaching to or slightly below the hocks; when the dog is in motion or excited, the tail is carried straight out or with a slight upward curve but never curled over the back or curved inward between the legs. A tail with a kink or curved at the end is very objectionable.

Gait

The Newfoundland has a good reach and strong drive, giving the impression of effortless power. In motion, the legs move straight forward, parallel to the line of travel. A slight roll is present. As the speed increases, the dog tends to single track, with the topline remaining level.

Mincing, shuffling, crabbing, too close moving, weaving, crossing over in front, toeing out or distinctly toeing in front, hackney action and pacing are all faults.

Faults

Legginess, narrow head, snipey or long muzzle, pronounced flews, short tail, long tail, tail with a kink, tail with curled end, fine bone, any show of ill temper or timidity, open coat, eyes showing pronounced haw, round, protruding or yellow eyes, splayed feet, down pasterns, mincing, shuffling, crabbing, weaving, crossing over in front, toeing out or distinctly toeing in front, hackney action, pacing, straight stifles, cow hocks, barrel legs, roached, slack or sway back, lack of webbing between toes, overshot, undershot or wry mouth.

Disqualifications

Bad temperament, short flat coat (Labrador Retriever type), markings of any other color than white on a black dog, any colors other than the traditional black or the Landseer (white and black).

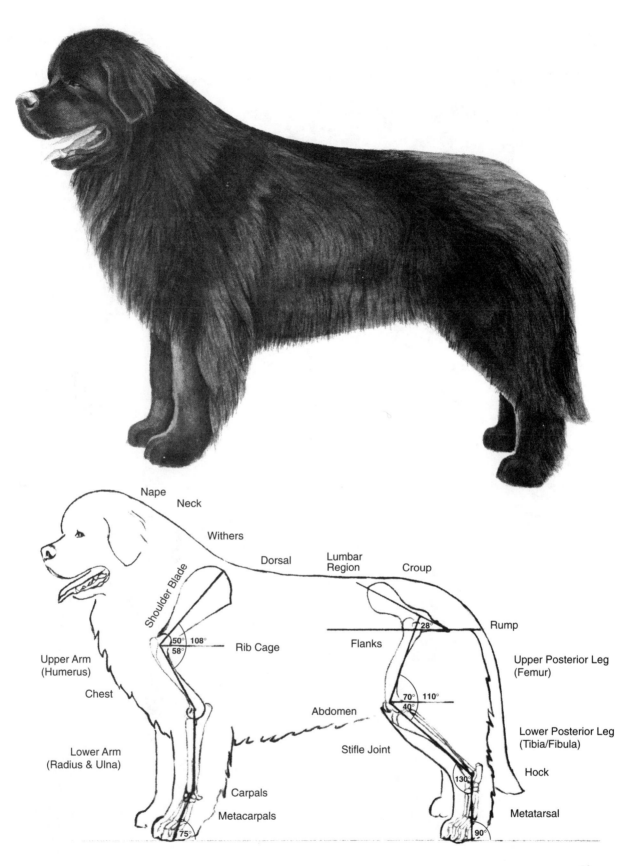

Nape

Neck

Withers

Dorsal

Lumbar
Region

Croup

Shoulder Blade

50° 108°

58°

28°

Rump

Rib Cage

Flanks

Upper Arm
(Humerus)

Upper Posterior Leg
(Femur)

Chest

70° 110°

40°

Abdomen

Lower Arm
(Radius & Ulna)

Stifle Joint

Lower Posterior Leg
(Tibia/Fibula)

130°

Hock

Carpals

Metacarpals

Metatarsal

75°

90°

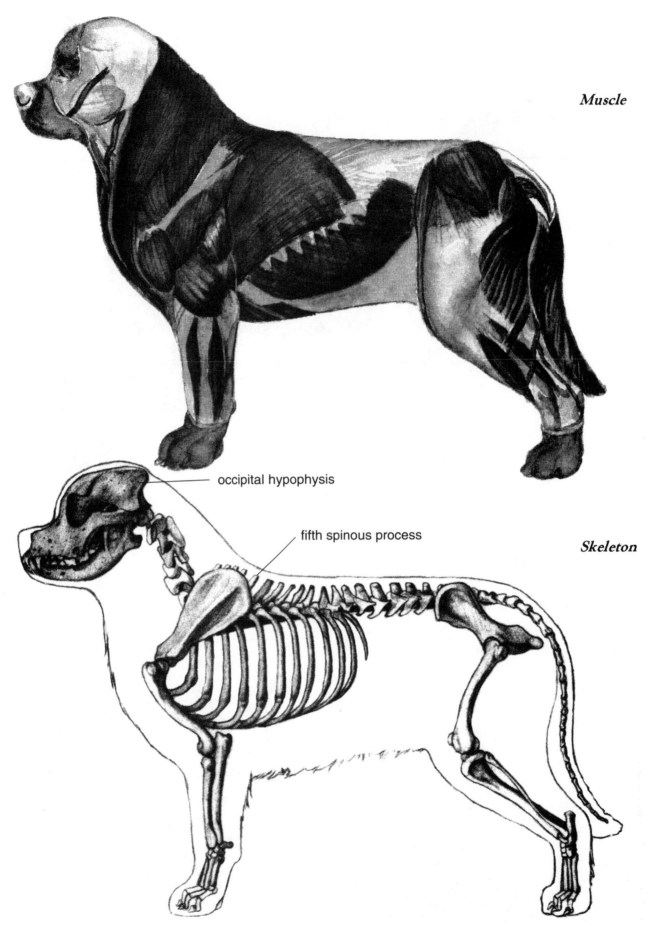

Muscle

occipital hypophysis

fifth spinous process

Skeleton

54

Cranium (lateral view)

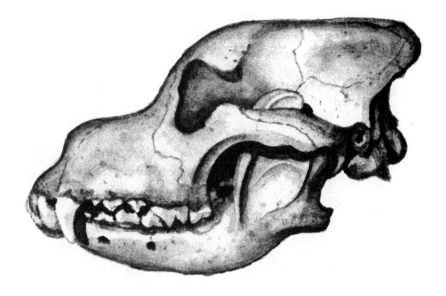

Regions of the Cranium

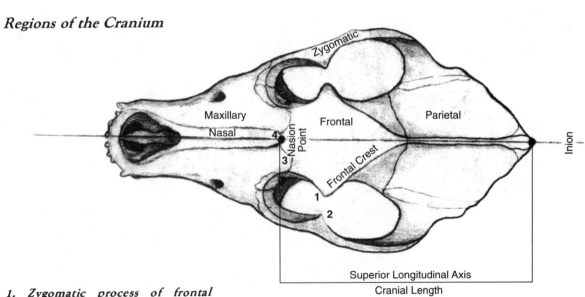

1. Zygomatic process of frontal (ectorbital point).
2. Frontal process of zygomatic bone.
3. Maxillary apophysis.
4. Nasal apophysis.

56

III. COMMENT REGARDING THE STANDARDS

Examination and comparison of the three standards allows us to make one important conclusion: there are no fundamental differences except for color.

The ideal Newfoundland is the same in all standards. Thus, it is natural to ask why, even within one country, there are at times substantial differences. It is obvious that breeders and judges must adapt to the above-mentioned standards, but too often they leave space for personal interpretations.

It may happen, for example, that some, while trying to strengthen a characteristic, interpret so much that results are caricature-like, while others allow characteristics to completely disappear, both are forgetting a very important concept held in consideration by lovers and students of the breed throughout the ages: "In the Newfoundland all must be harmony and proportion." Perhaps this would not happen, or it would happen less, if the standard were more precise. The Second World Cinological Congress, held in Monaco in 1934, unanimously hoped that the standards would adopt the following changes:

1. An unchangeable order in the description of the various parts of the body
2. A correct description of these parts
3. A point scale to evaluate them

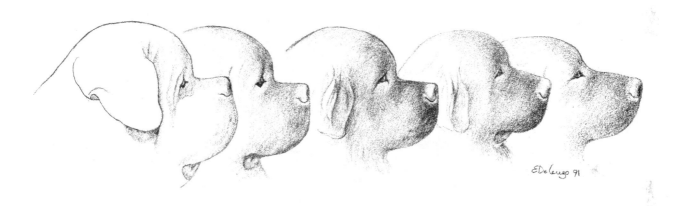

Variation of head types.

Furthermore, it gave a model of standards that was so very characteristic, so much so that in this era of computers, that a very precise identikit of the dog could have been made.

Obviously we do not intend with these words to take anything away from the individuality of single subjects. The concept of an individual subject implies that there are differences among members of the same breed, that no two members are ever the same. In any case it is important to differentiate individual variations within the same type and variations of traits within the same breed. Every variety possesses particular, important and affirmative characteristics that constitute the type.

One may hear words such as, "that dog looks like a hound," or "he looks like a Mastiff," or "he has the expression of a wolf." All of these subjects could belong to the same breed and have the traits of that breed, except for those details able to evoke a different image.

It is these same traits that must be better identified, described and illustrated in the standards, so that it is no longer a skeleton that one can dress as one pleases, and so that the standard can become a concrete guide.

In the history of every canine breed there exists a nebulous time in which uncertain images of very different ancestors appear. The founding of the breed coincides with the fixation of certain traits and type.

It could be that this founding was obtained through crossbreedings, which brought in different genes from those belonging to the original group, but nevertheless, from that moment on this set of traits and type is that to which we must refer.

It may happen that for certain periods of time breeders are not able to produce perfect animals. This must not, however, allow for the breed standards to become less strict or to follow fashions and tastes. Single individuals always have to be compared with the ideal. This protection of the ideal type is the way to protect the breed for the future.

Once this has been said, it is clear that it is the duty of every breeder to penetrate the most intimate mechanisms of expression of the type. This implies a series of comparisons between single specimens to discover similarities and differences between them, the knowledge of basic anatomy in order to be able to find and describe these similarities and differences, and the use of technical terms to constitute a constructive dialogue. It is also necessary to not lose sight of function.

General Appearance and Temperament

The Newfoundland dog is a large molossus with a strong, thick coat. His sweet and intelligent personality, his passion for swimming and retrieving, his strength and his courage have made him famous as a working dog used mainly for the noble purpose of saving people in peril in the water. It is useless to repeat the various stories of rescues that have occurred in the sea and in rivers or the aid that has been given to fishermen and sailors. It is more important to remember that this dog was used to pull lumber and sleds and as a courier. We can thus imagine him while jumping from one rock to

Ch. Christian of the Angeli Neri Kennels.

Ch. Erik v. Luxemburg, owned by O. Rinder

another, while diving, holding tightly in his teeth something to deliver, his back arched, his front legs pointed in indescribable effort. We see him pulling against the weight of his burden, and docilely waiting for the load to be set on his solid back. Thus, he must be built in such a way that allows him to fulfill these tasks. He must be robust, muscular, with a massive bone structure, very strong but always harmonious, balanced in his every part and free in his movement. Tall, in proportion to his transverse diameter, enough to be agile, but not so much as to make him lose his solid base.

The first thing we notice when looking at a good specimen is his size, his mass is more important than his height: a solid and strong body with ample diameters that must not give the impression of emptiness or narrowness. Equivocation over these terms, especially with regard to the race toward gigantism, has often caused great problems, first and foremost, the loss of balance and harmony. It is hard for subjects who are too large to maintain the proper proportions; the legs become too long, often not angled enough or the head often appears too small and narrow. We thus lose the famous "bear look."

All of this has a very precise meaning and should be investigated further, keeping in mind the constitutional doctrine. The reaching of certain goals, both through crossbreeding or selection, always means a change in the original physical type. If one thinks further about how hormones are able to influence the bone structure, and how much this hormonal mechanism influences the facial and cranial structure, it is obvious how this can create changes in the most important region of the body: the head.

The Head

Since studies about canine typologies began, the head has always held great importance in research. Scientists such as Buffon who considered the position of the ear; Curvier; Jean Pierre Megnin who formulated his classification (lupoids, braccoids, molossoids, graioids) in 1897; Corevin; Baron and Dechamber who, in 1921, subdivided the single breeds on the basis of their cranial-facial axis (concave, straight, convex), have always given the most phenotypical importance to the head. This climaxed in the famous quote of Guiseppe Solaro, "the head tells the breed."

Indeed, no other part of the body is so full of specific traits; the other areas are generally more important for the build. This is especially true for the Newfoundland.

One has only to think of the century-long tradition and the legendary character of this lifesaving breed to understand why it cannot do without a "face," that face! The Newfoundland's face, the harmony of shapes that in other parts of the body is indicative of the perfection of function, becomes the mirror of the interior equilibrium and tranquillity.

The wide and somewhat rounded cranium, with a wide forehead, framed by the sinuous line of the ears, the squared but cornerless muzzle, the soft and clean mouth that is soft on everything it touches, the serene intensity in its look are a synthesis of proportions that do not allow for defects or excessive unbalance.

One remains enraptured before a beautiful dog as one does before a beautiful painting, and one never tires of looking at him. Thus, to study the anatomical substrata of the powerful neck or the noble expression almost appears to be mixing the sacred and the profane.

However, we also notice that without a sufficiently descriptive terminology it all comes down to intuition mixed with personal taste. It is thus necessary to go back to those universal guidelines given by the standards.

As the standard states, the Newfoundland's head must be wide and massive. Its length, measured from the occipital apophysis to the superior anterior angle of the nose, is a bit shorter than the ratio of 4:10 of the height to the withers, about 38 to 39 percent. But the most interesting ratio is between the length and the width, taken at the level of the zygomatic arches and expressed by the following formula:

Total cephalic index = width x 100.

                length

This index allows us to divide the breeds into the following categories: dolichocephalic, or having a long and narrow head with a ratio less than 50; mesocephalic, with a ratio equal to 50; brachycephalic, or wide head with a ratio greater than 50. The Newfoundland, a molossus, belongs to the brachycephalic and possesses a cephalic index around 60 to 63. The head is divided into two fundamental regions: the muzzle and the cranium.

The ratio of these regions determines one of the fundamental aspects of the type and is defined by those ideal profiles that are referenced by the cranial-facial axis.

The superior longitudinal axis of the cranium is that which unites the Inion point (or center of the occipital protrusion) to the Nasion point (or meeting point between the frontal and nasal bones).

The longitudinal superior axis of the muzzle is the line of the nose, traced from the upper anterior corner of the nose to the transversal line that unites the two inside corners of the eyes.

The relationship of the axes can be one of parallelism, convergence or divergence. In parallelism these axes never meet, in the convergence they meet forming an obtuse angle inferior to 180 degrees, and in the divergence they form an angle superior to 180 degrees.

It is this interesting data, characteristic for every breed, that makes it immediately clear how a convergent axis brings the Newfoundland close to the St. Bernard while the divergent one brings him back to the hound or Bloodhound.

Relationships of Cranio-facial Axis

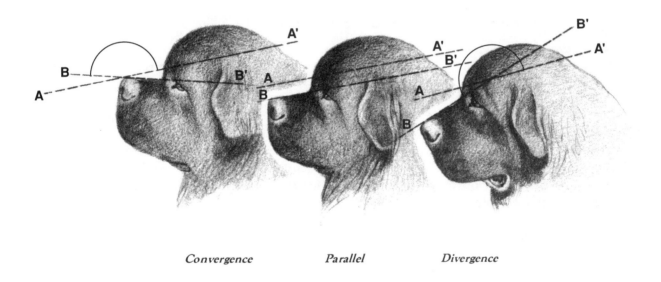

Convergence   Parallel   Divergence

These data are thus of the utmost importance in the definition of type, and every standard should give an accurate description. However, it is quite difficult to find this information even in texts that comment on the standard.

The only reference is found in the book *Le Terre Neuve* by Dr. Maurice Luquet, in which he comments on the Dechambre Classification, which puts the Newfoundland among the concave lines. Luquet writes, "In our day, if one referred to the standard and to the dogs examined at shows, we would think of him more as a subconcavelinear, halfway between the perfect straight line and the well defined concave."

This subject, one that should be discussed further, shows the importance of a well defined parallelism. In no case must one indulge in a divergence that has no meaning either from historical or

How the Newfoundland swims: importance of the cranial facial bones in the function.

functional points of view. It is a conformation that does not facilitate breathing while swimming and retrieving. It is enough to observe a Newfoundland while active to notice this. The position is invariably the same: withers and end of back slightly above the water, neck extended forward, head extended on the neck to maintain the nose far from the water.

A divergent axis would require a further extension of the head on the neck with consequent diminished breathing capability.

Another factor of utmost importance regarding type and function, always tightly intertwined, is given by the ratios of the diameters and by the conformation of the muzzle and cranium.

The Cranium

For a better understanding it is useful to review the interesting considerations of Studer regarding the birth of the Mastiff.

From ancient times, man tried to obtain breeds which, due both to their strength and jaws, would be able to fight powerful enemies and large animals, participate in hunts, and tame large and restless domesticated animals. To obtain such specimens, large dogs with well developed dentition [or development and arrangement of the teeth] were bred. These had a maxillary lever quite close to the point of muscle insertion, that is with the shortest possible branch from the epiphysis of the chewing muscles.

Such shortened jaws become heavyset and strong in dogs with well developed teeth. These circumstances required a great development of the jaw muscles, which in turn needed a large epiphyseal area. Consequently the bones of the cranium become accentuated, the sagittal crest is elevated, and the sides of the cranium fall in a roof-like fashion toward the zygomatic epiphysis; the cheek bones become abundantly developed and the temporal muscle finds an ample setting in the cranial fossae.

The cheek bones not only extend, but also become powerful and thick, giving a sufficient point of insertion to the masseter muscle. The inferior jaw bone presents indentations for these muscular insertions; it becomes massive, and its lower edge-by which movement is limited-is developed externally with a clearly convex shape.

Ordinarily, the point where the parts of the face conform to the parts of the brain is quite ample, and thus the forehead is wide and flat with a slight excavation of the median line.

Naturally, the Newfoundland is quite distant from certain exaggerated differentiations. It is important, however, to understand that this breed, which in the last century was classified along with the Mastiffs, must not tolerate dolichocephalic (elongated) heads, restricted frontal sinuses or receding temples.

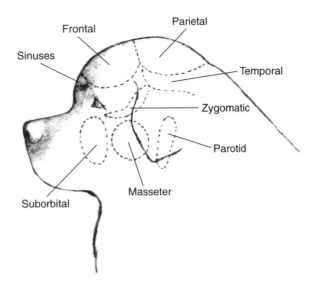

Regions of the Head.

The particular conformation of the cranium, with receding development in height as well, allows the temporal region to find perfect placement, without giving the head an excessive thickness such as that of the Rottweiler. In the same manner, a well proportioned masseter region is the base of a gently curved cheek. The ample and spacious forehead is a fundamental characteristic of the breed. Thus, while the width of the head is given by the bizygomatic (or high point of the cheekbones) diameter; its aspect is rounded or shaped as a dome. This is due to the expansion of the frontals both transversally and in height. A just proportion between these two aspects is necessary: if the height were too little, the head would appear flat. On the other hand, if it lacked width it would appear too vertical and narrow. The conformation of the frontal sinuses exists in relation to the qualities of the sense of smell in each breed.

Dogs with a well-developed olfactory sense, such as hunting dogs, who sniff the tracks with short and frequent breaths, show frontal sinuses smaller than those of dogs that capture odors at a distance, inhaling large quantities of air. The Newfoundland certainly belongs to the latter category and, in this case, morphology (type) and function come together in perfect harmony.

The width of the forehead and the distance of the two ectorbital areas (zygomatic processes of the frontal bone), determining the lateral diameters, influence among other things the position of the eyes which, as the standard specifies, must be set rather wide apart.

A correct development of the brow arch accentuates these traits, which are well seen from the front, with short, fine, shining hair that builds on the underlying bone structure creating a velvet-like mask with a dark-light effect.

The metopic frontal suture, the indentation that goes from the Nasion Point to the meeting point of the frontal crests, must not be overly marked so as not to destroy the softness of appearance.

In lateral perspective, the stop, or the frontal-nasal depression, is not as deep as that of the St. Bernard or the Great Dane. This is probably what the standard refers to when it says, "The stop must not be too pronounced." It must however rise with a good slope. The point at which the frontals rise from the nasal bones and from the maxillary apophysis of the upper jaws must be well-marked, developing into a gentle curve, rounded and further accentuated by the brow arches. The degree of the stop is determined from the cranial facial angle obtained by applying the side of a protractor along the nose at the frontal-nasal depression on the median line of the head. In the Newfoundland, its value is of approximately 130 degrees. At the level of the frontal sinus (sino nasal angle) it is 110 to 120 degrees.

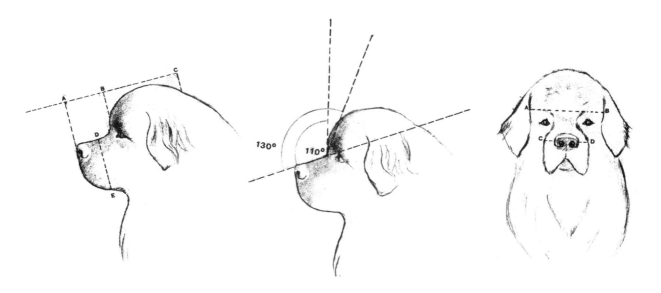

A-C = Length of head
A-B = Length of muzzle
D-E = Height of muzzle

130° = Craniofacial angle
110° = Sinonasal angle

A-B = Width of cranium
(Bizigomatic diameter)
C-D = Width of muzzle

Athos, owned by G. Sontacchi.

At the top of the cranium, the conjunction of the frontal crests is continued in the sagittal crest (moderately raised) that separates the two parietals and ends on the occipital bone.

Regarding this, the standard states that, "The occipital apophysis must be well developed." This point is evident because it is here that the ends of large neck ligaments and muscles insert; these components are important for pulling and carrying weight. It is important to note, however, that because of this, it must not appear as an excessive bony protuberance, which would indicate weak muscle development.

The Muzzle

The muzzle, or face, is the other important region of the head. It must be proportionate to the cranium; thus, if during a grasping action the cranium with its muscles represents the motor, the jaws are the levers upon which resistance and power meet.

In relation to an "ample and massive" cranium, there must correspond a "short and squared" muzzle for it to be solid and capable of function.

The length of the muzzle from the Nasion Point to the end of the nose is about 36 to 38 percent of the total length of the head. The muzzle height and depth are approximately equivalent.

The height relates to the good development of the upper jaw muscles, from which airways and great breathing capacity generate; this is quite important in a retriever whose ventilation under effort takes place with a closed mouth.

For the same reason, and even more importantly, the width of the muzzle, measured at the level of the first true molar, is the determining factor of function. This represents about 54 percent of the bizygomatic diameter.

The parallelism of the two lateral sides of the muzzle, which begins at the third premolar, is an important trait and determines the squareness and ampleness of the anterior platform. Seen from the front, it appears wide, but because of the slightly curved setting of the incisors it has softened margins. The muzzle thus has a cuboid aspect, but with rounded corners that perfectly complement the fluid lines of the cranium.

The superior nasal and superior maxillary bones must fuse harmoniously at the forehead and orbit. Prominent nasal bones damage this appearance and are to be penalized; the same holds true for a suborbital region that is chiseled, which indicates an improper development of the base of the cheek bone, of the jaw bone and of the masseter region.

The nasal choanae (passages), which is formed by the nasal, maxillary and incisive bones, is ample, and the nose in profile must appear straight. A curved nasal profile, typical of those breeds having a divergent cranial facial axis, constitutes a large defect and is in contrast with the functional anatomy of the Newfoundland.

As previously stated, the volume of inhaled air is very important for the Newfoundland; an ample and perfectly straight nasal cavity responds perfectly to these needs. Naturally, this would not be possible without an adequate shape of the nose that represents the terminal part of this organ.

The nose must be quite wide, well opened, neatly delineated, with lateral processes of the nostrils that are in line with the nasal plane. This is found on the same vertical plane as the anterior face of the lip plane and meets the longitudinal axis of the muzzle in a right angle.

The nostrils are ample, mobile and of moderate thickness in order to allow for good dilation when larger quantities of air are needed and as breathing accelerates.

The breathing while swimming: ample airway and mobile nose.

Sometimes one encounters protruding noses with an acute angle seen from the profile such as that of a pointer or a hound, lower in respect to the nasal cavity, and others, on the contrary, with a set back nose with a protruding nasal septum and thick wings; both are quite defective. The same can be said about those noses that, even having a correct profile, are small in proportion to the width of the face.

While the lower portion of the face is constituted by the mandible, strong and moderately curved with an ample intermaxillary canal, its profile is designed by the lips. In the lateral perspective, the upper lip is softly curved, rounded and full in the front, covering what is beneath it. It must not appear tense or thin, as is seen in cone shaped or pointed faces; neither should it be pendant, as in the case of other molossus whose lip gives the sensation of being heavy and fleshy.

The bottom lip must not fall; it must be adherent to the jaw and not turn outward. The outline of the mouth is soft, but must not form an evident commissure or closure or form hanging pockets.

On the anterior plane, the lips are separated by the median sulcus and are recognizable from a distance by the triangular space in the form of an inverted "V" that is well opened. Heavy lips are recognizable by a very narrow inverted "V."

Unfortunately, large lip development is confused at times with width and depth, which should be derived from the underlying bone structure as opposed to an overabundance of skin. At first glance, a face of this kind may appear strong from a side view, but, once seen from the front, it immediately reveals its true nature: a nasal cavity disproportionate in width to depth and labial disjunction.

Furthermore, since a set of genetic traits are often linked, one could associate insufficient cranial diameters, low and heavy ears, and open eyes with visible conjunctive, excessive skin, and so forth.

An overabundant lip accompanied by lower lip pouches has no functional meaning except to flood everything with saliva every time the dog shakes his head. It must be remembered that the Newfoundland is not a dog that drools if the lips are correct.

As color goes, the outline of the lip is preferably pigmented in the black and white and black with lighter pigmentation in the browns. Partial depigmentation occurs with aging but may also be found in younger subjects

The tongue may also be partially pigmented.

The Ear

The examination of the exterior profiles of the head cannot be complete without an accurate description of the ear. In the Newfoundland the ear can be justly considered the frame of a beautiful picture.

The ear is inserted with a large oblique base in the middle of the cranium either at the level of or slightly above the brow (supercillary) arch. The ear follows the outline of the head accentuating, from the front view, the typical earmuff conformation. Because the dog indicates his mood by the way the ears are carried, placement varies with different facial expressions. In an alert animal, the ears are carried higher and forward, making the expression of the brow and the volume of the head more powerful. When the dog is relaxed, they are held lower and further back. The ear is of triangular shape and has a rounded tip; the thickness is moderate, neither excessively thin nor heavy. When the insertion and the lengths are correct, it reaches the internal angle of the eye when pulled forward and lengthwise and does not go beyond the throat. Sliding along the head, the ear begins at the anterior insertion with a slight curve that follows the roundness of the temples; it accentuates on the zygomatic arch and then comes close to the masseter, which it delicately touches. This line is evident by the short and fine hair that covers the front half and the tip of the ear. It is certainly to this line that the standard refers to when it states, "short hairs without fringes."

On the other hand, the back part of the ear always presents fringes that must be trimmed when too long; however, they must not be completely removed because then the Newfoundland's ear would be similar to that of all other breeds, making the profile of the head and the insertion of the neck hard and sculptured.

The defects regarding the ear are mainly of insertion and dimension. An ear that is inserted too far down or too far back is similar to that of a cocker and damages the appearance of the head. Ears that are too small, inserted too high and too far forward devastate the fluidity of the lines and, in the presence of thick temporals, give the impression of a flat cranium.

The Eye

If the ear is the frame of the head, then the eye is the focal point that draws one's attention and gives full value to the contents. The expression would be worthy of thousands of attributes: noble, sweet, intelligent, patient, attentive, joyous, reflective, sincere, and these would not be sufficient to describe as much as one would like.

Apart from deeper meanings, one must individualize morphological aspects that make such an expression concrete. The eyes must be "small, dark brown, deep set, without visible conjunctive, and well spaced." It is from these indispensable characteristics that the much appreciated expression so typical of this breed is derived. This would not be possible without an adequate development of the underlying bone structure.

The distance of the eyes is determined by the ampleness of the forehead and nasal cavity. Narrow frontal sinuses would bring the eyes close together and change the expression enormously, making it appear wolflike.

Equally important is the orbital conformation. It is composed laterally by the zygomatic arches with its frontal process, above and medially by the frontal bone and below by the lacrimal bone that lies above the supermaxillary bone. This is where the eye is set, and this determines its position and depth. These bones are also determined through the structures connected to it, such as the orbicular muscle, the retractors of the lateral corner and the eyelid ligaments. A wide and massive head allows for the orbit to find the correct diameters and gives the eye correct position.

In relation to the median axis of the head, the eyes are situated in a subfrontal position, this meaning that the axis of the eyelid forms an angle of 10 to 15 degrees with the head. If the inclination were superior (lateral and ultralateral position), the expression would be similar to that of Nordic dogs; on the other hand, if it totally lacked angulation, the eyes would assume a markedly round shape. In relation to the nasal cavity, they are on the same plane. This gives them a sweetness and dimension of expression that would be lost if they were up too far.

Another factor typical of the breed are the eyelids. As seen above, the eye is small and deep set, an impression that is accentuated by the development of the supracillary (brow) arch. The eyelids must delicately follow the contour of the eye in order to protect it from air, water and foreign objects. Their shape is typical: the upper eyelid is arched upward, assuming in the attentive dog an almost triangular shape, still adhering perfectly to the eye. The lower lid is oval and follows the orbit without showing the conjunctive. It is the outline of the eyelid, adherent to the eye, that gives the dog his intelligent, thoughtful and joyous look. When the skin is too relaxed and the bone, ligament and connective structures are lacking, the eyelids no longer adhere to the eyes and they open outward with a skinfold that shows the ocular-conjunctival mucosa (haw). This can be situated at the temporal corner of the eye or at the central one, as in the lozenge shape, typical of the St. Bernard. In more accentuated cases, there can be cutaneous skinfolds that extend to the forehead and the cheek and to the eyelid ptosis of the superior palpebra (upper lid). All of these defects give the dog a melancholy or sleepy expression, nontypical in the Newfoundland. Also not typical are the expressions created by large, round, set forward or bovine eyes.

The edge of the eyelid must be completely pigmented along with the third eyelid or nictitating membrane; an even partial depigmentation damages the expression quite a bit. It must also be said that the third eyelid must never be so developed as to hide the eye. This defect, which aside from ruining the look can have pathological consequences, is more common in the Landseer ECT (European Continental Type), and makes one think of past crossbreedings with other breeds.

Convex Superior
Muzzle Border

Heavy upper lip with separation in
the shape of a tight inverted V

Mastiff type, overabundant lips with flews
(lower labial pouches

Hound type, overhanging nose
with ears low set and posterior

Lupus type
Stop and long-pointed muzzle

Eyes close, High ear set, converging lateral planes of the muzzle

Large, round protruding eyes

$$\frac{\text{incisors upper} \quad 3 \quad 3}{\text{lower} \quad 3 \quad 3} = 12$$

$$\frac{\text{canines upper} \quad 1 \quad 1}{\text{lower} \quad 1 \quad 1} = 4$$

$$\frac{\text{premolars upper} \quad 4 \quad 4}{\text{lower} \quad 4 \quad 4} = 16$$

$$\frac{\text{molars upper} \quad 2 \quad 2}{\text{lower} \quad 3 \quad 3} = 10$$

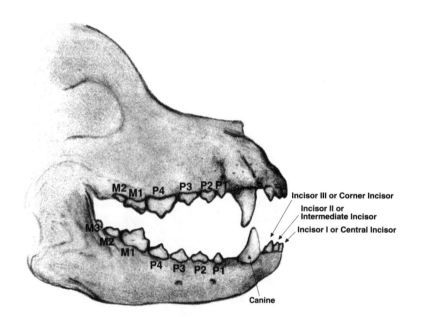

Once shape and position have been considered, no eye is ever correct without the right color of the iris. In the Newfoundland, the ideal color is dark brown, warm and deep; such an eye in itself gives security and is almost always accompanied by a sweet and balanced personality. Naturally all of the tones of brown, even if less intense, are acceptable. This is not true for yellow or light yellow eyes, which are objectionable. These colors are quite common in the browns and grays where they sometimes go unnoticed; however, they are immediately noticed on the blacks. From this comes the opportunity for a careful evaluation of crosses between the two colors in order to avoid black subjects with light eyes.

Teeth

There are 42 teeth in the adult dog, divided in the following manner: Upper incisors, 6; lower incisors, 6; upper canines, 2; lower canines, 2; upper premolars, 8; lower premolars, 8; upper molars, 4; lower molars, 6.

The upper jaw, starting from the center, has on each side: three incisors-incisor I or central incisor, incisor II or intermediate incisor, incisor III or corner incisor; one canine; four premolars P1, P2, P3, and P4, which is the larger upper tooth; and two molars M1 and M2. In the upper jaw between the corner incisors and the canine, there is a space called the interdental space, or diastema, where the corresponding inferior canine is inserted when the mouth is closed.

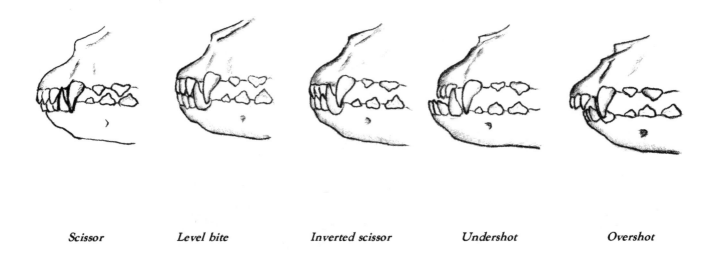

Scissor   *Level bite*   *Inverted scissor*   *Undershot*   *Overshot*

The same formula is true of the lower jaw, in which the largest tooth, however, is M1 or the first real molar. It also has one molar more per side. The upper P4 and the lower M1 are called carnivorous or lacerating teeth.

What is interesting about the teeth though is the closure, the insertion, the number and the size, a factor which cannot be ignored in a heavy retrieving breed such as the Newfoundland. As far as the closure of the mouth goes, the standard says that it may be a "scissor-like or level or even bite." In an orthognathous breed (one having a straight jaw without the lower jaw projecting), the upper jaw length is superior or equal to that of the lower jaw. The scissors closure, which is the most regular, calls for a disposition of the superior arcade incisors, which are further forward than the inferior ones, so that the lingual face of the first slides above the vestibular face of the second.

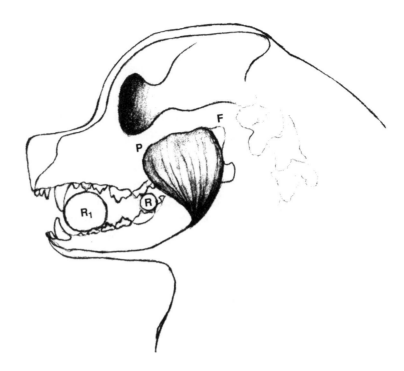

Actions of the Jaw:

Mastication
(Pf > Rf = second-degree lever)

Grasping
(Pf < Rf = third-degree lever)

The level or even bite occurs when the insertion of the teeth is such that they are superimposed one on the other; in this case their margins touch and are worn down more rapidly than with a scissors bite. It may also occur that in jaws of equal length, the vestibular-lingual relationship is totally inverted. The bottom incisors are then further forward than the top ones, this being called the antiverted or inverted scissors bite, which is still tolerated in breeds with short and squared faces.

When the jaws are not of equal lengths, the advancement of the longer one causes a loss of contact between the dental arches. This is called enognathism (upper prognathism or overshot) when the lengthening referred to is of the upper jaw; it is called prognathism (undershot) when it regards the lower jaw. Although prognathism is considered a typical trait in some breeds such as the boxer and does not cause mastication problems, enognathism, if accentuated to the point of brachygnathia (or parrot bite), can be a problem both in grasping and in chewing food.

Both of these characteristics are reason for expulsion in shows: they are hereditary and it seems that it may occur when breeding two subjects with unsymmetrical faces (short*long).

The number of teeth may vary in either direction. These anomalies frequently involve the lack of premolars and are to be evaluated while bearing in mind the importance of the teeth in question. Consequently, even if the absence of a P1 is acceptable, the absence of more important premolars or of molars is of greater importance. The dental examination must be done in depth so as not to overlook important teeth.

An aspect that should be carefully evaluated is the size of the teeth. The jaws of the Newfoundland must be strong and robust and the teeth adequate. The jaws behave as levers whose fulcrum consists of temporo-mandibular articulation. At the molar level, these joints behave as second degree levers (PF > PR); therefore, with this exceptional strength they are capable of breaking bones and other hard objects. At the level of the first premolars where the retrieving action occurs, these become third degree levers (PF < RF). This involves a minor force that is proportionate to the length of the RF arm, and that which the Newfoundland, a short and powerfully faced dog, needs in order to grip the arm of a person without hurting it. This action also involves the canines that prevent the body from slipping away with the mouth semi-closed.

The dog possesses a double dentition: the first one, known as deciduous teeth, is composed of thirty-two teeth and begins around twenty days of age with the eruption of the canines. This is followed in the next thirty days by the incisors and premolars P2, P3, and P4. P1, which is permanent, emerges at around four months of age, and at times, even later. The permanent teeth come out at the end of three months of age; at about four months the incisors are replaced and the M1 appear. Immediately following this, the adult canines appear and at around five months, the M2. The last tooth to emerge at about six or seven months is the third inferior molar.

Both the first and second dentures have progressive phases of wear and erosion of the margin of the incisors that manifest in wear of the central lobe and of wear of the whole rim. This wear can serve to assess the dog's age, keeping in mind that:

-At 1 year, the changing of teeth is finished and the teeth are clean and "unused."

-At 15 months, the inferior central incisors are flattened.

-At 18 months, the inferior central incisors show wear along the rims.

-At 21 months, the inferior intermediate incisors are flattened.

-At 3 years, the inferior intermediate incisors show wear along the rims.

-At 4 years, the superior central incisors show wear along the rims and the superior corner incisors are leveled.

-At 5 years, the superior intermediate incisors show wear along the rims.

-At 6 years, there is a progressive wearing down of the corner incisors and canines and a yellowing of the teeth.

This diagnostic method only suggests a dog's age because the use of the teeth is individual and tied to various factors: the type of diet or presence of parasites (fleas) that make the dog bite himself frequently. Alterations of the tooth enamel with yellowing or abnormal coloration may be caused by surviving distemper or treatment with tetracycline-based products too early in life.

Conrad degli Angeli Neri.

Summary

Based on the characteristic heads seen today we could present the traits in the following manner:

Fundamental positive traits:
1. Wide and massive head
2. Cranial-facial axis rigorously parallel
3. Correct muscular and skeletal development
4. Wide forehead
5. Squared face
6. Wide nose, at a right angle to the anterior plane of the lip
7. Small, dark brown, and well separated eyes
8. Eyelids that are closely fitted to the eye

Fundamental defective traits:
1. Narrow head
2. Poorly defined stop
3. Divergent cranial-facial axis
4. Bony cranium caused by underdevelopment of the temporal muscle in relation to the bone
5. Flat cranium due to lack of bone development in relation to the temporal muscle
6. Long or pointed face
7. Relaxed lips; pronounced lower lips; excessive flews
8. Small nose, meaty or protrudent on the labial plane
9. Eyes that are too close, light, round, protruding or with visible conjunctive
10. Enognathism or prognathism (overshot or undershot bite)

The Neck

As we will see further on when we discuss movement, the neck is of the utmost importance in the mechanics of motion of the dog because with its movements it acts as the center of gravity. It has as its base the seven cervical vertebrae and the very important muscles and ligaments that go from the head to the back. The shoulder, the sternum and the arm act as the motors of the cephalic-cervical (head-neck) balance beam. Its proportions must therefore be in perfect harmony with its function.

Ch. Zenith degli Angeli Neri, owned by S. Marcelli. Photo by F. La Rocca)

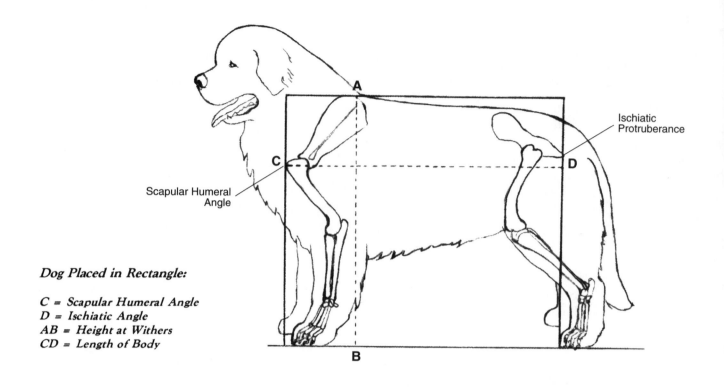

Ischiatic
Protruberance

Scapular Humeral
Angle

Dog Placed in Rectangle:

C = Scapular Humeral Angle
D = Ischiatic Angle
AB = Height at Withers
CD = Length of Body

Long-coupled dog.

Short-coupled dog.

In the Newfoundland the length of the neck, measured from the cervical to the first dorsal vertebrae, extended and in a horizontal position, is about 37 to 38 percent of the height at the withers. It is thus somewhat longer than in other trotting breeds, but without loosing solidity and muscular strength. When the dog is retrieving or pulling, both in the water and on land, it is very important for the neck to have robust muscular mass with strong insertions and a notable capacity for resistance. These are traits that cannot be found in a neck that is too long, which would be useful instead for dogs who need speed as a long neck acts as a facilitator for the sprint impulse. If the neck were too short, it would be less mobile and it would not be as helpful in the leaping motion of diving.

The neck should always be powerful with a circumference, measured midway between the nape of the neck and the withers, of about 83 to 84 percent of the height at the withers. The separation of the nape of the neck must be well marked and the upper profile must be convex because of the heavy muscle development. The neck is inserted into the shoulders with an ample base. Its axis should form, with the acromial process of the shoulder blade (or scapula), a 90-degree angle. This seems to be the best balance to help with movements upward and downward and changes of the center of gravity during activities.

Subjects are sometimes bred with long necks; although this may seem elegant and spectacular for show purposes, it is useless and even dangerous for function. In order to balance his heavy lever, the dog must hold his neck very straight, holding the front rigid, and putting weight on the hind legs. In the long run, these are situations that may result in gait defects and problems with the spine.

To make the aspect of the neck even more massive, there is a thick coat on the inferior border that reaches the chest from below the throat. This skin (or dewlap), soft and elastic, must never hang such as is the case of Mastiffs. It must be said that skin that hangs usually results from both general cutaneous relaxation and relaxation of the ligaments. Thus, while on the head too much skin causes wrinkles and eyelid ptosis (or sag), in the body it is often associated with lordosis, (or downward curvature of the lumbar spine or a weak topline), oscillating elbows, and metacarpals that are too flexed.

The Body

If, as has been previously noted, function must always be the guide and the meter of evaluating a working dog, this is even more true when dealing with structures deeply involved in the mechanics of standing and movement.

The body has a double significance: while the thoracic portion holds the pulmonary and cardiovascular system, the withers, back, flank and hindquarters constitute the organs of transmission of the machine that is the body in movement, where head and neck function as the balance beam and the legs alternate in the functions of propulsion and shock absorption.

In the Newfoundland, the length of the body, measured from the tip of the shoulder (scapula-humeral angle) to the tip of the buttocks (ischiatic protuberance) is a bit more than 110 percent of the height measured to the withers. This means that his body may fit within a rectangle.

This relation in lengths derives both from the backward curve of the ribs and from the proportion of the loins, which must be flexible. The measure of the intensity of the mass in relation to the length of the body is expressed by the following formula:

$$\text{body index} = \frac{(\text{length of the body} \times 100)}{\text{thoracic circumference}}$$

The Newfoundland presents values of about 78. Thus, we are dealing with a mesomorph that we prefer not to classify as a trotter or as a galloper, but as a swimmer. He seems, in fact, built specifically for this purpose.

The Thorax (Anterior Chest and Thoracic Rib Cage)

The important attributes needed in such an athletic animal are above all endurance and great cardiac and respiratory capacity. The chest must be well developed in all three dimensions: height (from the back to the sternum), width (at the level of the greatest dorsal diameter) and depth. The depth, measured from the manubrium of the sternum to the ninth fake rib, appears to be a very important measurement. It results from the distance between and the oblique alignment of the ribs. The width of the intercostal spaces and the backward curving of the ribs allow for a major expansion of the

Overweight dog with Lordosis (concave weak topline), down in pasterns and poor angulation.

Long-coupled dog. Light boned. Tucked-up abdomen with cifosis (convex) topline.

thorax during the act of breathing, under the action of the small and large dentate, serratus and the scalenus muscles.

An ample, well-curved, and deep thorax should observe the following formula:

$$\text{thoracic index} = \frac{(\text{width of thorax} \times 100)}{\text{height of thorax}} = 75$$

Ch. Dilysdegli Angeli Neri.

Such a thorax demonstrates a positive trait. Its height should surpass that of the elbow, but it should have such a conformation that does not interfere with the movement of the limbs; wide and rounded above, it narrows in the inferior portion, staying clear of the elbows.

Barrel thoraxes or narrow keel thoraxes, short or shallow are quite unacceptable in the Newfoundland.

The anterior and lateral borders of the thorax are determined by the superior margins of the limbs: the shoulder blade and the humerus. These outline the chest which is wide, muscled, and measures, from one tip of the shoulder to the other, about 35 percent of the height at the withers.

The angle of the scapula and humerus also determines the lateral profile of the chest. When these are straight with a wide scapula-humeral angle, it appears flat; on the other hand, when they are overly inclined, the lateral profile of the chest appears to protrude excessively.

The floor or inferior line of the thorax takes its form from the sternum, which continues through its xiphoid process to the abdomen, maintaining an almost horizontal line. A retracted, tucked-up stomach such as that of the Greyhound is a typical defect.

Further up and back, the thorax continues with the flanks, which must not be concave, but moderately rounded and short. This indicates a corresponding development of the thorax in an antero-posterior direction.

The Withers

The region of the withers is situated between the base of the neck and the back. This region includes the first five thoracic vertebrae. These have a spineous apophysis (or projection) in their upper portion that acts as a tension lever and that must, therefore, be tall and perfectly inclined. On these there is a meeting of the following: on one side the cervical ligament that begins at the head and is connected to the dorsal and lumbar vertebrae and the splenius and rhomboideus muscles that sustain the head and neck; on the other side the ileo-spinal muscle that from the iliac wing goes to the withers, neck and dorsalis maximus muscles.

A correct tension of the spine derives from the balance of these forces and consequently a good transmission of the impulses that originate in the hind region. The rhomboid and trapezius muscles connect the withers to the shoulder blade giving correct mobility. The withers must thus have a correct height and length, elevating harmoniously on the line of the back, which must be on the same level as the hind.

A dog with a lowered withers usually presents a narrow scapular-humeral angle, and appears thrust forward. One must be careful not to consider a withers tall just because of the rampant conformation of those dogs that present too wide an angle with straight shoulder blades and humerus, and which are taller in the front than in the back.

The withers is the reference point for measuring the height of the dog; the height is evaluated at the level of the fifth thoracic vertebrae, which is the tallest. In the Newfoundland, because of the position of the shoulder blades, it is not easily palpable; thus, one considers the most elevated margin of this process as an index. One must remember though, that even if the growth process ends at about one year of age, the structure of the withers is not complete until around 18 to 20 months when the ligaments and muscles are toned.

The Back

The back is made up of the last eight dorsal vertebrae, on which the remaining ribs and the four false ribs articulate. Thus, its length is a positive aspect because it indicates the width of the intercostal spaces, obliqueness of the ribs and a larger flexibility of the region.

The superior spinal apophysis maintain their backward inclination up to the tenth vertebrae and then assume the opposite forward inclination that is also found in the lumbar vertebrae. We are dealing with a structure that is particularly adapted to the function of transmission and support for which it was made and that finds its maximum efficiency in a straight topline profile. This is maintained such by the muscles and ligaments that balance the tension. When this balance is lacking, the back can be overpowered by the weight of the body, thus assuming a concave (slack) aspect that is called lordosis, or it can curve in the other direction, upward, taking on a convex shape called kyphosis (roached). While the lordosis is caused by a general looseness of the ligaments, at times a neck that is too straight reduces the action of the cervical ligaments. In a hind that is too high, kyphosis is caused, according to some, by a rickett-like condition with ossification of the intervertebral fibro-cartilaginous discs. According to others, it is caused instead by a disproportion between the anterior and posterior push. Both, however, reduce the impulse and are in contrast with the functionality of the subject.

Lower Back and Flanks

Formed by the seven lower back (lumbar) vertebrae, it has been defined as "the bridge that holds together the front and back." The flanks connect the lower back to the tail bone and consequently to the hind. Like a bridge, it must be moderately arched in order to better sustain the effort without sagging.

In the Newfoundland the flanks are somewhat lengthened which allows for better flexibility while swimming and which favors a slight undulation during movement. Naturally, it must never be too long and thereby lose solidity. On the contrary, it must be strong, wide and well muscled, characteristics that accentuate the convex aspect. A weak flank, as seen previously for the back, disperses the strength of the hind and is negative for function.

The Croup

The croup represents a very important structure in the mechanics of the animal because it is the center of transmission, where the action exercised by the posterior is projected upon the trunk and then transmitted forward. It has as a bone structure the two coaxials, formed by the ilium, ischium and pubic bones, and the sacrum, which is made up of the fusion of the three sacral vertebrae. This complex is called the pelvic belt or pelvis. From the unification of the ilium, ischium and pubic bones, the acetabulum is formed upon which the head of the femur is articulated. The coaxials are connected to the sacrum by a series of ligaments that maintain their stability.

Several muscle groups have an influence on this complex which, as we will later see, are connected to the movement of the hind quarters: in particular the psoas, the gluteus, and the ischiotibialis. Under their action, the hind acquires the function of a lever with its fulcrum in the coxofemoral articulation. The length and inclination (angle) thus have a very specific meaning. In the Newfoundland, this

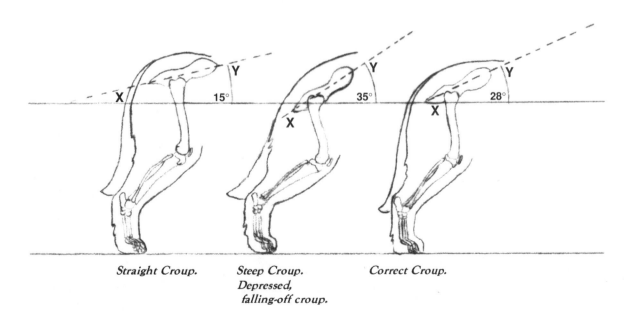

Straight Croup. Steep Croup. Correct Croup.
Depressed,
falling-off croup.

lever measured from the tip of the hip to the tip of the buttocks, represents about 33 percent of the height at the withers and supplies an ample lever to the power generated by the muscles.

The horizontal inclination of the hind, evaluated by the line that unites the iliac wing to the ischial protuberance is of about 28 to 30 percent. This inclination, halfway between the horizontal and the concave hind, allows for large movements of the limbs and the strength and muscular resistance needed for swimming.

Furthermore, the hind must be wide, proportioned to the diameter of the chest, which is needed in a breed that requires the development of power and resistance from a solid base. This relative width is also helpful for floatation stability during swimming.

The hind must be somewhat rounded with great muscular development.

In females, a wide and well-built pelvis provides an asset for reproduction.

The Tail

The tail is made up of caudal vertebrae, elevator muscles, flexor muscles and lateral adductor muscles. It follows the profile of the sacrum; its insertion is thus related to the upper inclination of the croup, corresponding to the line drawn from the iliac wing (crest) to the attachment of the tail,

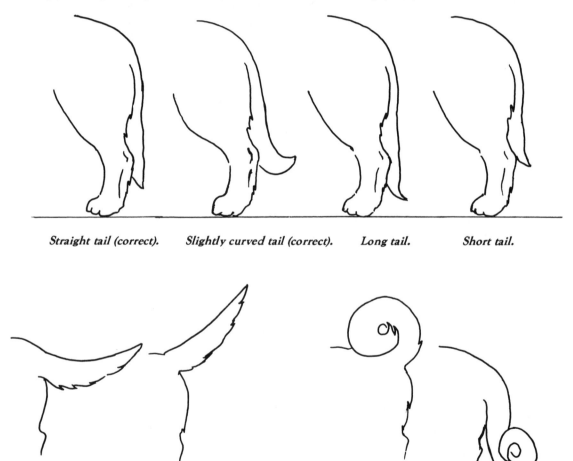

Straight tail (correct).   *Slightly curved tail (correct).*   *Long tail.*   *Short tail.*

Tail carry in movement or excited.   *Defective tails, curved back and ring tail.*

which is about 22 percent on a horizontal plane. Usually, a poorly inclined croup corresponds to a high attachment of the tail; if the hind is concave, the attachment of the tail is too low. If the hind is well formed, the tail presents a good insertion and functions at its best as a rudder while swimming.

The tail is held horizontally while swimming and is rigid; its lateral movement aids in directional changes. For this purpose it is also necessary to have well developed muscles in the tail, thus it must have a wide and strong attachment and taper off gradually.

When the dog is relaxed, the tail length must reach down to the hock joint or a bit lower. The profile is straight or with a slight curve at the tip. Normally it is held down; when the dog moves quickly, it is held instead at the height of the back. One must always keep in mind however that, like the ear, the tail represents a nonverbal expression in the dog. Thus, it could happen that it is held higher when the dog is excited, especially in the male, while a timid and distrusting dog holds it between the hind legs in a position of defense.

An important defect is a tail held curled on the back, such as that of the Nordic dogs. Other tails that are considered defective are those held in the shape of a ring and lowered, or which have vertebral ankylosis (or kink).

The hair on the tail is the same length all over and does not form fringes; it presents short and shinier hairs only at the attachment, which makes powerful and well inserted tails even more evident.

Front Quarters

By observing movement, it is easy to understand that the front quarters are mainly used for support. During the successive phases of weight bearing, the burden of much of the body weight rests on the anterior limbs with increased intensity relative to an increase in speed; its structure must thus be suitable for absorbing this pressure.

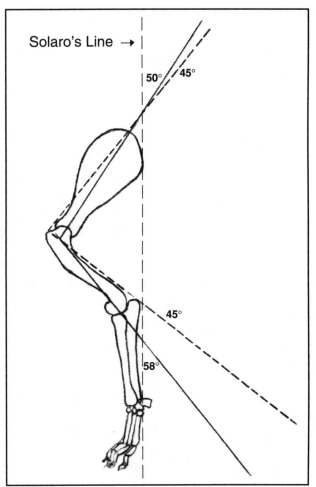

Shoulder angles using different reference points.

The shoulder, which is the proximal region of the anterior quarter, is the best example. It has the shoulder blade as a base. This is a flat, wide bone that is not connected to the body by a real articulation, rather by an elastic ligament complex that anchors it securely to the trunk, forming the scapula (or shoulder blade) girdle. The shoulder blade has more or less the shape of an upside down triangle, at the vertex or zenith of which is the scapula-humeral articulation. The acromial process (or spine) divides the scapula in all its length, determining its axis. It can be found by palpation, though it may be somewhat difficult because of strong muscle masses. By putting the dog in a stacked, erect position, its inclination allows one to evaluate the correct angulation of the shoulder. In the Newfoundland, which has well-inclined shoulder blades, it is about 50 degrees.

If one uses other reference points for evaluation, such as the tip of the shoulder, one would find different values that appear quite unrealistic. Its length must be measured on the same axis as well. This appears to be about 30 percent of the height to the withers.

A long and properly inclined scapula (shoulder blade) allows for a long stride and a good limb extension while swimming. However, a straight scapula usually corresponds to an overly inclined humerus; with the elbows posteriorly displaced, the center of gravity is moved forward, and the neck appears shorter. The result is a subject which is "thrown forward" with a heavy and nonflexible gait.

A positive trait of the shoulder blade is its mobility, not to be confused with looseness of the scapula girdle, which allows for abnormal movements with nonadherent shoulders and weaving elbows. It can make the following movements: flexion, extension, adduction, abduction, and circumduction. These movements occur principally with the aid of the trapezius, rhomboid, and serratus ventralis muscles of the scapula. The first two muscles, being adductors, bring the tips of the shoulder blades closer to the body, within the limits allowed by the corporal conformation. In the Newfoundland, these are quite far apart, both because of the width of the thorax and the thickness of the subscapula and large dentate muscles.

All of the muscles in the region should be well developed; the muscles which coordinate the movement of the arm and forearm are connected to the shoulder blade.

The Arm

Contrary to what occurs in humans, the arm of four-legged species adheres to the body to which it is connected for most of the upper two thirds.

The basic structure is given by the scapula (shoulder blade) and the humerus, a long bone that articulates by means of the glenoid cavity. These two together form the scapular-humeral angle and are closely tied together in such a way that altered dimensions or angles of one have repercussions on the other and vice versa.

The humerus, in the Newfoundland, is about as long as the shoulder blade, about 30 percent of the height, and its inclination on a horizontal plane is about 58 to 60 degrees. The scapula-humeral angle is thus about 108 to 110 degrees. These values refer to the real measurements of the bone, excluding the tip of the elbow, which also includes the olecranon.

As the angle of the humerus goes, we have just seen what happens when it is excessive. On the other hand, when it is not inclined enough we find ourselves looking at a dog that stands tall on the front quarters, with a straight neck, good looking, but with an affected, nonproductive gait. The center of gravity is moved back, which puts stress on the hind, causing at times a looseness of the vertebral column. There can exist a whole series of compensatory combinations between length and angle that does not allow for proper function.

According to Solaro, "A good indicative point to measure the proper inclination of the humerus is the tip of the elbow, dropping a perpendicular line from the most posterior part of the scapula to the ground. It should intersect the tip of the elbow."

Length and correct angles are the basis for correct movement; to these there must also be added solid bone structure and strong muscles, indispensable for the tasks performed by the breed.

As previously stated, a large part of the muscles that move the arm are connected to the shoulder blade. For the sake of simplicity we can divide them as follows: extensors (supraspinatus and infraspinatus) and flexors (large rotondus, coracobrachialis and deltoid). From the name it is easy to understand that these have the respective function of extending and flexing the humerus, a movement that normally occurs almost parallel to the median plane of the body.

When the elbow is moved outward (open elbow, out at elbow), this usually suggests defects in the forearm and metacarpal (barrel-legged). This is also true when the elbow is rotated inward (closed elbow) that is connected to pinched elbows.

The oscillation of the elbow that is seen during movement results instead, as previously stated from loose ligaments and muscles.

Also present in the arm region are the muscles that permit the movement of the forearm: in front there are the flexors (biceps, and anterior brachialis), and in the back there is the anconeus, which has the function of extending the forearm on the humerus, and thus is very important in swimming. These muscles must be well developed and are felt as a rounded mass, when sliding with the hand from the shoulder to the elbow.

The Forearm

In the Newfoundland, more than in other breeds, the arm acquires a particular importance relative to the other areas of the body. In the specific function of swimming it becomes, along with the carpal, matacarpal and foot, the oar with which the dog moves forward while floating on the water.

It is made up of the radius and the ulna that finish in the olecranon (elbow joint); this articulates with the humerus by way of the angular ginglymus, which allows mainly movements such as flexion

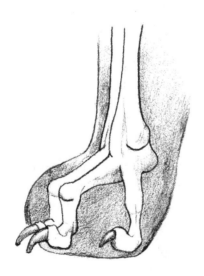

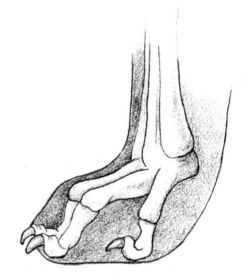

Cat-type foot. Correct.   *Hare foot. Defective.*

and extension, and in the dog also allows pronation (downward movement) of the paw and supination (upward movement) of the paw.

In order to be efficient and resistant, the forearm must present an adequate but compact construction. It is relatively short, about 30 percent of the height to the withers, but perfectly made for the amount of force that it must exert. It must not be thin or fragile but wide with solid bone structure, without being spongy with strong muscles and tendons.

It may seem superfluous to remember that in the arm, the motor muscles of a distal segment are situated with their center toward a contiguous proximal segment; therefore, while the muscles that move the forearm are situated near the humerus, those that circle the radius and ulna work for the metacarpals and phalanges. On the front face of the radius, we thus find the phalanges and metacarpal extensors; on the back side, we find the various flexors, most important of which is the oblique flexor of the metacarpal. Starting in two distinct fascia from the humerus and olecranon, this strong flexor reaches the pisiform and the metacarpal bones. It determines the carpo-cubital canal that must be well marked in order to indicate a more appropriate lever for the pisiform and thus a major strength of the forearm, the correct direction of which must be perpendicular to the ground. Apart from any pathological curvatures, any displacements from the vertical are mainly revealed in relation to defects in the surrounding areas. Thus a straight shoulder with an inclined humerus brings the forearm backward (underneath itself); on the other hand, a straight humerus makes it advance (outside itself).

The Carpal

The carpal follows the vertical line of the forearm. It corresponds to the wrist in humans and is made up of seven bones placed in two lines, one above the other. They are connected together and with the contiguous regions by a series of very complex articulations and ligaments. From this one can conclude that loose ligaments may easily alter the inclination.

The most frequent deviation is toward the inside, with outward rotation of the metacarpal and of the foot; this is called mancinism (pedis valgus) or toeing out; when the movement is outward, with the metacarpal and foot rotated inward causing cagnilism (pedis vara) or toeing in. Less frequent is the movement forward, or forward displacement. However, in young subjects, an anterior convexedness of the carpal is physiological and connected to the growth cartilage of the bone.

In the Newfoundland, the carpal must be wide, short, and very solid.

The Metacarpal

The metacarpal comprises the five metacarpal bones, each with a cylindrical and elongated shape, excepting the metacarpaleus, which is much shorter than the others. The metacarpal may be flexed, extended and moved laterally; these movements are of great importance for the mechanics of the animal: they are shock absorbers. Its inclination in relation to the carpal and forearm allows it to absorb and distribute the upward and downward pressures coming from actions and reactions of contact with the ground. In this way, these traumatic reactions are not passed on to the elbow and shoulder.

In the Newfoundland the metacarpal is relatively short but well inclined (72 to 75 degrees). It must be wide and very solid, both to hold the body weight and to have a better spread while swimming.

Metacarpals that are too long, too flexed, straight, or deviated from the perpendicular line constitute a defect.

The Foot

As in the case of the metacarpal, the foot has the function of a shock absorber. It is formed by five toes, each one formed by three phalanges and a nail, numerous tendons and plantar pads that are meaty and hard and that protect the foot. Of these five toes, only four have contact with the ground; the one that does not touch is the first, which is articulated at the metacarpal and which is shorter; it corresponds to the thumb in people. The foot is large and wide in order to support the body's weight.

The toes must be strong and arched in order to allow for good support and a strong hold when the dog must move on slippery ground. This structure gives the foot a rounded shape called "cat's foot" which is typical of the breed. The "hare foot" shape with the two central phalanges that are longer as well as open toes or flat toes caused by ligament and tendon weakness are considered defective.

As for the Newfoundland's foot, something must be said about its being webbed. It has often been said that the foot is webbed as an adaptation to the function of swimming. Although it is true that the membrane between the toes is well developed, and that while swimming, the dog opens its toes and uses them for a better hold on the water, the term webbed foot refers to the foot of other species such as the beaver or some aquatic birds, which have a true natatorial membrane. In the canine species, an interdigital membrane formed of thin fiber instead connects the toes. Depending on the breed, this membrane can be more or less accentuated. In the Newfoundland, as in other subjects with strong and arched toes, its development reaches the second phalanx, and is thus a useful complement for its function.

Hind Quarters and the Thigh

If the front quarters have support as their main purpose, the hind quarters are much more active in propulsion. The thigh, which constitutes the first segment, has the femur as underlying bone structure; the femur is articulated with its head in the acetabular cavity of the pelvis. The coxofemoral

Correct front.

Front toeing in.

Front toeing out.

Correct rear feet.

Rear toeing in. Cow-hocked.

Posterior toeing out.

articulation is the fulcrum through which the push is transmitted to the body; thus, its morpho-functional integrity is of utmost importance.

In respect to the bones of the anterior quarter, the thigh is longer than the others, about 34 percent of the height to the withers. The femur forms with the coaxial axis an angle of about 95 degrees, and is inclined on the horizontal plane about 70 degrees. The thigh must be strong and solid like the buttocks, which form the posterior margin, and must be thick. This indicates the development of muscles and consequently correct functioning. A subject showing a malformation of the hip, such as dysplasia, will take the weight off the hind quarters, using these muscles as little as possible. Lack of exercise causes a lack of development of the muscle fibers and consequently causes thin and underdeveloped thighs.

The coxofemoral articulation allows the thigh to flex, extend, adduct and abduct. In the Newfoundland, these combined movements are particularly evident while swimming and are useful to the dog for maintaining stability while floating. The thigh has a complex series of muscles; a few, such as the pectineus, act on the femur (flex). Most instead act contemporaneously on the thigh and leg, so that although the semimembranous and the semitendinous muscles, which are placed in the back and form the buttocks, are extensors of the thigh and flexors of the leg, the femoral bicep, tensor of the lateral fascia, and femoral quadricept, placed in the front, extend the leg and flex the thigh. Based on the intervention of the antagonist muscles, thigh and leg will be able to move separately.

The Leg

The leg is formed by the tibia, connected to the femur through the hinge-like articulation of the knee, and by the fibula, a long and narrow bone situated in the posterior lateral position. At the bottom, the tibia touches the hock and articulates at the astragalus. Its length is a bit superior or equal to that of the femur, and its inclination on a horizontal plane is of about 40 degrees. This provides for a correct angle and proportion allowing for a correct extension of the limb, making the muscles efficient both on land and in the water. The most important of these muscles is the surae triceps. It is formed by the gastrocnemius and the soleus muscles, which are connected to the calcaneus by the Achilles tendon, and it is one of the principal motors in the hind push. Along with the long peroneus tendon, this muscle works extending the metatarsus. Always on the posterior face are the superficial and deep flexors of the phalanges. Anteriorly, there are the anterior tibialis, the metatarsal flexor and the extensor of the phalanges.

Fana Prinzessin v. Luxemburg, owned by the Wassemberg Kennels.

Ch. Larissima's Baccardi (brown), Ch. Crawl (black) and West Side Igor (Landseer, white and black).

The Hock and the Tarsals

This component is formed by six short bones, disposed in two rows and solidly connected together. In the proximal row are the two most important bones: the astragalus and calcaneus. The astragalus presents a particular surface shaped in a spiral-like manner, and upon which it articulates, like a negative image, with the tibial cochlea. The particular structure of the articulation and the eccentric disposition of short and strong crossed ligaments allow, once maximum tension is reached, a sprint that aids the push. Equally important is the calcaneus that, aside from giving a sold insertion point for the Achilles tendon, is also used for the passing of the superficial flexor tendon of the phalanges.

The entire articulation of the tarsal must be very solid because it is upon it that all of the efforts and reactions to impulses converge. Furthermore, the dog carries the weight of its body on the hind quarters, both in the beginning of the gait and at the moment of jumping or diving.

Defects of positioning deviating from the median plane of the body are: varus (rotation inward of the tarsal) and valgus (outward rotation of the tarsal).

The Metatarsal

What has been said about the heel is true also for the metatarsal. Formed by the metatarsal bones, one of which is rudimental, it presents a more rounded section in relation to the front, which is wide and flat. The metatarsal constitutes, along with the tarsal and the phalanges, a second-degree lever from which the impulse of the posterior is sent. It has as its fulcrum the point where it touches the ground. Its resistance is in the tibial-tarsal articulation where the weight of the body is concentrated and the power is at the top of the calcaneus that the surae tricep acts upon.

The metatarsal must thus be short and very solid, with strong tendons that are perfectly positioned. When the dog is stacked, the metatarsal should be perpendicular to the ground and form with the leg an angle of about 130 degrees.

At rest, it is held slightly inclined forward and the tibio-metatarsal angle appears a bit more closed. If the metatarsal is too flexed, it will be positioned underneath itself. However, a too wide angle results in heels that are so straight that they tend to be inclined forward with serious functional disorders.

The Foot

The back foot is a bit less wide than the front one, but always solidly in touch with the ground and rounded. The fifth toe, or rear dewclaw, which may appear rudimental, is situated at the level of the metacarpal. It must be removed in the first days of life because it has no use and may cause distortions or traumas if it hooks onto something.

Perpendicularity

Discussions of the limbs have often mentioned the defects of perpendicularity with the ground. It thus is useful to define this term and to schematically see the main concepts. Essentially, the term means "the relation between the angle and direction of the limbs and the line that falls perpendicular to the ground." This will be examined for the front and back limbs, from a profile view and from the front and rear view placing the dog on a horizontal plane.

Front Perpendicularity from a Profile View

A vertical line dropped from the tip of the shoulder must reach the ground barely touching the foot. If the line falls too far forward, the subject is said to be "standing underneath himself;" if it falls too far backwards it is called "standing outside himself."

A vertical line dropped from the center of the humero-radial articulation must divide the forearm and metacarpal into two almost equal parts, touching the ground just behind the foot. In relation to this line, if the carpal is arched forward it is said to be "knuckling over;" if it is arched backwards it is said to be "down in pastern."

Front Perpendicularity from a Frontal View

A vertical line dropped from the tip of the shoulder must divide in two equal parts the combination of the forearm, carpal, matacarpal and foot. If the line falls toward the inside of the foot, the subject is said to be "open in front (or out at elbow);" if it falls outward, he will be said to be "closed in front (or pinched front)."

These terms are not to be confused with a subject that is "narrow and wide," which are terms that refer to the width of the thorax.

If the forearms are correct but the metacarpals are deviated outward "toeing out" occurs; if they are deviated inward "toeing in" occurs.

Posterior Perpendicularity froma Profile View

A vertical line dropped from the tip of the buttocks must barely touch the tip of the toes, with the metatarsal vertically placed. If the line falls toward the inside of the foot, the dog is said to be "standing underneath himself in the back;" if it falls amply forward of the foot, he is said to be "standing outside of himself in the back."

Posterior Perpendicularity from a Back View

A vertical line dropped from the tip of the buttocks must divide into two equal parts the combination of the tip of the hock, the metatarsal and the foot. If the whole limb is outside the line, the subject is called "open behind;" if it is inside the line he is called "closed behind." When the heels are rotated inward, and the feet outward, the subject is said to be "toeing out;" if the heels are rotated outward and the feet inward, he is called "toeing in posteriorly."

The Coat

In the Newfoundland, the coat represents a very important complement to function; in harsh climates, particularly during swimming it provides protection. It is a closed double coat made up of two layers; the outer coat, which is somewhat transparent, and the undercoat, which is woolly, waterproof and dense and keeps the water away from the skin. Length and distribution vary depending on the region of the body. The head, the side of the ears and the front of the legs are covered by a short, thick layer. It becomes longer and gains an undercoat on the neck and body where it measures about 3 1/2 inches. On the central posterior of the ear, throat, chest, inferior profile of the body and the

Markings: (1) Black dog with white chest blaze, white tail tip and white toes (acceptable). (2) Ideal Landseer markings. (3) Black dog with excessive white markings (defect). (4) White dog with excessive black markings and ticking (defect).

tail, it reaches a maximum length of 4 1/2 inches and forms thick fringes on the posterior side of the legs. The hair is straight and thin; when brushed against its natural line, it tends to return naturally to its normal position. An open coat that is raised and stands up as in the Nordic dogs or one that is lacking a second layer, such as in the Labrador, is considered a defect. This is also true of hair that is too wavy or kinky and disturbs the soft and flowing curve of the body.

Colors of the Coat

Three colors are admitted by the FCI standard:

1. Black: the dominant color is shinier where the hair is short. In other regions, the bottom layer makes it appear more opaque. The fringes, particularly if the dog is often in the water, may become reddish. On a black coat, a white marking on the chest, on the tip of the tail and on the feet is allowed.

2. Brown: the coat of a brown dog may be darker (chocolate) or lighter (bronze). As in the black, white marks at the chest, the tips of the tail and on the feet are allowed. In the brown dog, the skin is pink, as is the mucosa; the nose is pigmented brown.

3. White and black, or Landseer: the main color is white with localized black marks. These marks are preferably in the following regions: correctly drawn saddle, black croup that extends to the tail, black head with a white line that goes up the forehead. The beauty and symmetry of the black marks is held in consideration; the black marks must be clear on the underlying white areas; spotting (or ticking), which ruins this effect, is considered a defect. A subject presenting large, asymmetrical spots or a prevalence of black is considered mismarked. In the patched subjects, the nose must be black and the eyelids pigmented.

4. Grays are inadmissible according to F.C.I. rules.

The Problem of Color

Color has always been, even in the past, one of the most contested and debated aspects of the breed. If black is recognized by all as the dominant color in the Newfoundland, the other colors have evoked varied opinions depending on the country and the time. Even today, for example, Canada does not accept brown, while the United States recognizes gray as well as the three other European colors.

As far as the white and black goes, this has been the subject of much confusion and will need a bit of history in order to become clearer. In the 1700s many breeds were bred with the Newfoundlands of the namesake island in order to obtain tall subjects. At that time, the colors were more varied: black, brown, black and white, black and brown, black with reddish hues and highlights, and gray. In 1810, Teel stated that the breed had degenerated; and in 1840, Smith believed that the original dog was one with a black or bronze coat. In 1837, Sir Edwin Landseer created the famous painting, "A Distinguished Member of the Humane Society," which was to represent the famous dog Bob, winner of the Royal Humane Society's Gold Medal for having saved more than twenty-three people from the waters of the Thames. The model was Paul Pry, a white and black subject. In his paintings, Landseer always preferred this color, so much so that it took on his name.

In 1886, the first breed standard stated that the color was black with a white star. In honor of Landseer, a class for the not entirely black Landseer was also created. Many years later, the debate still raged. In 1932, the S.I.T. newsletter printed an interesting discussion that had appeared in "Our Dogs" between those who were for the mix of the two varieties and those who were against it. Colnaghi concluded the following: "The origin of the white in the Newfoundland is not certain. The white and black had a flat head, but was larger than the black. The mixture of the two varieties sought to obtain, and has obtained, greater height in the blacks and created a better head in the white and black, including the dome shaped cranium. The typical Newfoundland remains the one with a black coat. The white and black variety, or Landseer, is accepted. We believe that brown patches in the Landseer must not be admitted, and we further believe that there must no longer be a mixture of the two varieties."

Heim, Trager and Buckhard were of the same opinion. In the following years, the different opinions caused the breeders of different countries to behave in varying manners. As a result, the two varieties continued to be mixed in England, America, Canada, Scandinavia and Holland. In the rest of Europe, particularly in Germany and Switzerland where the breeding of the Landseer was common, the two colors were raised separately. The only exception was made by Otto Walterspiel who imported the black Storm of Sparry from England, using him with female Landseers and obtaining a variety more similar to the black.

Although pure breeding of the white and black variety had better markings and pureness of the coat as an advantage, it also provided an imprinting of atavistic genes that modified the subjects. These ancestral traits or types have a tendency to recur after disappearing for two or more generations (demonstrating a kind of intermittent heredity). These subjects produced a head less marked, longer and narrower, chiseled, tending to divergence, a face cone-shaped with a protruding nose and reduced labial volume, larger eyes, at times lighter and protruding. They were taller than the black but with more fragile bone structure and less angled; the coat was shorter with less undercoat, and the temperament was more excitable.

This variation in type was nothing but a genetic trail of the Landseer's origins, a return toward the basic ancestors; and it created an evident differentiation not only among the white and blacks and blacks, but also in the purebreds, and those crossed with the blacks.

In 1960, the FCI decided to separate the two varieties as the black or brown Newfoundland and the white and black Landseer. This decision, while favored by both Germany and Switzerland, was opposed by the Nordic countries and Holland. In the end, a solution was found: the European Landseer would become an independent breed called the E.C.T. Landseer (European Continental Type), with a different number in the classification of the canine breeds and with its own standard

Sexual dimorphism (males and females of the same species are different both physically and in behavior.

Ch. Zelda and Ch. Zeus degli Angeli Neri.

made by Germany. The Newfoundland breed would admit the white and black, or Landseer, but these dogs would have to be identical in every way to the blacks. The separation, in truth, was only partially respected. England, the United States and Canada, which did not belong to the F.C.I., continued to import the Landseer E.C.T. (European Continental Type) from Europe for selection of the coat, later exporting Landseer Newfoundlands. A further confusion was created because some of these subjects possessed the correct type, while others had the ECT type. Atavistic characteristics also appeared in some black subjects, offspring of the Landseer. In 1978, the F.C.I. assembly, held in Mexico and proposed by Germany, excluded the white and black coat from the Newfoundland breed, but in 1981, in Dortmund, this color was readmitted as a result of the intervention of Holland and Finland. Additional requests made by Switzerland to once again exclude this variety were not accepted.

Today's F.C.I. classification is comprehensive; its wording is as follows under the "Mountain Dog" type:

75) Newfoundland (CDN-GB): black-bronze-white with black marks (Anglo-American Landseer)
78) Landseer European Continental Type (D-CH)

It is quite natural to wonder why there have been such conflicts. When trying to understand the situation, note breeders of the blacks on one side, wanting to keep their dogs pure and wanting to avoid surprises of color and traits. Basically, the black breeders find no advantage in breeding with the white and black; the larger size, used as a pretext, can be obtained by selection and in any case should not be sought at the risk of type and harmony. On the other side, we have breeders of the white and black, who cannot avoid breeding their dogs with the blacks periodically in order to maintain the right type and correct bone structure. With a bit of good will, a solution may be found for everyone. First of all, the white and black and the black subjects presenting the E.C.T. type must be penalized. This, which appears obvious, is not easy to achieve. One owning a dog with a pedigree believes that it is a right to breed the dog as one wishes, and then register the product of that breedings. Too often however, the choice is casual with significant negative effects from the breeding between colors. The breeding of the white and black Newfoundland requires much attention so as not to break the balance between coat and type. The total freedom of breeding of the two varieties has brought about

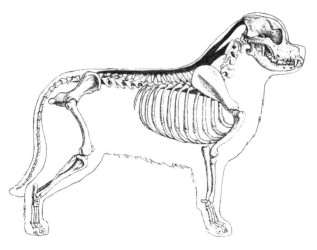

The Cervical Ligament.

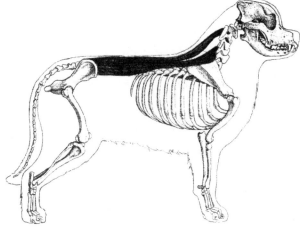

Ileo-Spinals Muscle.

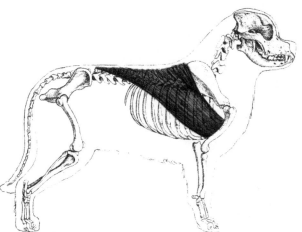

Grande Dorsalis Muscle.

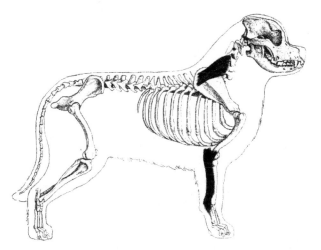

1. Angular Scapularis Muscle.
2. Oblique Flexor of the Metacarpal.

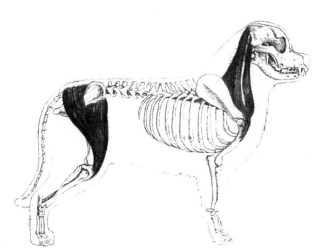

1. Brachio Cephalicus Muscle.
2. Tensor of the Fascia Lata Muscle

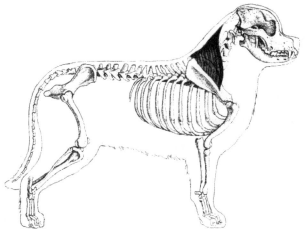

Trapezius Muscle.

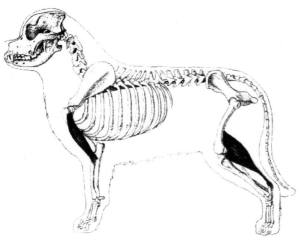

1. *Anterior Brachialis Muscle.*
2. *Triceps Surae Muscle.*

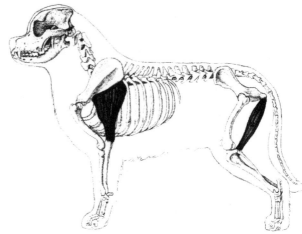

1. *Long Anconeus Muscle.*
2. *Semitendinous Muscle.*

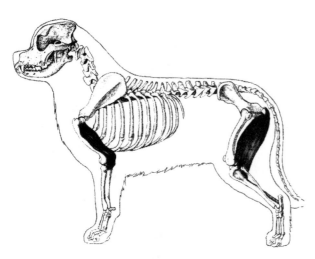

1. *Lateral Anconeus Muscle.*
2. *Semi Membranous Muscle.*

1. *Supraspinatus Muscle.*
2. *Deltoid Muscle.*
3. *Biceps Femoris Muscle.*

indiscriminate crossings. Today in Italy, we often find ourselves looking at those subjects that are defined as mismarked and considered defective: completely black dogs with white marks in regions not specified by the standard, metacarpals and forearms entirely white, entirely white chest, throat and stomach, white face and so forth.

This type of reproduction is the cause of regression without an aim at a precise scope and specific selection. Thus the need exists for an intervention that will allow cross breeding, but under strictly controlled conditions. Furthermore, the offspring of a Landseer and a black, as will be better explained later, are always carriers of the Landseer genes and potentially of other characteristics tied to it, and should be used only in the selection of this color. The black could thus maintain its pureness of type, to which the white and black could contribute at any time in which it is considered necessary. The first step to this goal would be to include on the pedigree the color of the parents along with their recessiveness. This already occurs in other countries and enables a more responsible choice for breeders.

Size and Weight

Size and weight have also often been the topic of discussion. Already in the 1800s, experts such as Mr. Mansfield declared themselves contrary to the idea of having continually taller subjects. The truth is, in past centuries dogs had been bred with island dogs in order to achieve spectacular height; this, along with cross breeding occurring on the island, also brought in new somatic characteristics and colors.

Personalities such as Heim, Buchner and Buckhard later stated the same things; Prof. Heim wrote, "Breeding with the primary idea of obtaining height is dangerous because one risks destroying the type and creating lymphatic dogs." Differing points of view were presented by the ideas of Doctor Gortlet, Landseer breeder, and of Mr. Brown who stated, "A large dog is better able to function in the water, so much so that there is no reason why we must not give the greatest importance to size!" Everyone agreed, however, that it was important to keep symmetry and proportion. More recently, M. Booth Chern wrote, "The size should be the medium one indicated by the standard or slightly larger, but it must never interfere with proportion. Size without balance and solidity has no value."

The values stated by the standard are a medium height of 28 inches in the male with a weight of 140 to 152 pounds, and 26 inches in the female with a weight of 121 to 130 pounds. This appears to be the best size to maintain the proper proportion between mass and stature. Naturally, a certain deviation from the mean is acceptable, but height above 30 to 32 inches rarely corresponds with correct proportion. These dogs are unbalanced and present the following characteristics: long legs, proportionately reduced transverse diameters, lengthened facial profiles. In the same way, subjects that are below this average do not possess the characteristics that categorize the Newfoundland as a large molossus. Once again, exaggeration of certain characteristics does not go along with the balance that is sought in the breed.

Furthermore, measurements must be precise and truthful. While weighing a dog is relatively easy, and all that is required is to observe the needle of the scale, the measurement of height provides the possibility of committing many errors that one must be aware of. The subject to be measured must be placed on a flat plane in a relaxed, standing position. The measuring stick must be perfectly perpendicular to the ground, and the transversal bar must be lowered to the highest tip of the withers, slightly compressing the hair.

Sexual Dimorphism

It is of the utmost importance to fully comprehend the meaning of this term because it sometimes happens that characteristics that have nothing to do with femininity and masculinity are confused with those that do. Sexual dimorphism is the physical or behavioral differences associated with the sex; males and females of the same species are different in appearance and behavior. The essential traits must remain identical in the male and in the female, although every good subject shows sexual characteristics in a secondary manner.

In the male, the head appears proportionately larger than in the female with a further development of the frontals and the brow arches. He presents a powerful head, larger nose, neck and muscles, and very developed bone structure.

In the female, everything appears more rounded and fluid without ever lacking substance. A narrow face, a poorly defined stop, a long face, or poor muscular and skeletal systems must never be confused with femininity. The female Newfoundland has all of the characteristics of the breed well in evidence, only they are a bit less pronounced and somewhat sweetened because of the natural sexual dimorphism.

Summary

In conclusion, with regards to the F.C.I. standard, there are certain defects that, particularly in the Newfoundland, are considered related to the construction or the type:

Defects of construction:
1. Vaccinism; cowhocked
2. Mancinism; east and west, toeing out, pinched elbows
3. Cagnolism; barrel legged, toeing in
4. Lordosis; slack topline; concave spine
5. Kyphosis ; roached topline; convex spine
6. Lacking or excessive angulation
7. Long or short tail

Typological defects:
1. Fragile bone structure
2. Long limbs
3. Narrow thorax (chest)
4. Inverted stomach (such as the Greyhound)
5. Tail held curved on the back such as in the Nordic dogs
6. Short coat, without the underlying layer, such as in the Labrador.
7. Atypical colors.

Like any other breed, the male subject must have normal testicles, well lowered into the scrotum. Monorchidism and cryptorchidism (absence of one or both of the testicles) is basis for disqualification.

IV. MOVEMENT

Mechanics and Kinetics

Movement represents the live expression of the somatic characteristics of a breed, and the study of the dynamics allows one to understand even further why the morphology form and function are so tightly intertwined. Every movement that we observe and that occurs with such naturalness and agility, making the analysis of it quite complicated, is the mix of a perfect game of balance in which muscles, bones and forces of gravity are the players.

The basis of the concept of movement is the concept of center of gravity. All bodies are subject to the force of gravity and each has its own center of gravity. This is the point where the lines of the forces of gravity, resulting from all of the particles in the body, converge. Thus, if one could keep a body suspended on its center of gravity, it would remain forever perfectly in balance. In the dog, the center of gravity is situated more or less at the meeting point of the two perpendiculars: the vertical tangent to the xiphoid apophysis of the sternum and the horizontal situated on the sagittal plane of

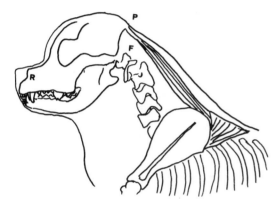

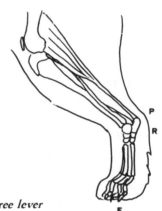

1. First degree lever.
3. Third degree lever.

2. Second degree lever

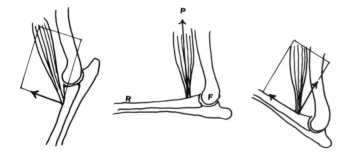

The concept of levers in the mechanics of animal limbs.

A framed moment during presentation in the ring.

97

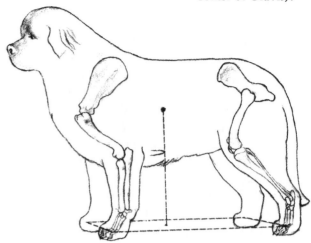

the body at half the height of the thorax. If we trace a quadrilateral shape, joining the points where the feet meet the ground, we would obtain a base for support. Only if the vertical plane that passes through the center of gravity falls on this base will the dog be able to maintain a position of static equilibrium. If the animal, while raising the front leg and pushed by the hind leg, moves its weight forward, this condition of balance will cease; the center of gravity is moved forward and the dog must take a step in order to maintain his balance.

From this, one can deduce that forward movement takes place under two forces: the hind push that begins the movement and the gravitational force, which, acting upon the center of gravity, continues the action. This diminishes muscular effort and occurs more quickly if the center of gravity is high. The movement will be greater when the limb upon which it depends is long.

A correct and narrow base and long limbs, typical of the dolicomorphs, will thus be the prerogative for speed, but this condition, which forces the subject to make an increased number of steps and jumps, will tire the animal in a short time. It can thus achieve the maximum, but only for a short while. Furthermore, long limbs have long muscles and bones that are relatively thin, capable of large movements, but useless for hard and long-lasting effort. In the same manner, a narrow chest with height development of the thorax alone would not allow for a solid hold on the ground while pulling and less floating stability while swimming.

On the other hand, transversal diameters that are too developed, such as a barrel thorax and excessively short limbs, are synonymous with elevated statics. The Bulldog is built to have a solid base, but could you imagine him jumping between two rocks? The Greyhound is agile and swift, but how long do you think he could fight the waves? Nature, more than man, created the Newfoundland, a breed different from others, by mixing perfectly all of the elements necessary for a useful dog, perfect for life on his native island. Thus, he must be a "miler" or long distance runner rather than a "sprinter," useful in work that requires strength and resistance along with agility. The structure of the mesomorph with its strong bone structure and powerful muscles perfectly coincides with this.

We have already seen how the force of gravity is important; now let us examine how bones and muscles function. These are basically levers that may develop further force and precision, depending on the disposition of the points of power and resistance in relation to the fulcrum. In the body of the animal, the power (P) is generated by the muscular action, the resistance (R) by the weight, and the fulcrum (F) is situated sometimes at the level of the articulations and sometimes at the ground.

We will thus have the following:

1. Lever of the first degree or balance lever, in which the fulcrum is between the power and the resistance; this is most advantageous as the arm of the lever is larger in relation to that of resistance.

2. Lever of the second degree, or lever of strength, in which the resistance is between the fulcrum and the power; consequently, the arm of the power is greater than that of resistance.

3. Third degree lever, or lever of speed, in which the force is between the fulcrum and the resistance. In this case, since the lever of power is always inferior to that of resistance, the movement of resistance will be larger than the amplitude of the muscular contraction; however, it is necessary to have a muscular strength superior to the weight of resistance.

Depending on the position in which the long axis of the bone is placed at the moment in which a muscle comes into action, the muscle can work with the power of different degree levers. For example, the posterior muscles of the leg put into action a lever of the second degree when, with a limb on the ground, the fulcrum is on the ground; a lever of the first degree is used when, with a limb lifted, the fulcrum is moved to the level of the articulation.

Muscles do not only present dynamic effects, but also static effects and act both as regulators and inhibitors. A stationary subject, perfectly still, is the result of varied muscular tensions that contrast with the force of gravity and that do not allow for closure of certain angles to balance one against the force of the other. The various movements are achieved through the intervention of agonistic, or

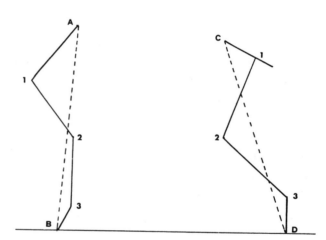

Mechanica Axies of Anterior (left) and Posterior (right) limbs.

straining, muscular groups, capable of producing the same actions, and of groups of antagonistic muscles, able to determine the opposite effect and to regulate the intensity and the speed of the movement with their tone.

When a muscular action force takes place, a movement of the long axis of the bone occurs. This movement's extent and velocity are proportional to the intensity of the muscular force exerted. Observing the angles of the limbs and uniting the proximal and distal extremities of their mechanical axis, one immediately perceives how the anterior limbs are better predisposed for support action, whereas the back limbs are suited to the push forward. This impulse, transmitted through the vertebral column and aided by the cephalo-cervical balance arm (or neck), is the basis of the movement.

Unlike people, who walk in an erect position and for whom the phases of suspension and elevation interest only one limb at a time, dogs are quadrupeds for which standing calls for both a synchronism of the anterior and posterior train and also of the diagonal biped; that is to say, posterior right-anterior left, posterior left-anterior right. This sequence is seen in the different gaits, however, with modified speed and tempo. It varies only in the pacing gait, a gait considered defective in the Newfoundland, and in which the limbs of the same side are brought forward contemporaneously: posterior right-anterior right, posterior left-anterior left.

The Walk

It is a slow gait, done in four beats. The touching of the ground is always on three limbs and the movements of the center of gravity are moderate both in a vertical and a transversal sense. The

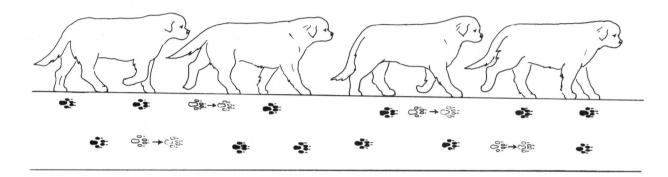

When movement accelerates, the limbs shift to single-track mode.

100

forward movement of the head, and the lifting of one of the front limbs are the initial phases of the walk related to the push of the diagonally opposed posterior. At this point, the front limb that is suspended will be moved forward and touch the ground in order to receive the weight of the body, while the hind leg that gave the push is suspended and moved toward the same anterior side. When this leg touches the ground, the second front limb is raised and the sequence begins once again on the other side. The tempo of raising is the following: anterior right-posterior left, anterior left-posterior right. In the Newfoundland, the walk must not be shortened, but normal or moderately lengthened; the back footprint does not, however, overtake that of the anterior footprint.

In the slow gait, the limbs move parallel to the body and the vertebral column shows a slight sinuous movement typical of the breed. The neck is held in an almost horizontal position.

The Trot

The trot is used often by the dog, even for short distances; similar to the walk, the trot does not require an excessive energetic expenditure. It is a diagonal gait, in two beats in which the weight alternates between one diagonal (anterior and posterior counterlateral) and the other.

In the small trot (which is a walking gait), the two beats are rhythmically alternated without phases of suspension; in the normal and lengthened trot (flying gait), the beats shorten their tempo so that all four of the limbs are raised from the ground. In the beginning, the diagonal two legs that are in contact with the ground project the body up and forward. There follows an instant of suspension during which the diagonal is changed, after which the other diagonal receives the weight and repeats the sequence. The center of gravity will be subject to major vertical and transversal movements, modest in respect to those of the gallop.

A correct angle and length between the anterior and posterior train is essential for the trot to be harmonious and balanced. During the slow trot, the Newfoundland presents a typical rolling of the

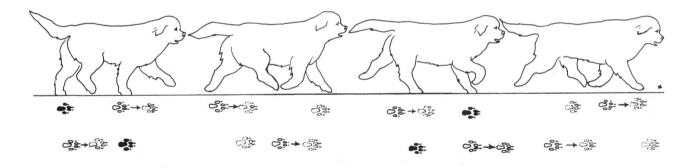

skin that reminds one of a bear, a rolling that stops when the gait gets faster. As the speed of the gait increases, the direction of the limbs, from high to low, tends to converge toward a central or single line (single tracking). This tracking must not be confused with an altered direction of the front limbs, caused by an outward rotation of the elbows, or of the hind quarters, which is shown by narrow movements with hocks that are close together.

The Gallop

The gallop is the fastest of the gaits as well as the most tiring. It is similar to a sequence of jumps. The head and neck balance beam and the vertebral column are actively used, and the center of gravity undergoes notable movements, mainly in the vertical direction.

Although the photographic analysis of the gallop reveals complex components that are not noticed by simply looking, we will try to make examples of the sequences, describing it as a jumped gait in three tempos: hind, diagonal two feet of the same side, counterlateral anterior followed by a suspension. After practically crouching on the back quarters, the dog projects himself forward and upwards, putting the weight first on one of the hind limbs and then on the other.

For example, the push begins on the left hind leg, immediately followed by the right hind leg, and with a slight downbeat, the front left limb while the body extends itself forward. Following in the trajectory he crunches down on the front right limb, which is now the weight bearer, and which pushed the dog away from the ground. A suspension follows after which the dog once again lands on the left hind leg and the sequence begins again.

During the gallop, because of the strong demands that are placed upon the bones, muscles and ligaments, especially in a heavy dog such as the Newfoundland, a perfect functioning of all of these systems is essential, without which the gait could not be powerful and loose. For example, when there are hip problems such as dysplasia, the push may be made with both of the hind legs together in the effort to bypass the functional deficiency.

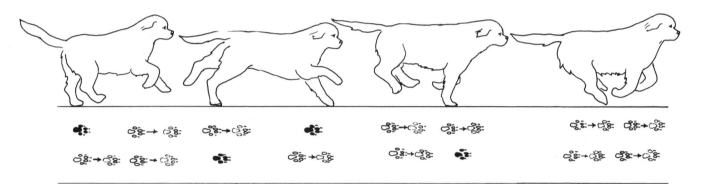

Ch. Mabel degli Angeli Neri in water training, owned by A. Pisaneschi.

102

The Dive

As with swimming, the dive is a natural movement for the Newfoundland though, when given the choice, he usually prefers to enter the water slowly.

The dive is essentially a long jump for which quite a bit of power in the whole hind train is necessary.

In the beginning, the dog crouches down on the pelvic limbs, flexing thighs and legs, the ischiotibial muscles (semimembranous and semitendinous), which serve as a first degree lever on the back part of the coaxial, rotate the axis on the fulcrum of the coxofemoral articulation, which raises the anterior section of the vertebral column. At this moment, the triceps come into play, which by means of the Achilles tendon with strong tension on the calcaneus, provokes the opening of the angulation of the hock and the forward and upward projection of the body. From the skeletal rays, the impulse is transmitted to the pelvis and to the vertebral column, while the cephalo-cervical balancer extends itself forward and is lowered along with the front limbs.

When the dog touches the water, the head is usually held high and does not go under water, already in position for the swimming that will follow.

Swimming

While swimming, the concept of force of gravity is commuted to the concept of floating. The body, immersed in the water, receives a push that sustains it. This keeps the body semisubmerged according to a line of flotation from which the head, extended forward, the upper part of the neck, the withers, and at intervals the upper part of the back, the hind and the tail emerge.

Swimming. An underwater photo.

103

Differently from other breeds, the Newfoundland always holds a horizontal position in the water. In this position, the limbs are moved alternatively such as while walking without having to bear the weight of the body, but with the precise goal of moving forward, gripping the water.

The sequence is the same: anterior right-posterior left, anterior left-posterior right, but the execution of the movements is quite different.

The front legs assume an important role as propellers. The forearms are flexed on the humerus as much as possible and brought upward, after which they extend forward, down, and finally backward. In this movement, there is participation by the thick, wide metacarpals and of the feet, which allows for the best use of the intradigital membrane that holds the toes apart. A strong action on the water pushes the body forward. After this, the limb returns to its flexed position.

The author's Ch. Christian degli Angeli Neri Kennel.

104

Apart from muscles of the shoulder and arm, other muscles come into play in order to have a better "grip" on the water while swimming; in particular the anconeus muscles and the flexors of the metacarpal and of the phalanges must be robust and well developed. At the same time, the hind quarters work in a similar manner: they are alternatively brought down and forward exerting a strong push on the water that is completed with a final sprint during the moment of maximum extension. As for the anterior train, the muscles of the thigh and leg, along with the flexor tendons of the metatarsal and of the phalanges, must be solid and well developed.

At the same time as the limbs propel in an anterior and posterior directions, they also make lateral movements that help to correct deviations in the straight floating line.

An important role is played by the tail, which is kept horizontal and rigid and that acts as a rudder in changes of direction. The loin, which is slightly lengthened, favors the flexibility of the vertebral column and aids movement.

Every motion in the water is made with balance and efficiency. In comparison to movement on the ground, swimming is not only a question of covering a certain distance, but also of having the right push on the liquid mass for a productive propulsion with the least effort. Swimming is never frantic in this breed, but calm and rhythmical, in order to be able to last for extended periods of time. It is as though nature had taught these animals how to conserve energy. Thus, they can swim for a long time without loosing strength while pulling or retrieving. The double water repellent coat that isolates the body like a wetsuit also permits immersion in harsh climates and for long time spans without loosing body heat.

All of the above elements come together to give the Newfoundland the functional image of *the water-rescue dog*.

Let us now forget theory and try to imagine a scene that occurred many years ago. It is the story of a storm, like many others, and of the everlasting fight of man against the sea. But this time, in addition to the man there is a large dog, not quite like the ones that we know, shiny and well kept, but very similar: strong, courageous and with the same wonderful instinct.

We see him as he jumps from one rock to another, searching for a point from which he can dive. The solid and compact foot, the muscular shoulders, and the wide chest help to prevent him from slipping. The dilated nostrils smell and analyze through the air that which is happening nearby. Above the roar of the waves, beyond the fog and the salty air, he senses the presence of men in danger.

The sailboat has dropped its anchors, but it is in danger of wrecking itself on the rocks. On the deck are a handful of frightened men; on land another handful of men watch helplessly. The dog barks insistently many times. He shows his desire to dive. Then, an idea shines in his eyes.

A word is all he needs for this idea to grow in those intelligent eyes. The jaws close tightly around a rope. He is ready to dive, not a high jump for which lightness and height are necessary, but a long jump that requires maximum power. If he were to land too close to shore, he would not have time to begin swimming; the waves would throw him against the rocks. So, the dog stands on his hind legs, extends his neck to the utmost. The massive head is pushed forward; powerful is the push from behind that is passed on from the hocks to the hind and the back to project his sixty kilograms (or 130-odd pounds) forward.

Soon, he emerges from the waves with the rope still tightly clenched in his mouth. The wide masseters and the well developed temporals allow him this steady hold, along with the power of will typical of the breed. Rhythmically, without tiring himself, like an expert mountain climber who begins the climb, he begins to brave the seas. The rigid tail is used for direction; the corrections in route are made by the legs and arms. But the fight is still long and arduous. Well-opened airways, capable lungs and an excellent heart provide the large muscles with enough oxygen under stress.

In the end, the rope is handed over. Salvation. A bridge between land and sea is made that would otherwise be impossible. For the dog, however, it is not yet the end. He now has to go back to the land and patiently seek out a low rock, a small ledge, the right moment for regaining the ground. He must have courage, timing and agility to avoid being tumbled by the waves.

The sailors, thankful for being rescued, will bring a Newfoundland along on the next trip, and in case of need, they will send the faithful helper to land with rope. But only gifted dogs with certain qualities will be able to accomplish this task, and it will be people who will have the task of keeping these traits alive through time.

This is an old story. Today's experts have another very important task to fulfill: that of always keeping function in mind. It is hard for people to weigh changing some traits for esthetic reasons, which is always a subjective reason, against changing those traits that in nature are selected only by function.

Water! My enduring passion.

V. CHARACTER

One aspect of Newfoundlands that most interests those who are close to the breed is personality. This is a combination of such peculiar and important characteristics that it is a typical trait of the breed.

If we go back and examine the evolution of different breeds, we notice that often serious damage is done to a breed by ignoring this aspect. This is most often because of the desire one may have to enhance the somatic traits, such that a perfect coat is preferred over intelligence, the harmony of lines is preferred over resistance, the way the dog carries himself is preferred over the balance. However, it is sometimes the exaggeration of certain tendencies, wrongly interpreted, that creates neurotic animals incapable of correct reactions. One thing must be clear: personality is inherited just like exterior traits, and it is thus of utmost importance that breeders and judges give it the right weight. Every standard, along with the description of the physical traits, should always describe clearly the personality and attitudes of the breed in relation to its function. In this regard, the Newfoundland standard states the following: "...large dog used in pulling and in the water, possessor of the instinct to save and devoted companion. Extraordinarily sweet and docile...." and the American one adds: "Sweetness of character is the hallmark of the Newfoundland, it is the most important single characteristic of the breed." It is obvious how both feel the need to explain his intelligence and good spirit even before his love of water and retrieving, which are nevertheless fundamental characteristics of the breed.

There is, in fact, something in these friends of ours that transcends the already beautiful relationship between man and dog. Since the beginning of time, the dog has been our companion as a hunter and shepherd in peace and in war. Accepting his role with humility and dedication, he renders us service with his natural egocentric impulses and survival of his species: the love of hunting, of retrieving, of chasing, of fighting. Time after time, the objective was the untamed, the herd, the enemy.

In a dog used for rescue, all energy, attention and effort are made instead toward man. It is in this total love of mankind, which in nature is found only in the bitch trying to save her puppies, that the Newfoundland overcomes his identity as a dog to become the hero that we all know. It would be easy at this point to go on and on about the thousands of stories written about him, but this is exactly what I want to avoid because I am afraid that this mystical aura has often created problems for our friend. Who, after reading of his acts, is not inclined to make of him just that kind of a companion? The problems begin because the Newfoundland is not a dog for everybody. He can give a lot, but he also needs to receive much in exchange. What a disillusionment for the uninformed to find that the faithful guardian, abandoned to boredom and loneliness, will seek distractions by running away! What a bad impression one makes when one is not able to control his strength when walking with him! And what if the dog is only brought to the water on rare occasions and runs the risk of drowning his owner with the frantic motion of his large paws?

Angry, betrayed in their expectations, these individuals conclude that the dog is too large, that he is dirty, that he ruins the plants in the garden, that he must be brushed, fed, taken care of and that they do not have the time. They eventually get rid of him or confine him in a kennel under the care of unknown hands that are rarely able to give him love along with food. Such is the story of Alpha, Beta, and of many others, victims of human superficiality and inconstancy, idealized dogs that were not loved enough.

The Newfoundland cannot live without love and feeling for his owner. He does not need a spacious home or rich food, but family life and a profound relationship with man. This is exactly what some do not know how to give. If a child needs to be loved in order to develop his intelligence, so the dog needs to meet the right person who will be able to understand him and allow for the full development of the mores of the breed. Just as giving birth to a child is not sufficient to merit being called a parent, so buying a puppy is not enough to be an owner. I would not like to be misunderstood on

The loving relationship between dog and owner is of fundamental importance.

A companion of their youthful games.

this point that emphasizes mainly responsibilities and obligations before rights. For the dog, the true owner is head of the pack, a friend, a hero. It is sad to delude the dog in his expectations. This is especially true for the Newfoundland whose main goal is his love for man.

If the hunting dog is satisfied by walking with someone carrying a weapon, if the Greyhound is happy just chasing the hare, if the shepherd concentrates his attention on the animals in his care, if the guard dog monitors his territory, then the Newfoundland is essentially the companion who cares for the well being of the family. How could he live outside of it? He does, however, know how to be discrete. While he appears to be sleeping, his brain follows small habitual noises, analyzes odors, evaluates messages and informs himself on what is happening. There he is, ready to jump to his feet if necessary when that sixth sense, present in simple creatures and born from the attention for thousands of details, warns him of danger.

I remember my mother used to tell me about a game she used to amuse herself with, when, as a young girl she used to walk on a narrow ledge until her Newfoundland, Urano, would push her back from the edge, putting himself between her and the danger.

Always standing vigil, he looks after children, he observes before acting with a patience that allows him to wait for the right moment to intervene. Serene and balanced, he doesn't easily lose himself in barking or fighting. Only if attacked will he respond with courage, but without going beyond the acceptable, regaining his poised temperament immediately. All of these characteristics, along with the love for swimming and retrieving, create the perfect image of a dog that may be used for saving drowning people.

Faithful guardians.

Piero Scanzini in his book, *The Useful Dog*, analyzes the components of character, finding the following principal attributes:

Reactions	Docility	Courage
Resistance	Temperament	Defense impulse
Fighting impulse	Mordacity	Vigilance

Analyzing more deeply these terms, we will try to penetrate the mind of the Newfoundland as much as possible.

Reactions

This term refers to the resistance that the dog offers to unpleasant external factors. The tough animal reacts against the impulses that he perceives as obstacles, while the fearful one instead retreats at the first difficulty.

I am sure that most people are aware of this development of reactions. Watch puppies as they play: they chase each other, full of the joy of life. At times they run into objects or into each other with such force that one fears the consequences but, though they might get back on their feet limping, they rarely abandon their games, they are always ready to face new experiences.

It is this high self esteem that causes the Newfoundland to have a great and tolerant attitude towards situations, people and animals. He acts toward another dog in a serene manner without making too much show of certain behavioral patterns. You will rarely see an adult raise his hackles or put his tail between his legs. It is always this security that stimulates his curiosity toward the rest of the world. Unfortunately this behavior is confused at times with naiveté. What a mistake! Every good Newfoundland is able to demonstrate, and continues throughout his life to demonstrate, how untrue this is. An equally great mistake is made by those who confuse this trait with hardheadedness, connecting to it the negative attributes of humans, when instead it demonstrates noble and positive clearness of thought.

The subject that has this trait well implanted is "neither victim of instincts, nor of training, but has a strong individual capacity for reflection; he thus has a great personality." This is extremely important for a dog who saves lives. He must not retreat or be intimidated by difficulties or by the crazed frenzy of the drowning person. He must, with strong willpower, reach the shore. Furthermore, he must be capable of making decisions on his own, evaluating each situation.

Thus, he never acts mechanically. For this reason he must fully understand what and why we are asking him something. When he has understood this, he will be able to make the best use of it. This is why it is important to teach and exercise him in those tasks he is to undertake. The Newfoundland must be trained, never tamed.

Docility

This term means voluntary submission to the will of man. It must absolutely not be confused with cowardice because the dog offers what he has to his owner of his own free will. He does not obey because he is forced to or because he is afraid not to, but rather to please those he loves. Obviously, the dog must only be trained by its owner. It would not be fair to force him to obey someone he does not know, and in any case, it would only be possible if the dog became attached to this person.

The greatest proof of his docility is demonstrated when he comes when called. Here I can only imagine the protests of those who do not have obedient dogs. "My dog goes where he wants to. If I call him, he doesn't come; if I chase him, he runs away and amuses himself by making me run." My dear friends, everyone harvests that which is sown. Even the most docile dog becomes confused when faced with human incoherence. Try to remember how you acted with him when he was a puppy. You took him for a walk and once you decided to let him go, you started reading the newspaper or chatting with a friend. After a while, the puppy returned happily. He smelled you and looked you in the eyes, and when he understood that you were too preoccupied with your own business and that there was nothing that he had to do, he ran away seeking a friend with whom to play. Unfortunately, as soon as he found one, you finished the conversation, finished reading the paper or smoking the cigarette and noticed that it was time to return home. You may have wanted the puppy to come right back to you, but at that moment, he was too busy elsewhere. When you noticed that he would not come, you yelled and punished him, when love and comprehension would have been more useful. At least

Nike van Het Heidemeer, owned by Enrico De Cenzo.

for the first few times, the dog should be praised every time he comes back, so that he understands that you are happy to have him by your side. You must also have respect for his curiosity and love of life.

The Newfoundland is a courageous dog. Because he is not afraid, it is only normal that when freed from the leash, his natural inclination is to wander toward his own kind or toward passing people. When his freedom is taken away he can only explore the world by running away as soon as he can. What would you do if you were never able to take a vacation, have a dinner out or indulge in your favorite hobby?

Courage

I believe that everyone will agree with this aspect of his personality. Courageous is he who voluntarily faces a danger for the well being of others. Well, the Newfoundland is the most classic example. But even when he is not engaged in a heroic act, he shows this virtue in everyday life.

Courage is demonstrated by his calm, his patience. Any dog that is frightened is under the stimulus of the adrenal glands and such a dog may take on defensive attitudes that could be avoided. The Newfoundland's look is instead friendly, the look of one who is honest and one who expects loyalty. If you attack him, he will neither fight back nor escape. He waits and contemplates the hostility that he does not understand. When attacked, he does not pull back, either in front of animals or people. This courage is not aggressive, but is permeated by moderation so that it can be put to use in the best of ways.

Resistance

Aside from physical resistance, the term resistance includes the psychological capacity of always finding new forces within oneself. It is obvious how this quality must be heightened in a rescue dog that is also a swimmer. Physical resistance is bolstered by the build of the Newfoundland. Solid bones, powerful muscles and a wide thorax are all anatomical requisites of the breed, but the Newfoundland's calm and reflection are also useful. As with any able swimmer, he does not use all of his energy immediately, but he rations it to be almost inexhaustible.

Temperament

Temperament is identified by the speed of response to an outside stimulus, in vitality. It seems correct to defy certain critics who define the Newfoundland as "a couch potato" or "lazy." Surely those who say this have never seen him play hide and seek in the trees. In any case, you are probably familiar with those annoying dogs that spend their lives running between two gates and barking at shadows, or others who would not, for anything in the world, miss the leg of a cyclist. Well, the Newfoundland is not one of these dogs.

He is a philosophical thinker, movement with no objective does not interest him. If he were a person, you would not see him on a stationary bike; instead try inviting him for a walk or a refreshing dive. He will happily jump up and hop along ahead of you.

He is mature as a puppy and young as an adult. The soul of the Newfoundland never grows old, and is renewed in thousands of little details for the joy of those who love him.

Defense Impulse

It is the speed with which the Newfoundland intervenes in the defense of his companion that makes it obvious that he has a certain sense of property and a certain diffidence. This impulse, which pushes the dog forward angrily if someone raises an arm in the direction of the owner, would have negative consequences if it were too developed in a rescue dog. It could lead to a self defense response toward one who is drowning. This instinct is deep and needs a strong stimulus in order to be brought out.

This is what Hegel demonstrates. One night, while taking his habitual walk on the leash, he encountered a drunken man. He was quiet when he saw the man wobbling or when the man began speaking meaningless sentences. But when a hand menacingly gripped the arm of his owner causing her to scream in fright, he raised himself on his hind legs, in all his height, and the drunkard found himself glued to the wall with two large paws pressing against his chest and a black face breathing on him in quite an unfriendly manner.

Fighting Impulse

This quality is the pleasure of fighting, and is totally contrary to the nature of the Newfoundland. He must not become overly excited, because he would not be able to conserve the calm and lucidity necessary for fulfilling his tasks. Furthermore, it would be impossible for him to do team work with other dogs when this is asked of him because the fighting impulse would cause them to fight with each other.

Mordacity

Even more than the last trait, this aggressive feature is the antithesis of the breed's sweetness and balance. It is a violent impulse that is often born not from courage, but from fear. Examples of this are those dogs that jump toward the Newfoundland with straight hair, bared teeth and loud barking. They would behave quite differently if their owner were not present on the other end of their leash. They would probably put their tail between their legs and try to pass unobserved. Mordacity is always a significant defect in the Newfoundland.

At this point, I would like to call the following to the attention of breeders and judges: During the judging process, the dog must be serene, the look in his eyes should be curious and friendly. He must allow one to touch him. If a dog is mordacious, an analysis must be done; if in doubt then he must be seen again, leaving the judgment suspended. If he reveals an obstinate alteration of character, he must be disqualified independently from all of the exterior characteristics that he may possess. If he is mordacious with other dogs it can be tolerated, but care must be exercised because this may be the prelude to other more negative aspects. The Newfoundland must know how to work in a group.

The breeder, in turn, must be careful not to have these dogs reproduce. How would he be able to give the offspring to someone who has small children? A similar dog is unpredictable and may react in an unpleasant manner on any occasion. The true Newfoundland instead is always balanced and patient. For example, if a child tumbles on him while he is sleeping, the most that the dog will do is

Tender first approach.

112

to lick him in the face. If one would inadvertently step on his paw, he will simply change position. It would be tragic to lose such virtues.

The breeder has a further task that is of utmost importance and should not be underestimated: the first experiences of the puppy occur at the breeding kennel and are determining factors for the rest of his life. Contact with man, smelling him, receiving food from his hands and being open are all aspects that act positively toward his future balance. It would be negative to raise him in solitude, to mistreat him or to have him always hear angry voices.

This concept, which is true for all breeds, becomes essential for a rescue dog. He must love people; it would be terrible if he were afraid or felt repulsion and aggressiveness. How would he be able to overcome these feeling to the point of risking his life for a person?

Vigilance

This quality is interpreted as the aggressive reaction to the stranger who invades his property. Our dogs do not like to attack man. If someone rings the doorbell, they welcome him kindly after having warned of his presence. But if someone enters without warning, their behavior is different. They stay close to him barking and prevent him from moving around by blocking him with their large size.

Someone had doubts regarding this particular trait and stated that at times the dog had been friendly with people entering the home to test him. I am certain that in these cases the dog was aware of the "test" or may even have perceived the absence of danger through his very fine sensibility. It has been demonstrated that dogs notice fear through sweating and perhaps also through other channels unknown to us. In any case, I don't believe that any honest Newfoundland would allow his house to be robbed under his nose; in fact, stories of postmen and plumbers held back by the large guardians are not rare.

In cataloguing and defining each of the above psychic traits, I did not want to make a qualitative comparison with other breeds. Depending on the function of the animal, the same quality or characteristics may be positive or negative. It is important that those who want a dog to carefully examine their needs and expectations, so as to find the ideal dog.

This is also true for those who already own a dog and who must accept his character. This is why an animal should not be given as a gift. Furthermore, though it may represent the nicest gift for a child, a dog must never be considered a toy, rather a companion with very precise needs that must be respected. These first responsibilities will aid the child in coming out of his infantile egocentrism to

A hole for two: A friend is always a friend.

become an adult. Often, children make thousands of promises of collaboration and help, and will then forget all of them once the enthusiasm has passed. Be careful to avoid having the animal pay the consequences of this superficiality that may be excused in a child, but not in an adult.

The decision to buy a dog must not be taken lightly. Though it may seem excessive, it is comparable to the decision of having a child. One assumes certain responsibilities for this creature that will certainly impose changes in one's lifestyle. He did not ask to come with us; it is we who chose him from among his brothers, taking him into our home. We have responsibilities toward him, and the most important is to guarantee him a happy old age in the family in which he lives.

I understand that asking this in a consumer society, which tends to disregard the family, where too often there is not enough time for the young and space for the old, is a utopian view. But nobody is forced to own a dog, even less a Newfoundland with his needs and personality. It is possible that in teaching children the love for a puppy and the respect for an old dog, you may one day be grateful. In any case, be sure that a Newfoundland, intelligent and good, will never be consumed by loneliness or be forgotten.

A group photo of the Angeli Neri Kennel. The author with Ch. Dilys, Ch. Zelda, and Ch. Zenith.

114

VI. BREEDING

The birth of a litter is always an important event in the chronicle of a breed. Whether the birth occurs in the noble surroundings of a well-known kennel or is the singular experience of a small, private breeder, its product will increase the zoological population, mixing and blending into it. Every litter thus has the possibility of either positively or negatively influencing a breed. The decision to have a particular subject reproduce must, therefore, be taken with utmost seriousness and with earnest thought. Producing a dog is easy, breeding one is not.

Those who want to dedicate themselves to the activity of breeding should be very conscious of their role and responsibilities. In breeding, man takes the place of nature and its ancient knowledge, and he imposes his own desires and aspirations. It is a delicate matter, not without risks, which requires a great deal of good sense along with a pinch of humility.

Most breeders share a common experience: they meet a dog, the interest for its breed grows. The breeder studies the dog breed, confronts it, and so on, until he has a clear vision of what he wants: his personal ideal, always present, but hard to reach. Mauro de Cillis wrote: "In order to make an idea live, be it a painting or a dog, one must first be able to envision it." Nothing is more true! The breeder must have a very clear idea of what he wants to achieve and he must work with tenacity and awareness toward this idea. He must also maintain great balance, in order not to give in to excesses or deficits that are out of the standard and that could interfere with function and type. The goal of a breeder should not be that of seeking excellence, rather that of maintaining a good average, or to be able to maintain a harmonious type in the most homogeneous subjects. This means creating a kind of stamp for a kennel such that the traits of each dog originating from there is like the signature of a painter's work. In this way, a kennel truly achieves meaning.

But how does one reach these goals? With time, patience and some technical knowledge; one cannot improvise breeding.

The Pedigree

One of the most important aspects of the pedigree is knowledge of the genealogies that one has to work with. However, if we said that the study of ancestors through a pedigree represents basic research, we would be telling only half the truth. The pedigree, the Certificate of Registration in the Origins Book, has a different language for everyone: for people new to the breed, it seems like a sequence of important names without meaning; for others, it is the place to look for ideal ancestors in order to create better bloodlines. For still others, it is the search for certain kennels that bring forth particular traits. In truth, it is not the names or the classifications as champions that count, but it is instead the possibility of substituting a clear image with precise characteristics to each name, those characteristics, which the breeder seeks or wants to exclude, that he can only know through the individual representatives of the breed and their descendants throughout the years.

The richer the amount of information and emotions felt toward individual subjects, the deeper and more fruitful the research will be. The breeder thus has an ideal map of the genetic situation of the breed. The pedigree becomes an interesting chapter of history, full of important information which in the end reveals data and interpretations on the genotype of the subject.

In simple theory, a subject receives 50 percent of the traits of the father and mother, 25 percent of the traits of the four grandparents, 12.5 percent of the traits of the eight great-grandparents and 6.25 percent from the great-great-grandparents, and so on.

Practically, as one understands through the observation of genetics, these percentages are largely tied to casual recompilation of heredity in the moment of formation of the zygote and to the complex phenomenon of dominant and recessive genes.

The phenotype, or the exterior manifestation of traits, is the result of these complex interactions. Although it expresses the contents of the genotype with some approximation, it is never certain. The

Tommy and Clara getting acquainted.

Family portrait: Ch. Zeus, Astrid and Raissa, owned and photographed by F. La Rocca.

job of the breeder is that of finding and slowly pulling out characteristics that are wanted until they are fixed in the bloodlines and, at the same time, trying to eliminate defects.

There are three methods of breeding:

-Reproduction between subjects that have no common blood (outcross)
-Reproduction between subjects that are not close family members, but which share some common blood (linebreeding)
-Reproduction between close family members (inbreeding)

Each of these methods pose both positive and negative aspects, but in the right proportion they can each be used advantageously.

If outcrossing risks diluting certain traits that are already well fixed, and inbreeding risks bringing certain defects to the surface, the art of the breeder consists of knowing how to measure the extent of these risks, weighing them against the relative advantages through precise research. One must not leave one's type in order to introduce a pleasant characteristic, because one would risk losing both the type and the characteristic as well as creating great confusion. One must try with patience to find the desired characteristic in a similar type.

Whether one uses one method or another, the concept that must be followed remains the same: finding the greatest affinity between two partners, regarding those characteristics that represent the ideal of the breed. A male and female that do not share common ancestors, but that look alike and come from parents and grandparents that also look alike, have greater probabilities of creating similar traits rather than two brothers who do not look alike at all and come from nonhomogeneous lines. Naturally, the capacity of evaluating the degree of affinity of two subjects is tied to experience, preparation and, above all, the sensitivity of the breeder that is realized in the choice of the dogs that reproduce.

The Reproducing Type

The concept of a reproducing type is usually tied to the stud dog, rather than to the bitch. He is able to influence the breed because of the number of puppies produced.

One must not overlook, however, the importance of a good bitch. The cloth of any kennel is essentially woven by the quality of its bitches. It is quite easy to obtain great stud dogs, but the potential for reproduction of an exceptional bitch is something that must be treasured.

116

What factors help us to recognize the best reproducers? Their phenotype are the first thing to attract attention, but this has no value if the capacity for reproducing it is lacking.

A stud that obtains prestigious results, but has no offspring with these same results, will not be a good reproducer. The same can be said of a bitch that never had great exemplars among her offspring. These must be considered the fruits of fortune. The results are quite different when the wanted characters are manifestations of homozygotes, and even more so when these are able to strengthen themselves through the affinity of the two partners.

One must be careful not only to look at the titles of the parents but also at those of the children; future test breedings of those children will also be quite helpful.

Two factors that must always be kept in mind when choosing dogs to breed are character and genetic instinct.

It is obvious that character represents a very important coefficient of type, so much more in a breed used for rescue. A beautiful but aggressive dog is not a Newfoundland, and thus must be carefully avoided by breeders.

In the same manner one must not give too little value to the capacity for natural breeding. This mechanism, which is at the base of natural selection, is often underestimated by man who resorts to artificial insemination in cases of difficulty. It is especially in this situation that artificial insemination must not be used because the risk is that of bringing out these negative characteristics even more resulting in future subjects that will not breed naturally.

Artificial insemination, with frozen sperm, could be very useful instead for selection, allowing us to use, after a protracted period of time, the sperm of valuable stud dogs whose thoroughbred capacities and lineages may only be evaluated after a number of years had passed. This would additionally allow a breeder to widen research to include those instances where stud dog and bitch live at great distances, reachable only by plane, with its risks, or in countries with quarantine laws.

Some Genetic Concepts

The genetic baggage (genotype) is enclosed in the nucleus of every cell that, along with thousands of others, constitutes a living body. This influences the expression of the different characteristics (phenotype) during development. In the nucleus there are chromosomes, narrow filaments of DNA (deoxyribonucleic acid) and proteins upon which genes or hereditary units are placed, each of which occupies a fixed position and determines the showing of specific traits based on one or more variables (or allele).

Every species has a specific number of chromosomes, so, while a man has forty-six, a dog has seventy-eight. The chromosomes are presented in couples in every cell of the organism except for the reproductive cells. Understanding the concept of transmission of traits is based on this precept.

Indeed, while in the normal multiplication process of the cells (or mitosis) a duplication of the chromosomes occurs-which remain the same number in the new cell-in the procedure that leads to the formation of the sperm in the male and of the ovule in the female (or meiosis), the pairs of chromosomes do not duplicate but are instead divided. The reproductive cells of the male and the female will thus carry half of their hereditary belongings until the moment of their union.

When the sperm and the ovum meet to give life to the new subject, the number of chromosomes once again becomes even: half from the father, half from the mother. At this point, dominant and recessive genes come into play.

As previously said, the pairs of genes that pertain to a certain trait may be the same for an entire species or different even within the same breed. Every subject could thus have pairs of identical genes in his cariotype, such as in the homozygote, or different ones, such as in the heterozygote. In this last case only one of the allele expresses itself phenotypically (dominant) and the other remains hidden (recessive).

The recessive character manifests itself when the subject bears a homozygote for that particular trait, or possesses an identical pair of recessive genes. This is obviously tied to the need for the

Georg and Gulliver and Great-Bear of the Angeli Neri Kennels.

presence of the gene, in a manifest or latent form, in both of the parents. For example: two heterozygotes Aa are able to produce: 25 percent of AA (dominant homozygotes); 50 percent of Aa (heterozygotes); 25 percent of aa (recessive homozygotes). The Mendelian percentiles of heredity are verifiable on a large enough number of products, and are in any case the basis of different genetic forecasts. These concepts are much more complex in reality because a characteristic is often influenced by more than one gene.

Heredity of Color

The color of the coat is tied to the presence or the absence of certain chemical substances called melanins that are deposited as granules in the skin and the hair. The black subjects possess large grains of black or dark brown eumelanin; the browns instead possess smaller grains of yellow or reddish feomelanin.

Type, distribution and density of pigments are each determined by a series of genes. Though there are about twelve genes related to color in the canine species, there are five that interest the Newfoundland.

1) Aguti Series-Present in the breed with two allele: A, dominant black and at which is manifested with small seal like patches on the feet and face. The possible allelic combinations are: AA (black), Aa^t (black), a^ta^t (opaque). However, in some cases it seems as though there also exists a dominant at.

2) Black-brown Series-It is tied to the B and b allele, stimulator and inhibitor of the black pigment respectively. The homozygote BB is thus a black dog, and can never produce brown offspring. The heterozygote Bb is also black, but bred with another black heterozygote or a brown, can also produce some browns in different percentages. The brown is a recessive homozygote and can to generate some blacks (heterozygotes) only if bred with dogs of this color.

3) Dilution Series-It presents two variations: D and d. The dominant D indicates the normal color without dilution, the recessive d indicates dilution of the coat. In the presence of recessive dd homozygosis, the dilution gives different results depending on whether the cariotype also contains the B gene of the black or b of the brown. In the first case it produces gray subjects; in the second beige subjects occur. Like the brown character, the dilution factor also influences the color of the eyes, the nose and the foot pads, which are lighter.

118

4) Patched series-This series contains different allele. In the Newfoundland these are basically dominant S that gives a single color and recessive sP that gives the patched coating. The "white and black" or Landseer coat appears in the recessive homozygotes sP sP that also posses the BB or Bb combination for the black color. In the case of the presence of bb, the dogs is brown and white. Because this color is not admitted, the above combinations must be avoided. In the same manner, one must pay careful attention to preserving the correct extension of the white that constitutes about two thirds of the coat. Selection for the position of the patches gives uncontrollable results. The patches on the chest, feet or tip of the tail in single colored dogs are tied to the presence of minor mutants of the S allele.

5) Dotted series-This trait, which is not welcomed, is determined by the dominant allele T, the non-dotted, by the recessive t. The selection can bring about a perfectly clean white and black coat, because the characteristic is dominant; however, in the mating of the Landseer with the black, it is

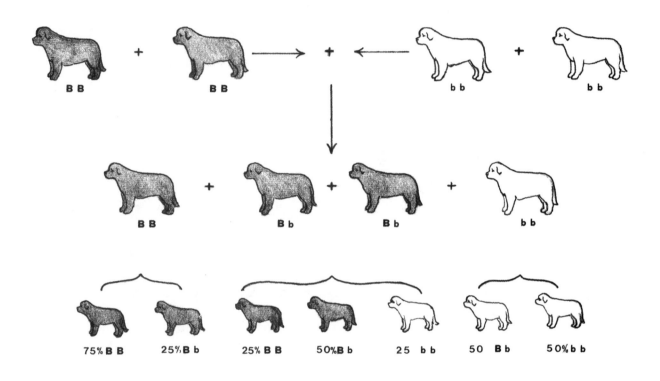

Mendelian Heredity Chart—Dominant and Recessive—Valid for the colors brown and white, black

not possible to know the results because one does not know whether these single-colored subjects are carriers of T or t. Extensive "ticking" may occur in these cases.

Hip Dysplasia

Hip dysplasia is a hereditary malformation involving the coxofemoral articulation. It is characterized by an altered development of the acetabulum (or cup shaped socket of the femur) of the head and neck of the femur, which results in a morphofunctional problem and successive osteoarthritic reactions.

The acetabulum is formed by the ilium, ischium and pubic bones that fuse around the twelfth week of life creating the hemispherical cotyloid cavity. It is in this cavity that the head of the femur rests. The shape and dimension are such that the cavity and bone fit perfectly. This structure is held in its correct position by the rounded ligament of the articular capsule.

This disease is not evident in the first months of life. During growth, the predisposed subjects first develop a looseness in the ligaments, probably because of diminished tissue turgor caused by hormonal (hyperestrogenism) and metabolic factors. With a deficient containment, the relationship between the acetabulum and the head of the femur undergo variations. The growth and ossification process, no longer guided by the correct functional asset, is disturbed by the pulling of the capsular ligament on the cotiloideus edges and of the round ligament on the acetabular cavity. The consequences are a gradual opening and flattening of the acetabulum and a successive deformation of the head and neck of the femur.

The acute inflammatory process, which can occur between three to nine months of age, is not always related to the degree of alteration. All of this can happen without any symptoms, or it can manifest itself with severe limping even in cases that are not severe.

Usually, once this phase has passed, a certain balance is instituted that allows the dog to lead a normal life, regardless of potential osteoarthritis. Fortunately, even severe cases, which in other breeds would cause immobility, rarely have such serious consequences in the Newfoundland. This should calm those who have found this defect in their subjects, but it should also make one think seriously before allowing these subjects to reproduce.

It is sufficient to think about the percentage of risk in puppies that come from different combinations, calculated by Bornfors as follows:

-Both parents are dysplastic:	80 percent
-One parent is dysplastic, the other normal	58 percent
-Both parents are normal	30 percent

The risk is further diminished if the grandparents were also normal.

Dysplasia has been subject of various genetic studies, with the goal of preventing the problem, but it is still quite complex.

It is at times attributed to a recessive gene, and at times attributed to a dominant gene with incomplete penetration. In reality it seems to be the expression of a multifactored polygenic heredity, which is why it is so hard to eliminate. A series of other causes have a determinant role on its phenotypic expression: weight, diet, either hypervitaminosis or a of lack of vitamins, traumas, physical exercise, and so forth.

Thus, one is never certain whether or not the situation of the hips faithfully reflects the genotype. In any case, only a serious program of control through the x-ray of all reproducing dogs and the exclusion of those who carry the disease can reduce the malformation's incidence by diminishing the concentration of the implicated genes.

The x-ray method of research of the FCI, to which The Italian Newfoundland Club adheres, has five parameters of readings: normal, almost normal, admissible, medium dysplasia and serious dysplasia. The subject must be at least eighteen months old for the tests to be accurately performed.

A very interesting method is that of Dr. Malcom Willis. He takes the analysis to a deeper level by comparing the subject to the average of the breed, taking into consideration the various radiological and morphological aspects onto an ample scale of value. The evaluation is comprehensive of nine descriptive points of the two separated hips with relative scoring.

Nevertheless, the results of the various techniques are always subordinate to the willingness of breeders and owners to have their dogs tested. Comprehensive testing of this matter would involve research extending to the entire population with true statistics and the potential of creating a DNA test, which is the best way to evaluate the genetic situation of such a complex hereditary pathology.

Mono and Bilateral Cryptorchidism

Cryptorchidism is the failure of one (monorchidism) or both of the testicles to descend into the scrotum. The testicles are formed at the sides of the vertebral spine during the embryonic stage.

Stimulated by hormones, they migrate in the fetus from the abdominal cavity by following a ligament, the gubernaculum testis until they come close to the internal inguinal ring. At the time of birth they are still in the abdomen, but in just a few weeks they go through the inguinal canal, becoming palpable in the scrotum at about two months of age. If this does not occur within five to six months, it indicates an abnormality.

When one or both of the testicles are not able to follow the entire sequence, they give birth to abdominal, iliacal or inguinal cryptorchidism, depending on the position in which they are situated. Testicles that do not descend degenerate and become atrophied; this is also caused by a higher temperature inside the body. Thus, while sterility is total in the case of bilateral retention, a monorchid subject is not only able to procreate but can also transmit the defect to his offspring. Furthermore, because this defect can only occur phenotypically in the male, female carriers are implicated in its diffusion without being able to be identified.

Genetically, cryptorchidism behaves like a recessive autosomal factor with variable penetration. According to some genetic engineers, the particular case of monorchidism could be tied to a polygenic complex that is expressed only when several genes are joined in an individual.

Subaortic Fibrous Stenosis

This serious pathology consists of a tightening of the diameter of the aorta just beneath its valve. The diagnosis may be done by carefully listening to puppies that are between two and three weeks of age. In the United States, where this disease occurs more frequently, puppies are always examined.

Aortic stenosis causes a stagnation of circulation in the left part of the heart that in turn influences the vessels of the lungs. The consequence is fluid in the lungs and thus coughing. The dog may die suddenly without any symptoms, usually between six and eighteen months of age. In less serious cases, the animal can live a full life without showing any sign of cardiac insufficiency.

Congenital Defects of the Eye

There are four congenital defects of the eye that involve the Newfoundland: ectropian, entropian, overdimension of the third eyelid and eversion of its cartilage.

ENTROPION: This term indicates introflexion of one or both of the eyelids toward the orbital cavity. It can be limited to the lateral angle or it can involve the whole eyelid. It gives the dog considerable pain because the eyelashes, which often additionally present an altered direction (trichiasis), irritate the eyeball by rubbing against it. This can lead to blindness in the most serious and long lasting cases.

When irritation or inflammation begin, surgery must be done immediately.

ECTROPIAN: This is the opposite defect from the first one mentioned. In this case the eyelid is turned outward. Thus, the conjunctive is exposed to the action of outside factors such as wind and dust that cause chronic conjunctivitis.

In this case plastic surgery is also essential.

CONGENITAL OVERABUNDANCE OF THE THIRD EYELID AND EVERSION OF ITS CARTILAGE: These abnormalities occur in the nictitating membrane, located at the medial canthos of the eye. It is formed by a T-shaped cartilage covered by an epithelium, rich in lymphatic tissue, which continues in the conjunctiva.

Normally the nictitating membrane is perfectly adapted to the eye, and is not very visible. The tear gland, which is located at its base, cleanses the eye and keeps the corneal surface moist.

When the nictitating membrane presents an abnormal development or an outward folding of the cartilage, it is easily inflammable and can cause chronic conjunctivitis.

The veterinarian must perform surgery in this case also, conserving the pigment of the external edge as much as possible.

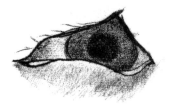
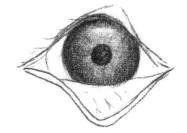
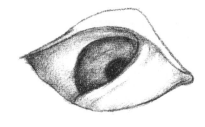

Entropian

Ectropion

Congenital of the third lid, overabundance (nictitating membrane

CONGENITAL DEFECTS OF THE EYE

Other hereditary conditions that merit interest include prognathism, enognathism, elbow dysplasia, caudal anomalies. Their means of transmission is still quite unknown, thus the only way of diminishing their occurrence consists of avoiding the reproduction of those subjects that are afflicted by them.

In conclusion, one must not forget that an excellent subject that has quelled one or more of these problems through plastic surgery might transmit the problem to his offspring.

Reproduction and Birth in the Newfoundland

Now that we have examined genetic factors that influence reproduction, let us try to answer those questions that any owner of a female might ask.

At the base of everything is the initial choice, a carefully thought out decision. This opens the doors to wonderful experiences that can also require sacrifices and work. Many times people have asked me :"Is it better to own a male or a female?" Poor knowledge and prejudice have rated the female lower in the past, so much so that she was given less value. As a breeder I have not noticed any difference, believing the concerns to be unjustified. It is a pleasure to notice that these prejudices are now beginning to disappear, which indicates a more mature knowledge of dogs. Naturally, one who wants a larger size and who is decisive and strong enough to have authority will get along better with a male,

Puppies of the La Venaria Reale Kennel.

122

but there is much sweetness and elegance in a female along with great concentration capacity and a will to learn.

Thus, while keeping in mind necessary exceptions, we will see that the pros and cons will be equal, so that the choice is always dictated by individual preference.

Many will object to this: "And the physiological problems?" Therefore, let us address them in order to clear away any doubts or fears.

The Estral Cycle in the Female Newfoundland

Unlike breeds of smaller size that are earlier developers, puberty usually does not occur in the Newfoundland until at about nine to twelve months. At this age, the coordinated action of the nervous system, the hypophisis and the gonads determine the arrival of the first heat. From this moment on, the cycle is repeated about every six months throughout life, following a biological clock regulated by hormones. It is a very delicate mechanism that must not be altered with external factors for the purpose of convenience.

Let us now try to understand what a heat is, which causes so many to choose a male for fear of problems.

Every semestral cycle consists of four phases:

PROESTRUS manifests with an increase in size of the vulva, followed by hematic losses that, differently from the human species, do not indicate that the involution of the uterine mucosa has occurred. Rather they indicate a phase that precedes ovulation and the relative preparation of the uterus to receive the products of conception. This phase lasts about nine to ten days. During this period, although the female attracts males, she will not allow them to mount her.

ESTRUS also lasts about nine to ten days. Ovulation occurs toward the second day with the free-

ESTRUS CYCLE

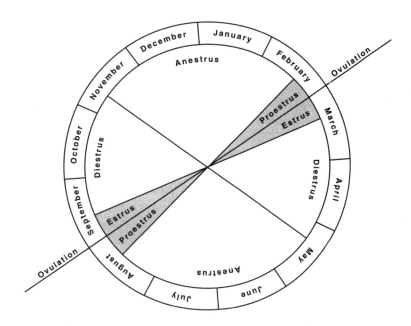

ing of the ovum that remains fertile for more than four days. In this period the female accepts the male and invites him with characteristic behaviors such as playful stiffened posturings, jumps and the lateral movement of the tail (flagging).

DIESTRUS follows the end of the heat and lasts about eight weeks. The uterine mucosa undergoes pseudogravidic modifications. It is at the end of this period that the symptoms of the so called "hysterical pregnancy" may occur, which include occasional lactic secretions and behavior similar to that of a pregnant female.

ANESTRUS occupies the whole period of sexual rest before the next heat, or about three months.

We could say that the heat, made up of proestrus and estrus, lasts about eighteen to twenty days and occurs about two times a year.

Usually the first period falls between January and March and the second between August and September, but this influence of seasons is often altered by domestic life or life with other females.

Clearly the possible "annoying" time only lasts for a short time. In any case, the behavior of the female dog is very different than of the female cat. The latter often cries and undergoes personality changes; the dog usually remains calm. Thus, it is not that difficult to keep her away from potential courtiers.

As far as the blood flow, it is usually quite small, and because this is a breed with long hair, the frequent self cleaning are enough to avoid stains on floors and carpets.

Now that this first problem has been addressed, a few words to those owners of a female who do not want the burden of a litter: it is not at all true that a female must have at least one litter of puppies during her life to avoid serious illnesses such as breast cancer.

Apart from the doubts and uncertainties that have always gone along with these ailments, it is not understandable why there is such alarm for something that is not scientifically proven. I have often seen bitches that had many litters end up with lumps all over their chests. I have also seen virgin dogs reach the age of fourteen with absolutely no problems. There is no evidence that not having puppies causes this problem; the reasons are more likely to be a poor diet or genetic predisposition.

As far as the "false pregnancy" goes, it is caused by an altered hormonal balance, rather than by a true desire for maternity. It is not rare that females that have had these symptoms in the past are not able to produce puppies when bred.

There are also females who refuse to mate. This usually concerns the "only child syndrome"; dogs that have grown far from their companions and are very attached to their owners. These dogs are accustomed to escaping all males and they behave toward the unlucky chosen male like true "animals," showing with satisfaction how good they are at defending their honor.

Naturally, this is not always true. It would be wise, however, to always allow for a good psychophysical development through games and encounters with others of the same species.

Based on these considerations and on an honest evaluation of one's dog, any owner can decide freely about any reproduction. It is a real pity to see, at times, great subjects that are not bred while others, carriers of serious defects, reproduce repeatedly. One must put egoism aside: one cannot only love one's dog without loving the breed that gave this creature the physical and personality traits that we love so much.

The Age of Reproduction

As I have already said, the female Newfoundland goes into heat for the first time at around ten months of age. A gradual increase in the size of the vulva and frequent cleanings indicate that the moment has arrived. At this age, in theory, the time of fertility begins; the body, though, is not yet ready.

The bones are still in the phase of growth and one must wait for the female to be two years old before the bones are totally formed.

If one thinks of the incredible amount of minerals and nutrients that the fetuses require of the mother, it is easy to understand that ailments could result from a premature pregnancy

I would like to add that two or three pregnancies, well spaced and supervised, do not create a problem; more than this could cause a premature aging. These should be distributed between approximately two and a half and seven years of age.

Beginning with the first heat it is a good idea to write down the various dates in order to be able to know, at least approximately, the date of the next heat unless there are irregularities. It is easier this way to notice the discharge from the first day. This is quite important to calculate, when needed, the best period for conception, which is quite short.

If the male and female live together there should be no problems: it is the two partners who choose the right moment. When it is necessary instead to reach a male that lives far away, it is important to be aware of the optimum days that usually occur between the tenth and fourteenth days.

There are some laboratory exams to diagnose the estrus, such as the vaginal smear and progesterone tests. These are quite useful, especially for those who take long and expensive trips, driven by the desire to find good subjects that may strengthen and better the breed. One must not forget that three or four days of travel are not much compared to the time necessary for the care of a litter, and that the expenses and labor are the same if one raise excellent subjects rather than mediocre ones. Thus, it is evident that the choice of the stud dog must be well thought out and not casual.

The Coupling

Once the choices have been made and the best time has been considered, the two partners finally meet. At this point, the union may be concluded in a simple and natural manner or some difficulties may arise. Usually it is the female who is aggressive, and may even cover her partner with bites. This could be caused by an incorrect calculation of the cycle or, more often, to those external and home-life factors previously mentioned. In this case, some necessary help can be given by holding the female and calming her with your voice.

The presence of the owner and a familiar location are of great psychological help to the stud dog.

In relation to the type of coitus and the anatomy of the canine species, a certain amount of supervision is useful. The coupling can last from ten to thirty minutes during which time the male and female remain attached in a permanent manner (tie). Strange or sudden movements of the female could be damaging to the stud dog.

The mount must be repeated two to three times during a three-day period, also keeping in mind the availability of the subjects. In this way it is easier to encompass the moment of ovulation.

Once conception occurs, it usually causes a rapid ending of the estrus; although it may at times continue for a few more days. Thus, the female should also be monitored after the mount to avoid additional fecundations from undesired males.

The Pregnancy

Once the coupling has taken place, the long wait begins, which actually is not very long. The duration of pregnancy is about sixty-three days. I have noted cases varying from a minimum of fifty-nine days to a maximum of sixty-nine days (when there was only one fetus), but usually the time is about sixty-three days. In any case, one must be patient because it is not possible to perform a pregnancy test on the bitch.

Theoretically, one should start feeling the fetuses at around twenty-eight days by palpating the abdomen. In truth, this is quite difficult, both because of the size of the breed and because the female resists such manipulation.

At around forty days, if the number of puppies is normal (seven to eight), one notices a certain rounding just behind the ribs that grows rapidly with the passing of days. From the forty-fifth to the fiftieth day, an increase in the size of the abdomen becomes evident and it is possible, by placing a hand on it, to feel the movement of some of the puppies. Some doubts may remain where there are only a few puppies.

During pregnancy one also notices an increase in appetite. It is important, though, not to exceed in feeding, but rather to pay attention to the quality and nutritional value. As far as protein needs, the portion of meat should be increased from 500 grams (or approximately 1.1 pounds) to 700 or 800 grams (or 1.5 to 1.75 pounds). It is also beneficial to provide milk, eggs and fresh cheese to the female. Cereal intake should vary only moderately.

With a healthy and balanced diet there should be no further needs; however, one can also provide a good vitamin and mineral complex. A good complement to the diet is a calm lifestyle, perhaps in the open air and a sufficient amount of exercise. In some females a change in personality also occurs, in which she becomes even sweeter and calmer.

Toward the fiftieth day, a growth of the mammary glands occurs as they become endematous and very distinct in two parallel rows. A few day before the birth, especially the pluripara (or bitch that has already had two or more litters), they begin to secrete colostrum.

A similar secretion may also occur in the nonpregnant female toward the end of the diestrus, along with a false pregnancy.

At this time, though, a symptom exists that is quite reliable: the thermal course. We know that the normal temperature of a dog is about 38 to 38.5 degrees Centigrade (or 100.4 to 101.3 degrees Fahrenheit). Toward the last five to six days of the pregnancy, this temperature drops by about 1 degree Centigrade (or 1.8 degrees Fahrenheit) about twenty-four hours before the birth. When the delivery begins, the temperature immediately returns to normal.

This factor is of the utmost importance and all owners must be aware of it. It could allow one to make a correct diagnosis capable of saving the mother and the offspring with rapid intervention. If the temperature of a female, which is thought to be pregnant and has presented typical prebirth behavior, descends to 37 degrees Centigrade (or 98.6 degrees Fahrenheit) and returns to normal without giving birth in the following few hours, the aid of a veterinarian is indispensable.

The Delivery

As the moment of birth grows close, some preparation is necessary. What should one prepare for the happy event?

First of all, one must chose a calm room. There should be a bed in a corner made out of a waterproof mat of 120 by 120 centimeters (or approximately 45 by 45 inches) and covered with old sheets. There should be a table near the bed with a scale, pen and paper, colored yarn, scissors, antiseptic, and a basket full of surgical sponges and pieces of cloth.

Many instead use a wooden bed with protruding edges to prevent the mother from lying on her puppies (a whelping box).

During the last stage of pregnancy, the bitch will search for a cave.

Guided by an old instinct, she seeks a hiding place for her puppies, and she can often be found digging enormous holes in the ground. The first contractions alert her that the time has come and she responds in the way that nature has taught her. One must not stop her in her quest. It has been demonstrated that, in certain cases, the delay or interruption of the births was caused by the mother who was put in a strange environment and in a situation that she did not like. Thus, one must leave space for her will; meanwhile show her the bedding that has been prepared. It is a good idea to give her a few sheets or blankets that she can reorganize as she pleases. She might immediately accept her new "room," but in most cases she will continue her search. She may visit, among others, the place we prepared for her, as though evaluating her choice. It could happen that she prefers the house to the garden or, at times, even the bed of the owner. In any case, it is a good idea to take preventive measures.

When the dog goes into labor, she breathes hard and walks around in an agitated manner. Often a viscous liquid is secreted from the vulva, which is caused by the rupture of the mucus plug. At this point, the birth might begin within a few hours, but it can also occur a day or more later. In such cases, the preoccupation of the owner is the concern that all is going well. I must keep repeating that checking the temperature is a necessity. Until the actual birthing occurs, it should be around 36.8 to 37 degrees Centigrade (or 98.24 to 98.6 degrees Fahrenheit). If it returns to 38 degrees Centigrade (or 100.4 degrees Fahrenheit) and no puppies have been born, one must be alarmed.

The bitch must be, in any case, constantly supervised. Most of the time she will be the one seeking the company of her owner. Here we can see how our domestic animals have far distanced themselves from their behavior in the wild, and what a strong feeling of love and trust they have developed for man, when he is for them the good and faithful companion. Often, the female likes to be caressed and seeks this contact by touching your hand with her paw.

When the dilatory phase of the labor ends and the neck of the uterus is wide enough to allow the passage of the fetus, the expulsion phase begins. The bitch has stronger contractions. Most of the time,

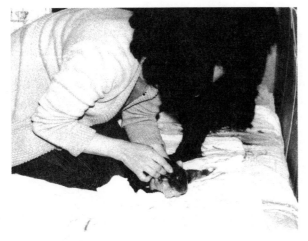

The first puppy is born still enveloped in the amniotic sac; we quickly free him.

The puppy begins to breathe while the mother eats the placenta and cuts the umbilical cord.

A piece of colored string will allow one to distinguish between the various members of the litter.

Under the watchful eye of the mother, the puppy is weighted; this is essential for control of the growth progress.

Conquest of the best position is the first battle in life. (Photo by F. Orebic)

she lies on her side; at other times she is in an almost seated position as though she were defecating. At times she stands and moves. Thus, one must be very careful to notice an interruption of breathing and shivering, accompanied by a lifting of the tail. Soon, you will see the amniotic sac, almost as large as a tennis ball, on the edge of the vulva. When this breaks, it releases fluid. You will soon see the head of the first puppy, followed very quickly by its total expulsion. The head-first presentation is the most common, but puppies born hind-first also occur often (40 percent of the time). Immediately, the mother cuts the umbilical cord with her teeth. At this point, one must be careful that an overly anxious mother does not damage her puppy. Therefore, hold the umbilical cord tightly between your fingers, near the abdomen of the puppy, while the mother bites it. At the same time, check that the puppy is alive and that its nostrils and airways are free. If it is still enveloped in the amniotic sac, you must free him rapidly.

A stimulating massage with a warm piece of cloth may be useful, or in the case of difficulties, an injection of respiratory stimulants. Usually the bitch provides to all the needs of the newborn; she licks it and gives it vitality and soon the puppy crawls toward the source of its milk. In the meantime, the placenta is expelled and the mother quickly eats it, leaving the bed clean. This is a natural instinct that seems to give hormonal substances to the mother that aid in the secretion of milk. The greenish color of this material must not preoccupy you; it is completely normal because of the presence of residual pigments from the marginal hematoma.

While the puppy keeps warm close to his mother, tie a piece of colored yarn around his neck to distinguish him from the others. The piece of yarn, which has enough resistance to avert an accident, must not be too tight or too loose, allowing for the passage of a paw. It must be frequently changed because of the rapid growth, usually at every weekly weigh in. In the meantime, write down the time of birth and the weight of the newborn.

This information, which is not just a matter of being precise, is very useful for evaluating the progress of the delivery and the later growth of the litter.

Almost always there is more than one puppy; having only one puppy is quite rare. The normal litter is of about seven to eight, but ten to eleven is not considered abnormal. After a time that varies from a few minutes to an hour or more, the female once again begins acting in the previously described prebirth manner. Often the birth of a second puppy is immediately followed by that of a third. After another interval, there are another two or three puppies in rapid succession or at regular intervals of about one hour. When the time span between the birth of two puppies is more than three to four hours, it is not rare that there are one or more stillborns; in this case their death may have been caused by a lack of stimulus of the uterine motility or it may have been caused by the long labor.

The entire birth process usually lasts about six to twelve hours for a normal sized litter, but anything can happen. In a personal case, a female, after giving birth normally to five puppies, was calm for twelve hours, after which she gave birth to a stillborn, followed by another two live puppies.

The zonular placenta in the dog: The villi project into the marginal hematoma where they are bathed in maternal blood. This blood undergoes modification to become the so-called "marginal green band."

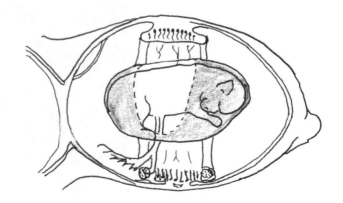

From the following chart one can find information relative to a litter:

First	00:45	red female	grams 550 (19.40 ounces)
Second	01:30	red male	grams 555 (19.58 ounces)
Third	02:48	blue male	grams 510 (17.99 ounces)
Fourth	03:05	yellow female	grams 365 (12.88 ounces)
Fifth	04:05	blue female	grams 510 (17.99 ounces)
Sixth	04:15	green female	grams 560 (19.75 ounces)
Seventh	06:25	orange female	grams 490 (17.28 ounces)
Eight	06:37	orange male	grams 610 (21.52 ounces)
Ninth	07:30	green male	grams 540 (19.05 ounces)
Tenth	07:50	white male	grams 360 (12.70 ounces)
Eleventh	08:45	white female	grams 550 (19.40 ounces)

During the birth, especially if it is lengthy and there are many puppies, give the bitch some beaten egg with coffee (if she is used to having it) or with milk. Water should be placed where she can drink and should be offered to her because it is unusual for her to leave the bed before everything is over.

Every puppy should be identified and weighed. When the number of puppies is high, they should be kept at turns in a warm basket nearby the mother, but separated from her so that she can give birth more easily. One must also be careful that all of the puppies are able to suck enough colostrum in the first few hours of life, as it contains necessary antibodies.

After the delivery, the bitch, exhausted and quiet, will rest with her puppies, licking them in turn to help stimulate their intestinal functions.

The total absence of pushes indicates that the uterus is empty; if contractions of a sort should persist, and one remains in doubt after touching the abdomen, it is best to have an x-ray done.

A few hours after the delivery, invite the female to go outside to relieve herself if she hasn't already. In these first few hours, the motherly love, enhanced by the presence of prolactin, make her very attentive and anxious about her new puppies; consequently, keep away animals or unknown people that may cause her to feel jealous or frightened.

Allow her to spend a considerable amount of time with her puppies feeding them and licking them, and pay particular care to her diet. Meals should be given more often (four or five times a day)

Kluna v. Kilombero of the Moicani Kennel while she feeds her puppies.

in order to give her necessary food without making her feel heavy. In the course of breast feeding, the female produces an amount of milk equal to one and one half to two times her body weight. Her dietary needs are doubled in the first and second weeks and are tripled in the third, obviously keeping in mind the number of the puppies. For an average of six puppies, the amount of meat should be at least one and a half kilograms (or 3.3 pounds) to which you may add milk, eggs, cheese and a good vitamin and mineral complex.

Here, I refer only to the natural delivery, believing that inherent problems of dystocia (or uterine inertia) should be evaluated on an individual basis in the competent hands of a veterinarian.

Particular attention must also be given to the postpartum period.

It is a good idea to take some precautions and, as always, check the temperature of the bitch. In the first two or three days, a slight increase of the temperature (39 to 39.2 degrees Centigrade or 102.2 to 102.56 degrees Fahrenheit) is normal. If the temperature should rise above 39.5 degrees Centigrade (or 103.1 degrees Fahrenheit) or reach 40 degrees Centigrade (or 104 degrees Fahrenheit) one must worry about a postpartum infection or a mastitis, which must be treated with appropriate therapies.

The Puppies

At the time of birth, the baby Newfoundland is all head with small and disproportionate legs. The eyes are closed as are the ears, which appear turned upward and show the contour of the internal lobe. The average weight is between 400 and 600 grams (or 14 and 21 ounces) more or less, but what matters most is the vitality, a characteristic that should always be noted. It is not rare that small puppies are more vital than large ones.

After the mother has cut the umbilical cord with her teeth, invigorating the puppy with powerful strokes of the tongue that will make it roll around, the puppy begins moving in the direction of the heat of the mother's body, the source of food. By moving its head it crawls forward and finally conquers a nipple and stops its search. It is incredible to note the force with which a puppy is able to suck. Soon the simple suction is accompanied by a rhythmical arching of the neck that aid it in pulling the nipple toward it and working with its little paws on the mother's breast.

The First Eight Weeks of Life

In the first fifteen days, the life of the puppy is divided between feeding and sleeping. Food and heat are his only needs, which a healthy bitch, with a good character and good food, should be able to provide without trouble even in the case of a large litter.

The typical sounds emitted by the sleeping puppies, interrupted only by a few yelpings emitted by those who lost their place or have woken up hungry, indicate that all is going well. A longer cry, especially if coming from more than one subject, could instead signify that there is not enough milk or that it is not nutritious enough, that the puppies are cold or that in any case something is wrong. One must find the cause of the screaming and provide the necessary remedy without delay.

If the mother is ill or requires surgery she may not be able to breast feed. It is then necessary to use artificial milk. There are several products on the market that are quite good; if these are not obtainable, one can use fresh cow's milk with three egg yolks per liter (or a bit more than a quart) and a cup of concentrated meat broth plus fifteen to twenty drops of Tricrescin (Note: Because this product is not available in the United States, check with your veterinarian for the recommended substitute.). One must remember that the milk of the mother contains more proteins and fats than cow's milk, which is richer in sugars. However, the important thing is to avoid exaggerating the portions in the beginning. The quality of the food, which even with the supplements is never the same as the natural one, the necessity of using a baby bottle, which at times allows for too much milk to come out forming large lumps in the stomach, or the excessive zealousness of the breeder could all have tragic consequences for the puppy, which cannot overcome serious indigestion.

A factor that must be remembered if the mother is not able to care for her offspring is the necessity of assisting in the bowel's evacuation by massaging the abdomen and the genital area with a warm,

The first 8 weeks.

moist piece of cloth. Luckily, the necessity of this is quite rare in the Newfoundland. However, a breeder must bear in mind the capacity of the bitch to raise her puppies, this being one other index of the health of the breed.

Around the twelfth day, the eyes begin to open; first one can see small openings that open upon the world. In the following two or three days, the puppies begin to observe their surroundings while standing on their unsteady legs, and soon the wonderful encounter that has tied man to dog over the past centuries occurs.

It has been written that nature gives puppies a fundamental code :"If an animal is smaller, chase it; if it is larger, run." Well, as soon as the puppy can focus on the large, erect animal that stands above him, the puppy does not hesitate: abandoning the rules, the small tail wags in a sign of friendship. Without doubt, our smell, fixed in his memory during the dark days of his existence, teaches him to recognize us as a friend.

These are the bases of imprinting, and I never tire of reminding of the importance that this factor has in breeding. Continual good contact with man is essential, especially in the Newfoundland, a rescue dog.

At fifteen days, another factor contributes to strengthening this tie: feeding. For the first two or three days, one may use meat flavored baby food (three quarters of a teaspoon, twice a day). This food is very well accepted though it is new. I would be lying if I were to say that it is easy to place small portions of food in the mouth of an excited puppy. Experts may be able to do this with a teaspoon; others allow the puppy to suck on their finger, though half of the food ends up on the puppy's face. The puppies think about cleaning each other.

Soon, the baby food is substituted with fresh meat of good quality and finely ground, beginning with fifteen grams (or .53 ounces) twice a day and increasing the portion rapidly.

Starting from this moment, it is fundamentally important to maintain the balance of calcium and phosphorous coming from meat with adequate portions of vitamins also containing magnesium and other minerals. It is also important to have water available and offer it often, because a bowl left on the ground soon becomes a place for water games. Depending on the number of puppies and the quality of the maternal milk, one may also have to add milk integrated with the previously listed nutrients. The broth is substituted with a jar of baby food per liter (or approximately 1 quart) of milk. With

Early and frequent contact with puppies is the basis of imprinting—a kind of learning in the young based mainly on maternal attachment and acquisition of basic behavior patterns.

Feeding time.

the use of broth and baby food, one avoids acid diarrheas that are often present at this time. At this age, the puppies already have their first baby teeth, which appeared at about sixteen days. If left in proximity of the mother's filled food bowl, they immediately show how well they can use them! In any case it is better to avoid going too fast, which might cause large digestive and intestinal problems for the entire litter.

Around the fourth week, the first carbohydrates are also introduced, consisting of rice, pasta or well-cooked bran. It may also happen that the mother may regurgitate the food she has eaten near her puppies so that they can eat it. This is a natural instinct that many good bitches retain and that must not be cause for disgust. With this method, nature provides the puppies with a whole series of enzymes and gastric fluids that they have not yet completely produced.

At three weeks, one must do a careful microscopic examination of the feces that often reveal the presence of ascarid (or roundworm) eggs. The infestation is usually picked from the ground, but at this age it can happen by transmission of these eggs from mother to child in a transplacentar way during intrauterine life.

The complex migrations that these undertake throughout the organism, with particular concentration in the intestine, the liver, and the lungs (entero-hepato-pneumo-enteric cycle), cause massive infections, retardation of growth, rachitism and a predisposition to other illnesses. One must take timely action to avoid their diffusion. It is enough to use a specific worming medicine (for example, Conbantrin [(Note: Because this product is not available in the United States, check with your veterinarian for the recommended substitute.]), giving it in a single dose, and repeated at two or three week intervals, depending on the level of infestation and additional microscopic examinations.

Growing very quickly, the puppy is about to reach one month of age. At four weeks his weight should be about 3 to 3.5 kilograms (or 6.62 to 7.73 pounds). In thirty days he increases in weight by six times, and it will be much greater in the weeks to come, reaching 9 to 10 kilograms at two months (or 19.28 to 22.08 pounds). This requires one to think about the necessary care that such a fast growing organism must need. An excess or a deficiency, which would go unobserved in an adult, can be the cause of serious and at times irreversible problems. Everything must be carefully controlled, from diet to exercise. A healthy life in the open air, in a large area with lots of sunshine, enough sleep and play, a fresh and well balanced diet distributed at regular times—this is the perfect recipe for good growth, without ever exaggerating with vitamins.

Example of a whelping box with overhanging borders.

At this time, the puppy's day becomes much more interesting and is directed toward relationships. The games with other members of the litter, the relationship with the mother and other adult dogs, and the contact with the breeder represent a school of life that a healthy and balanced dog undertakes with curiosity and interest. With the games of running, hiding and fighting, the muscles and tendons strengthen, guiding the growth of bones in the right direction. Frequent naps alternated with movement contribute to stimulate the appetite.

Even if the mother still feeds the puppies up to fifty days, breast feeding assumes more of a psychoprotective function and we could define it a dessert.

The real nourishment is divided into five meals throughout the day in the following manner:

8:00 - fresh whole milk, grain, b-complex
12:00 - cereals, pasta or rice (very well cooked), fresh meat, vitamins, minerals, 1 tsp. of corn oil
4:00 - fresh whole milk, biscuits
8:00 - cereals, pasta or rice (very well cooked), meat or fish, minerals
11:00 - fresh, whole milk, dried bread, ground, skinless apple or carrot

The food should be given individually (especially meat and vitamins) so as to avoid some puppies becoming too fat while leaving others without enough food. There are puppies that devour everything in seconds and others that eat slowly. One must also keep in mind any potential individual needs while preparing portions. The portions of food, vitamins and minerals and the times of vaccination and worming are indicated in the chart on the following page. The doses of vitamin A and D are quite reduced. A dog who spends enough time in the sun and has a correct diet, with an intestine and liver in good condition (an absence of worms or viral infections), normally produces enough vitamin D. Giving too much of this vitamin may be dangerous. It might be better to ask oneself whether possible posture defects are not caused by life in an apartment, long walks on the leash, too much weight to bear, or a lack of minerals. Every diet must be personalized, and one must always keep in mind the place where the puppy lives and the season.

Choosing a Puppy

At two months, the puppy is ready to begin a new life with his adoptive family. It is a delicate moment for everyone: for the breeder who wonders about the preparation and capacity of the future owners, for the owners who want to make a good choice but often do not have enough experience, and for the puppy which sees all rhythms of life change at once and sees the disappearing image of the security given by mother and brothers and sisters.

A collaboration based on trust and a common love of the breed provides the best results. The dog lover does not consider this change in property as mere business that is concluded with a sale. There is an exchange: the breeder, following the growth of his products with care, can give the best

FEEDING AND TREATMENT CHART IN THE FIRST TWO MONTHS

PERIOD DOSE	MEAT	MILK	FRESH WHOLE MILK	PASTA OR RICE
WEEK 1		maternal		
WEEK 2		maternal		
WEEK 3	baby food for 3 days 10 grams (.35 oz.) . ground meat	3 bottles of 80 grams (2.82 ounce)	3 egg yolks or baby food in 2 liters (2.114 quarts) milk	
WEEK 4	50 grams (1.76 ounces) divided in 2 meals	3 bottles of 150 grams (5.29 ounces) each	4 egg yolks 1 baby food in milk	well-cooked rice in 2 liters (2.114 quarts) milk or broth
WEEK 5	100 grams (3.53 ounces) divided in 2 meals	3 bowls of 200 gr. each		1 cup twice daily
WEEK 6	160 grams (5.64 ounces) divided twice in 2 meals	3 bowls of 250 gr. each		1 cup daily
WEEK 7	200 grams (7.05 ounces) divided in 2 meals	3 bowls of 250 gr. (8.82 oz.) each		2 cups
WEEK 8	240 grams (8.47 ounces) divided in 2 meals	3 bowls of 250 gr. each		2 cups
WEEK 9	250 grams (8.82 ounces) divided in 2 meals	3 bowls of 250 gr. each		2 cups

PERIOD	VITAMINS	MINERALS # OF MEALS	WORMING	VACCINATION
WEEK 1		6		
WEEK 2		6		
WEEK 3	*idroplurivit 10 drops in 2 liters (2.114 quarts) of milk	1 pinch 5	* conbantrin (21st day)	
WEEK 4	*adisole (concentrate) 1 drop per dog	1/2 teaspoon 5		
WEEK 5	B-complex (1 tsp) *adisole (2 drops)	1 tsp. 5		
WEEK 6	*adisole 2 drops	3/4 Tablespoon 5	*conbantrin (46th day)	
WEEK 7	B Complex (1 teaspoon) pva *adisole (4 drops)	1 Tablespoon 5	in case of worms *Droncit or *Mansonyl	
WEEK 8	*adisole 6 drops	1 Tablespoon 5		
WEEK 9	B-complex (1 teaspoon)	1 Tablespoon 5	feces exam	

*Candur   *Cel *trivalent *adisole(10drops) * Note: If this product is not available in the United States, check with your veterinarian for the recommended substitute.

advice and carefully evaluate the results of the breeding; the owner should then use the experience of the breeder and his constant comparisons with the other members of the litter.

It is quite different when the purchase of a puppy is done quickly, pushed by the impulse of seeing him in a store window. A dog is not a car. Its choice must be made with calm, studied according to the profile of the breed, preceded by visits to various kennels. Only in this way will one notice eventual typological differences, increase one's knowledge and make an intelligent choice.

Although no serious breeder is able to guarantee you a future champion at two month of age, an offspring of excellent subjects, with selected and homogeneous bloodlines, has a greater probability of resembling its parents. It is likely that a waiting time may occur with a puppy from a kennel, but this is better than looking back with sorrow on an impulsive choice. If the desire should vanish in the meanwhile, the lack of available puppies can only be considered a fortunate circumstance.

Growth

If the genetic baggage constitutes the base in the construction of the new being, all of the negative and positive influences that occur in the first year of life complement it. It is enough to observe the growth curve of the Newfoundland to realize what rapid changes occur in only a few months. It is in this stage that life-lasting mistakes can be made, at times for lack of attention, more often for an excess of zealousness and almost always because of inexperience.

The most delicate phase is usually that from three to five months of age. During this time, the puppy must undergo two important events: adaptation to its new environment and growth of its adult teeth. We must keep in mind that all of this is cause for stress and, as we will see, must be followed in the right way, without excesses.

At this age, the skeleton is formed mainly by a protein matrix and is not able to support excessive weight. Consequently, diet and exercise are very important to correct development.

Unfortunately, many owners want to increase the rate of growth by feeding large quantities of food, hyperdosages of vitamins and high protein foods, all of which can cause excess weight and unbalances. Some of the pathologies most common in the young dog of large sizes include secondary hyperparathyroidism, osteocondritis dissecans (OCD), panostosis and hip dysplasia; each may be found as a consequence of these owner excesses, and if not the only cause, one of the major aggravating factors.

The other factor that must be carefully controlled is movement. Everyone knows that in order to grow and to develop a good muscular system the organism needs exercise, but the quality of this exercise becomes of fundamental importance. In nature, puppies play with each other by running and fighting, and then by sleeping. The movements are as different as the terrain upon which they play, and these different movements and terrain give the limbs good structure. Living with people does not always allow for these optimum conditions. For example, the situation of a puppy growing up in an apartment is quite different: his movements are limited to some walks on the leash, low in number and

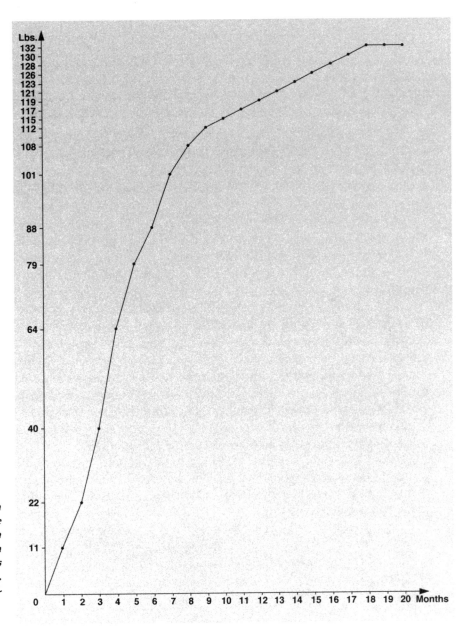

Diagram of the growth curve in a male Newfoundland in the first 20 months. Numbers from top to bottom indicate weight in kilograms. To convert kilograms to pounds multiply by 2.5. Numbers from left to right indicate months.

*Pouch Cove's My American Dream at seven months,
owned by F. Orebic.*

too long in duration. The need for climbing up and down stairs, the pulling at the leash, and constantly walking on shiny and slippery surfaces may cause posture problems that are usually treated with massive amounts of calcium and vitamin D, which are both useless and damaging. Just a few weeks of this treatment is usually enough to make the dog lose its appetite, and then the owner has a new problem to deal with.

All of this would not occur if the puppy could grow in the way nature dictates, with a garden, even a small garden with grass and hard earth, with areas of sun and shade.

It would be even better to have a companion to play with. In this way the various changes that occur in its body, and that surprise the inexperienced owner, have the best conditions in which to develop.

While at two or three months the puppy looks like a woolly bear, at around four months it looses its undercoat and a stronger and shinier coat develops. This new coat goes all along the back from the attachment of the tail, the sides, and the thighs, leaving a few discolored marks here and there. In the meantime, the face get longer while the cranium seems to loose its proportions.

At five to six months, the large puppy is linear and unbalanced, and there is a certain lack of equilibrium between the front and hind quarters. Making a judgment at this age is much harder than for a forty day-old puppy. One must wait until nine or ten months to start seeing some positive traits.

Toward nine months, the proximal growth cartilage of the long bones will seal, and the distal ones will seal at around twelve months. After this age, a lengthening of the bone is no longer possible and moderate increments in size are caused be muscular and tendinous development. At this age, the head gradually becomes proportioned as does the ear, which in the puppy seemed exaggerated and large. In addition, the coat becomes richer with fringes and undercoat, and contributes a new powerful and harmonious look to the dog.

At eighteen months, our Newfoundland may be considered an adult but its growth continues until about two and a half years. The long walks, not indicated in the first months, become after eight or nine months a healthy training that allows the dog to acquire freedom of movement and agility. Naturally, these walks must take place during the cooler hours of the day in hotter months or even substituted, where possible, with swimming.

138

Nutrition

The diet of the dog has always been one of the most debated subjects both by breeders and veterinarians. Through the years, the various theories have been exalted, changed, debated, reaffirmed, without any of them becoming a basis for the subject.

In the beginning of the century, some dogs were fed with soups, bones and leftovers because of economic necessity. This brought an increased number of proteins to their plates, at times creating diets principally consisting of meat, which could be the cause of serious consequences both in growing subjects (secondary hyperparathyroidism) and in adults (kidney exhaustion).

It thus becomes a good idea to reiterate a question, "Is the dog a carnivorous animal?" It depends on what one means by this term. Research done on wolves in the 1980s demonstrated that based on the analysis of excrement, wolves primarily ate small rodents: rabbits, mice and squirrels.

In nature, the first parts of the prey that are eaten are the intestinal contents. Here is a whole series of nutrients, at times already digested and rich in enzymes, that go to integrate the diet of the carnivore: seeds rich in oil and containing large amounts of essential fats, sprouts, berries, fruit and naturally those important vitamins and minerals including vitamin A and D (liver), vitamin C (kidneys) and calcium and phosphorous (bones). When the prey would be a young ruminant, he would even find milk and "cheese," a useful integrator. One must also remember the eggs that many birds lay in nests close to the ground and that are easily reachable and quite well liked. To test this, it is enough to bring our dog to a hen house, next to an unsupervised egg. He does not wait long before eating it without considering the hard-to-assimilate egg white and shell.

From this, one can deduce that the pure carnivorous animal has never existed. One thus may understand how the diet of the dog must reflect as much as possible that which nature provides, including an ample supply of those components that result in a well balanced diet.

Although it is not possible to delve deeper into this subject for which an entire book on diet is necessary, we can take a glance at principal nutritional elements:

-Proteins: Essential components of all cells; they have a principally plastic function and are a necessity for growth and maintenance of the structures of the organism. They also play an important role in the production of enzymes, hormones and antibodies. They are composed of about twenty amino acids of which about ten are essential and not produced by the organism. Their need in the adult animal is of about 22 percent of the dry portion of the food. In the period of growth this percentage increases to about 25 to 30 percent. Proteins are contained in meats, cheeses (100 grams (or 3.53 ounces) of cheese contains about the same amount of protein as 100 grams (or 3.53 ounces) of meat but with twice the calories), in eggs (an egg corresponds to 35 grams (or 1.23 ounces) of meat but has double the energy and four times the amount of fats), and in milk (100 grams (or 3.53 ounces) of milk corresponds to 20 grams (or .71 ounce) of meat with five times the fat.).

-Carbohydrates: These are sugars, starches and cellulose. While the first have the main function of giving energy, the cellulose is eliminated and plays an important role for intestinal mechanics. Carbohydrates represent about 40 to 45 percent of the dried portion of the diet and are usually rice, pasta, toasted bread, cereals and vegetables. Starches must be well cooked to be digestible by a dog.

-Fats: These are made up of a combination of glycerol and fatty acids. They store and give energy; they transport and hold the liposoluble vitamins; they participate in the construction of the cellular membrane and of other important structures. They must be present in 5 to 10 percent of the portion of food and may be animal fats (lard, butter) or vegetable fats (olive oil, corn oil). Carnivorous animals use both saturated and unsaturated fats well, due to their capacity to emulsify fats because of their ample biliary secretions, but it is important to respect a certain balance between the two. The unsaturated fats are present mainly in vegetable oils. Amongst these, linoleic acid, contained mainly in corn oil, is indispensable. The fatty acids give the coat a good shine and prevent exudative dermatitis, dandruff, alopecia, external ear infections and interdigital dermatitis.

-Vitamins: These represent, even in minor quantities, an essential part of the diet. The problems that arise from an insufficiency of vitamins are well-known, but today, an inverse situation occurs in dog breeding from hyperdosages. These are mostly caused by vitamins A and D, liposoluble and thus hard to eliminate once introduced into the organism. In a healthy, fresh and well balanced diet, all vitamins should already be present in sufficient amounts. A glance at the chart allows one to see how often the given doses are well over the advised limit. It is evident that a moderate dose in order to avoid potential deficiencies from altered absorption or from an increased need does not cause damage. Often though, without noticing it, some owners add together different elements containing the same vitamins to reach absurd levels of the vitamins. It may also occur that these elements are given at the same time: integrated foods, cod liver oil, calcium with added vitamin D, and as if this were not enough, injections of an identical product. Such a treatment for a few weeks causes long term and often irreversible consequences. Therefore, before using a product, it should be carefully evaluated and its components analyzed.

-Minerals: These components could be needed in high doses including calcium, phosphorous, magnesium, potassium, sodium and chlorine, or in traces such as the metallic minerals iron, zinc, copper, manganese, selenium, iodine and so forth. These are indispensable for the process of the organism, and they intervene in many vital functions (basic-acid balance, regulation of the osmotic pressure, myocardial contactability, catalyzing reactions and so forth.). The interest in these minerals in breeding is mainly directed toward those factors that intervene in the skeletal development. A correct calcium to phosphorous ratio appears to be of fundamental importance. In nature, the carnivorous animal balances these values by feeding himself muscles and bones. This is not so for the dog that lives with people because these products are excluded from his diet because of the justified fear of intestinal perforations. Meat contains a low amount of calcium (9 milligrams per 100 grams) in a 1:20 ratio with phosphorous, when instead this ratio should be of 1.2:1. An altered blood level is the consequence, verifiable through a blood test, which stimulates the parathyroid glands to draw the calcium from the bones, demineralizing and weakening them. This pathology, called secondary hyperparathyroidism, osteofibrosis, or "all meat" syndrome becomes more serious as the amount of meat increases. It can be avoided by giving some foods rich in calcium such as dairy products. One can also introduce chicken necks to the daily portion of food, slightly boiled, which are of no danger because of the soft and fragile bone that they contain. In any case, it is always be important to integrate the diet of the growing dog with a mineral supplement containing magnesium and other elements. For a correct osteogenesis (or bone development) a balanced administration of minerals is more important than that of vitamin D, which a healthy organism can work out itself.

MINERAL	GROWTH	MAINTENANCE
calcium	320 mg	119 mg
phosphorous	240 mg	89 mg
potassium	240 mg	89 mg
sodium	30 mg	11 mg
chlorine	46 mg	17 mg
magnesium	22 mg	8.2 mg
iron	1.74 mg	0.65 mg
copper	0.16 mg	0.06 mg
manganese	0.28 mg	0.10 mg
zinc	1.94 mg	0.72 mg
iodine	0.032 mg	0.012 mg
selenium	0.006 mg	0.002 mg

VITAMINS	GROWTH	MAINTENANCE
A	202 UI	75 UI
D	22 UI	8 UI
E	1.2 UI	0.5 UI
K	60 UI	24 UI
thiamin (B1)	54 mcg	20 mcg
riboflavin (B2)	100 mcg	50 mcg
Pantotenic acid	400 mcg	200 mcg
Nicotinic acid (PP)	450 mcg	225 mcg
Pyrodoxin (B6)	60 mcg	22 mcg
Folic Acid (Bc)	8 mcg	4 mcg
Biotin (H)	6 mcg	—
Cianocobalamine (B12)	1 mcg	0.5 mcg
Choline	50 mcg	25 mcg

After this easily understood information, there follows a practical scheme of diet I have used for years. With this diet I do not expect to achieve abnormal results, but only to allow my dogs to express their genetic potential, live a healthy life, and serenely reach the age of 13 to 14.

Diet at Two Months

8:00: 300 grams (or 10.58 ounces) milk, 1 egg yolk (4 times a week), 10 drops of Vetidasole or similar (check with your veterinarian).

12:00: rice or pasta soup, quite thick with meat broth and vegetables, 120 grams (or 4.23 ounces) raw meat in small pieces, 1 teaspoon minerals, 1 teaspoon corn oil

4:00: 300 grams (or 10.58 ounces) milk with cereals

8:00: rice or pasta soup, 120 grams (or 4.23 ounces) meat (or fish or half meat and half cheese), 1 teaspoon minerals, 10 grams (or .35 ounce) brewers yeast

11:00: 300 grams (or 10.58 ounce) milk, dried bread, carrot or apple to chew on.

The meals will be reduced in the following manner: at 3 months the 11:00 meal is eliminated; at 5 months the 4:00 meal is eliminated. After 15 months, the meals occur twice a day. The portion of rice goes from 200 grams (or 7.05 ounces) to 400 grams (or 14.11 ounces)-weighed raw.

The portion of meat is increased in approximately the following manner:

3 months: 350 grams (12.35 ounces)
4 months: 450 grams (15.87 ounces)
5 months: 550 grams (19.40 ounces)
6 months: 600 grams (21.16 ounces)
7 months: 700 grams (24.66 ounces)
from 8 to 18 months: 800 to 900 grams (28.22 to 31.75 ounces) a day.

After 18 months the portion of meat is reduced to 500 to 600 grams (17.63 to 21.16 ounces) daily. It is always a good idea to vary the type (chicken, turkey, beef, fish) and to alternate partially with other proteins (cheese, eggs, and so forth). The meat must be cut in pieces to aid the function and motility of the stomach and to avoid torsion. This is also true for giving meals twice a day: it prevents distending the ligaments more than necessary. There are various theories regarding this, but as far as diet is concerned, nothing is certain and everything changes. It seems to me, though, that certain thick and inconsistent soups that are fed once a day are deposited in the bottom of the stomach as in a bag, and do not help to prevent the feared "bloat."

There are also different opinions with regard to milk. Personally, I consider it a complete food and I advise giving some to adult dogs also to maintain the activity of lactase enzymes. A dog that is no longer able to digest it often reacts with attacks of diarrhea. If it is tolerated, you can substitute milk for one of the meals on a hot day when your dog appears lazy and lacks appetite.

As far as vitamin and mineral doses go, the table of daily needs compared to the individual growth chart is useful for a fairly precise integration. These portions are to be considered purely indicative and used for comparisons. However, the various charts and rations, determined through very careful studies, represent statistical results while the actual use should be directed toward individual subjects with different needs.

Once again, common sense determines the right measurements: a healthy dog eats a good portion with appetite. If he leaves some of it and is in good health, diminish the portion. If, on the other hand, he finishes all of his food and seems to be looking for more, try to increase it a little bit. Metabolisms vary. Even in humans there are people who seem to be insatiable who do not gain an ounce while others gain weight with only the smallest excess. In order to determine to which category your Newfoundland belongs, raise the abundant skin on the back. If it is elastic, there are no problems; if it seems thick because of the presence of an underlying fat fold, reduce the diet.

Finally, I would like to add something about prepackaged foods, which are more and more in use today. Without denying their convenience and the good intentions of the dog food industry in producing very specialized products of the best quality, I believe that none of us would agree to eat canned meat for an entire lifetime. Thus, why should we put our best friends in this situation? Besides, the use of variety presents a great advantage: that of not bringing errors to an extreme. A diet that is always the same can, with a minor unbalance, provoke serious problems over time.

Ordinary Cares

Although correct growth and a healthy diet represent the basis of your dog's health, it is also important to keep other influences under control in order to keep it in the best possible condition.

Parasites

There are basically two types of parasites: internal and external. The external parasites include fleas, lice, ticks and mites. Fleas represent mainly an annoyance for the dog who feels itching, but their presence can result in dermatitis and lesions in the event of allergies. On the other hand, ticks and mites can have more serious consequences. Ticks, aside from causing massive infestations and dangerous anemia, aid in the transmission of piroplasmosis and rickettsiosis, serious conditions that degenerate the condition of a dog rapidly and may cause death if there is not a quick intervention.

The optimum results of a proper diet.

Various types of mites can cause sarcoptic mange, both generalized and auricular (or ear) dermatitis.

The best prevention against the external parasites is a systematic control and interventions that aim at eliminating the infestation of the habitat. Moderate antiparasite treatments on the dog may be necessary in certain seasons of the year.

The internal parasites include roundworms (ascarids), hookworms (ancylostoma), tapeworms (cestodes), heartworms (dirofilaria immitis), whipworms (trichuris vulpis), and threadworms (strongyloides stercoralis). As it is not possible to elaborate on such a vast subject in this book; I advise you to inform yourself about them and about the necessary remedies. I can only remind everyone that each parasite must be fought with a specific method and that often the diagnosis requires microscopic examination. The use of periodic treatments with polyvalent products, even as a preventive measure, is not advised and is often harmful because of the toxic effect of these products.

In the case of heartworm, transmitted by mosquitoes and which, like leishmaniasis, is more and more common today, it is instead necessary to take preventive measures in regions that have a significant risk.

Vaccinations

The viruses against which a dog is normally vaccinated are distemper, infectious hepatitis, leptospirosis, kennel cough, parvovirus and rabies. Except for the rabies vaccination, which, in Italy, is done at six months or, even better, at one year of age, the other vaccinations are usually administered at around eight or nine weeks. When one buys a two-month-old dog, it should have already received the basic vaccinations. However, one must remember that fifteen days are necessary for the vaccinations to be effective. Thus, a certain caution is necessary. One must avoid exposing the dog to potential contagious situations, particularly places that are frequented by other dogs (for example dog shows). At twelve to fourteen weeks, the booster vaccinations are given, which are then repeated once a year.

Without wanting to excessively alarm people, be aware that in certain cases weak dogs or dogs that are particularly sensitive could develop reactions to the vaccinations that may be serious. I want to remind owners that there are homeopathic treatments useful in preventing such reactions. This type of medicine, which is now becoming popular among veterinarians as well, should be better known. It may also be particularly useful in other areas, especially during the growth period when balancing health depends on the basic health of individual organisms.

Grooming

The shine of the hair and the shape of the coat are mainly derived from the biochemical composition of the organism, but adequate external treatment is essential to maintain optimal conditions. Many consider grooming a large dog such as the Newfoundland a difficult task. In reality, it becomes quite easy when grooming is frequent and efficient. The dog must learn from a young age to be groomed once or twice a week. In this manner he learns to remain still lying first on one side and then on the other and finally to remain standing for the finishing touches.

While combing him talk to him quietly and pet him. He will be pleased by your attentions and let you continue what you are doing without complaining. This procedure will thus become a pleasurable time of relaxation for both. Things are very different when a dog is not groomed often. He will not like this novelty, especially when the fringes and the undercoat, which have been ignored, are knotted. Intervention with scissors, which is very damaging, may be necessary at times. If this should happen, one must remember that a knot must not be cut straight, but divided in stripes in the direction of the lengths of the hair and then separated manually or with a comb.

A neglected coat may also interfere with the breathing of the skin and result in inflammatory reactions and lesions. The grooming must thus be regular with particular care during those periods in

The importance of exercise.

which the dog changes coat, and the undercoat practically collapses. Many use a hook brush for this operation, but this only acts superficially for a long-

haired dog such as the Newfoundland; thus, under an apparently cared for coat, knots continue to form. Instead, the ideal is a steel comb with long teeth that allow one to disentangle the hair in all of its lengths; the brush is then used for the final touches.

Often it is necessary to eliminate excessive hair that is formed between the toes and that eliminate the rounded look of the feet. In the summer, it is also important to check daily that burrs are not between the toes that can perforate the skin and penetrate deeply to cause serious infections.

If the back fringes of the ears are too long, they can be thinned, avoiding a sharp line that would give the look of other breeds.

Cleaning the ears with a bit of cotton and baby oil completes the grooming. It is important to avoid using Q-tip® cotton swabs that may irritate the hearing cavity. If the dog should shake its head or hold it tilted to the side, note that a burr may have penetrated inside the ear and immediately call the vet. Such behavior may also indicate a simple ear infection, perhaps caused by parasites. The shaking of the head can also cause an otohematoma (or a hematoma of the ear canal) because of the trauma. This is a hematic buildup between the skin and the cartilage that has great swelling as a symptom. This can be surgically removed; although personally I prefer encouraging its reabsorption through the application of a prescribed topical lotion. Use one recommended by your veterinarian.

Baths with shampoo should not be too frequent because they remove the coat's natural protection. After every swim in salt water, it is a good idea to rinse the dog with clear water to help him dry faster and to avoid a reddening of his hair.

Shows

What is, or what should, be the main goal of showing? The specific regulations of the Italian Kennel Club (ENCI) define it as a "canine manifestation in which dogs are judged for their beauty and exterior conformation, in relation to the official standard of the breed to which they belong." These terms define precisely the goal of such shows: comparing a dog with the standard and with others of his breed, and selecting the best examples.

For the dog lover it mainly represents a meeting place and a way to verify the breeding programs. For many owners it is instead a first experience that might remain the only one, or it may involve them in a growing passion.

144

How should a newcomer behave? What must he do for the show?

It is important to pay attention and to remain calm. A dog is very sensitive and can detect our nervousness simply by the way we hold the leash. Some dogs are born to become champions. In the ring, they are perfect: head held high, attentive expression, legs well placed. The walk is their specialty: an elegant and contained trot, a fluid and shiny waving of the coat. Others instead prefer to show their behind to the judges and look at the owner questioningly," What's up? Why did you bring me here? And what are we supposed to do?" And, if one tries to calm them, the least they do is jump up and lick you in the face or lay on the ground belly up.

All of this is understandable, but what does the judge think? He needs to see everything in those few seconds that he can dedicate to each dog and does not have time to wait. He must give a judgment that is the fairest according to his conscience. Every part is methodically and carefully examined: head, teeth, back, position, general impression—and it is not always easy.

"How is the hind quarter of that subject which walks without fluidity? And the anterior train of that other subject which is dragging its owner? Are its elbows wide or is it caused by its gait?"

And how does the showing of the teeth go? No dog likes to have a stranger's hands placed in its mouth, and some do not even like it when it is their owner doing it. So a benevolent battle begins: the dog throws itself to the ground, the collar comes off, someone intervenes to help, but before one

A relaxing moment during a show.

Ch. Debbye degli Angeli Neri, owned by C. Del Bue.

can do so, the owner is able to open the dog's mouth and the judge sees only its tonsils, which was certainly not what he wanted to see. Ever hear about overshot, undershot, lack of molars? So here they are together, trying to sort out this problem.

Every dog should receive a bit of training; it is useful for living in society; if one also wants to show him, it then becomes indispensable. In particular, he should learn to walk on the left side of the owner without pulling and to stop in a standing position. He must allow his mouth to be examined and he must also learn to be civil in the company of other dogs.

At this point let's try to put ourselves in the dog and the owner's shoes. After a long trip, they arrive. From the previous day our friend noticed the air of preparation and became more and more excited until the moment of departure. When he finally comes out of the car, what he sees is the most exciting thing that can possibly exist for him. In the entrance there are a lot of people and dogs, but while man tries or pretends to lose himself in the crowd, the animal inevitably feels the presence of the other dogs. His greatest desire is that of getting acquainted, of smelling them. Instinctively he understands what others expect of him: if they want to be friends or enemies, if they are males or females, young or old. At that moment though, he can't comprehend why the owner won't allow him to meet these others. The owner wants the dog to stay still, to hold his tail down, to show training that may not have been received, and so he continues to jerk on the leash, not allowed to fulfill his canine desires. Not allowing him to do his "research" may cause him to do it later, perhaps when he's in the middle of showing he may stop, stick his nose to the ground and follow a trail that he found. Instead, fulfill his curiosity, allow him to go close to other dogs, walk him quietly, give him water. Allow him to rest quietly without bothering him. About this, many things should be explained to people who go to see dog shows. Even though a Newfoundland may not react, it is not fair to have him receive hundreds of pats on the head.

There are also the owners who are maniacal about perfection. They do not allow their dog to lie down, fearing that leaves or dust may ruin the masterful grooming. If the judging is late, it is also possible that the dog, tired and bored with the pretenses, may lie down in the middle of being judged. Let's not forget that a well-cared for coat only needs a few brush strokes before entering the ring in order to look perfect.

Finally the time has arrived. The subjects are called based on their class: champions, open, puppies. The representatives of each class are then examined alone. The subject thus waits on the edge of the ring awaiting his turn. The dog must be left alone, and at the sign of the judge quickly presented. At the moment of examination he needs to be placed (stacked) correctly, being careful that uneven ground might make him look taller in the back and that would make him appear thrown forward.

The correct method to examine teeth and bite.

146

I am opposed to certain forced presentations: I believe them to be unnatural for the Newfoundland and I believe that they also do not allow the judge to see the real profile of the spine. One should be careful though that all four legs are correctly placed. If, for example, one of the forequarters should be further back than the other or moved outward, have the dog take a small step forward.

Those who are strong enough may even pick up the whole anterior train and replace it on the ground in the correct position, such as is done for the small breeds. It is absolutely negative that the dog smell the ground. In order to do this, he opens the anterior limbs, the withers lower and the spinal profile is no longer horizontal to the ground.

When the head and expression are being judged, it is a good idea to have the dog be attentive. In this manner, the ears are pulled forward, the cranium is more rounded, the forehead more marked, and the whole effect is very positive. At times, the judge may try to achieve this himself. It is also possible to seek outside help, as long as it does not disturb the other dogs. When the dog is interested in a person on the outside, it is enough for him to move slowly around the ring, the dog will follow his every movement, thus obtaining the desired effect.

After this the judge checks the teeth. What he is interested in is the bite, thus the mouth must remain closed and only the lips must be raised. He then goes on to evaluate the depth of the thorax, the bone structure, the solidity of the back and flanks, the texture of the coat and the development of the testicles in the male. In order to do this, he touches the dog gently, and this must occur at all times without reaction by the animal. This is very important in the evaluation of the character. A Newfoundland which is untouchable because of aggressiveness or fear is worse than one that is monorchid, rachitic or lame. If many breeds have undergone psychological deterioration, this is because of those who saw in them only nice looking "objects" without a brain.

After the examination has finished, the subject must show its gait. It is almost always quite difficult for the judge to have the subject walk in the right direction. He must see the movement of the limbs from the front and from the side. Thus the handler must have the dog walk away from the judge in a straight line and return on the same line; a triangular figure may also be requested. The dog must absolutely not pull; if this should happen, stop him, and then move again holding the leash short but not taut. The pace must be a normal walk or a relaxed trot. If the dog should begin cantering, try to accelerate in order to make him change the leading foot. In some subjects however, especially those who are a bit overweight, ambling is a habit and a defect.

Once the individual subject has had his turn in the ring, every dog receives a judgment and a qualification. European show classifications have the following lettering: AB (fairly good), B (good), MB (very good), ECC (Excellent). If there are various subjects they are then compared in order to create a qualification. In the national shows, the judge can assign CAC (Attitudinal Championship Certificate) to the male and female qualified as first; in the Open Class, ECC is assigned; in the international shows, aside from the CAC, the CACIB (International Beauty Championship Attitude Certificate) may be assigned.

In order to be an Italian Champion, the Newfoundland must obtain four CACs, two awarded in international shows and two ECC Firsts in the Open Class in a show organized by the Italian Newfoundland Club. The titles must be given by at least five different judges.

In order to be an International Champion, the dog must have obtained four CACIBs in three different countries and with at least three different judges. One of the CACIBs must be obtained in the country of residence.

An important consideration must be made: because everyone likes to win, one tends to give greater importance to the order of qualification, when instead the qualification and judgment are more important than the order. Although the first should be the obvious consequence of the second two, it is through these last two that we understand how our dog has been judged, what he was able to show of himself, and what impression he made on the judge. The important thing is to accept whatever judgment is given. The look of the dog is not always the same; there are elements of shape and

A day's outing on the river.

details of a particular presentation that may vary from show to show. Thus, it is not a good idea to get discouraged if success is not achieved or to rejoice too much for a victory. Mainly, it is important to keep gaining knowledge about the breed. Certainly, a good preparation is the best way to attain objectivity and this is the real goal to which all of us must aim.

VII. TRAINING

Anyone thinking of the Newfoundland immediately imagines this great hero saving a man in great danger in water. This image has been created through centuries of living with seamen and has reached us through a series of traits that came together for a specific reason. The notable strength and impressiveness, balanced by a sweet and calm personality have become the support for two particular instincts: an innate ability for swimming and a great passion for retrieving.

It is enough to observe the behavior of a puppy of only a few weeks to notice it: an object of any dimension brings out his desire to retrieve it, hold it, and transport it. One way of greeting the owner or any newcomer is that of bringing him something, sometimes a leaf or a stick, sometimes objects of clothing. Some puppies also have the instinct of grabbing the owner by the hand and leading him. As we have already said, it is an admirable instinct that must be allowed.

The proverbial passion for water is always present. Anyone who wants a Newfoundland must share this passion at least in part; if not how could he tolerate a companion who tries to swim in his water bowl or prefers to play in puddles rather than to avoid them?

If the choice is right though, and water is the passion of both man and dog, they become an inseparable couple. They learn to understand each other more and more, and give each other satisfaction, reinforcing the initial relationship until it becomes a perfect understanding.

All of this has a base in the training, a term that many do not understand and identify as an abuse, a way of having the dog become submissive. This is absolutely not true. For he who loves animals, training is essentially a wonderful dialogue with one's dog, a reciprocal exchange of respect and comprehension. Teaching him with joy means showing interest in him, giving him a way to understand us, and of pleasing us, which is what he primarily wants. So, step by step, all of the exercises of a training program further strengthen the relationship between the two and cause them to be inseparable companions who work with the same goal in mind.

It is important though that the training of the Newfoundland be done by the owner. The dog learns for love; in front of a stranger he could be hardheaded. It therefore seems quite unnecessary to me to have him come to love another, or even worse, to obey for fear. It would be like sending a child off to boarding school because one does not feel like, does not know how or does not have the time

The passion to retrieve is already evident in the puppy.

149

Inseparable pair.

to educate him. There is not much work to do, just a few minutes a day, but consistence and patience are essential.

I can assure you though, that training is a very useful exercise. Calm is important in the delicate moments of the task, because anger may ruin the work of many weeks and make the dog stop idealizing its owner. Thus, constant self-control is necessary and allows one to come out of this experience as a better person.

At What Age Should Training Begin?

The relationship of trust at the base of training must begin as soon as possible. The dog must see you as the leader of the pack, feel safe with you, know that you are stronger, because in this way he is guided and protected. This superiority, though, must not be an abuse because he must also know that you are fair with him.

I think that the first contact between the puppy and the owner when he reaches his new home are of utmost importance. Imagine, for example, this scene: your two month old puppy comes to your house for the first time. The family greets him with joy; the children scream. Grandfather looks for his positive and negative points; the next door neighbor comes to take a look. All attentions are concentrated on him, but in the wrong way. The puppy may appear timid and remain lying down in a corner, or he may begin inspection of his new home. At a certain point he smells the ground, maybe he goes to the door and cries. Everyone watches him, but no one understands him. He lies down and goes to the bathroom. At this point the children laugh; the mother runs to get something to clean up, thinking that problems have begun. The grandfather thinks that this new arrival needs a lesson; the friend advises rubbing his face in his excrement and give him a little swat on the behind. The father doesn't know what to do, and the puppy? Well! The puppy thinks that this is the right place to go to the bathroom. But he is wrong! After sleeping and eating he looks for this place again and right when he is about to go to the bathroom, he gets a slap on the behind. The dog thus thinks that he is being punished because he is going to the bathroom, that his owner is unfair, and that next time he will hide his urine, maybe on the carpet in the living room floor that absorbs so well.

150

Look, A water bucket for bathing!

Things instead should go this way: During the trip home someone will pet and reassure the puppy. They should make him feel the warmth and smell of their body. This person should be the one that wants him the most and who will primarily dedicate himself to the dog.

As soon as he arrives, he must find a calm place, a bed, a bowl of water, and something to eat. Thus, he knows that there is a place to drink in his new home, and that you are aware of his needs. Be careful though! Your puppy is a Newfoundland; the water should be given in a bowl that he cannot spill, otherwise the most likely occurrence is that once he has spilled his water on the floor, he will lie in it.

While he inspects his new home you will follow him, and as soon as he looks at you, talk to him very sweetly and with a calm voice; after a few seconds he will begin wagging his tail. This is a sign of friendship. Naturally, after a while he will smell around and look for a place to go to the bathroom. Immediately place him outside. Stay with him, and as soon as he has gone to the bathroom, pet him and bring him back into the house. This operation must be repeated for a few days, every time that the puppy wakes up or eats. Don't forget that he is like a small child and has more frequent bathroom needs than an adult.

If he should go to the bathroom in the house, behave in the following manner: if you don't see him doing it, ignore what happened and clean up with strong deodorants. If you notice it right away, even if you remembered to take him outside, take him by the skin of the neck, shake him a bit and say with a strict voice "NO!" and put him outside. From these first approaches the dog will begin to understand the tones of your voice; he will understand that there are some limits to what he is allowed to do, but that these limits are made by a fair person who cares about him.

Talk to your dog often; pet him. One surely obtains more from a Newfoundland with sweetness rather than with forcefulness. Careful though: demonstrate sweetness, not weakness. Each of these things that you teach your friend will be useful to him in the future. These lessons enable him to be appreciated and accepted even by those who do not particularly like dogs and they allow him to stay with us everywhere. This will make him happy. Also, dogs get lonely. And certainly a dog who is used to pulling on the leash, crossing the street, chasing cats and chickens, a dog who does not come when called, who likes to pick fights with other dogs or to jump on everyone to greet them, is not a relaxing companion, and may also get us into trouble.

"I love you!"

Concentration is an important factor in training.

Thus there are things that must be taught and behaviors that are unacceptable and that must be punished. However, it is of utmost importance not to act out of anger. A gentle slap on the behind accompanied by an annoyed and disappointed tone of voice are enough and do not damage the dog physically. In the same way it is very important to know how to praise him. Petting must not be mechanical, but a gesture of deep love. Your voice when praising him should show satisfaction and pride; it should make him feel that you are very happy with him. Most of all, you must not contradict yourself, do not use different terms. One must not try to force the dog into thinking like us, but you must bring yourself to his psychological level. You must be sure that the dog has understood well what you want from him.

There is a sentence that I will never forget that comes from the *Practical Training Manual*, written by A. Fatio:

152

If you had a maid working for you, from a country whose language is totally different from yours, and you tell her to sweep the kitchen, she will look at you curiously, trying to guess from your face what it is that you are asking her. If you interpret this as laziness or unwillingness to work and you slap her, you will create in her a very simple association of ideas: the order and the slap. Every time that she hears you asking her to sweep the kitchen, she will react by covering her face with her arm, even though she may be very intelligent. If, on the other hand, when you ask her to do this for the first time, you place the broom in her hands, and when telling her the second time you show her the broom, you will see that the third time she will get the broom by herself, looking at you to make sure that she understood well.

This is the basis upon which one must work. There are always little things that you must do in order to have the dog understand what it is that you want from him and to make it a pleasure for him to obey you.

The Recall (3 months)
The puppy must learn right away to be called by his name. He must find it pleasurable. Thus, it is important not to change it once the choice has been made. It is possible that he already has one; if possible, it should be kept. As soon as he is with you, you should call his name and immediately afterwards say, "Good," in a sweet voice. If he comes toward you, pet him under the throat or on the side, then let him go.

The secret to having an obedient dog is to respect the need for freedom that every living thing needs. The puppy is naturally lively and curious; he needs to run, and play. One cannot expect that he must always be at our side without allowing for all of the above. Thus, before beginning the recall exercises, seek an open space where there is no danger from cars. Bring your puppy there and allow him to play. If he should go too far away from you, call his name, catching his attention by clapping your hands or moving your arms, run as though you are playing with him or throw him a ball.

Once you see that he has played enough, call him, following the name with the command "Come." As soon as he obeys, pet him. Press his side against your leg, patting him affectionately on the ribcage, making him feel how nice it is to be together. At times we can also give him a little treat; not always, however, because otherwise he obeys only for that and it is enough for him to smell you in order to decide whether to come or not. He must come for the pleasure of being with you. Immediately after, release him with the word, "Go."

It may happen that he does not come back immediately. So, after calling him, quickly go away from him. The dog will follow for fear of losing you. If he overtakes you, change directions; he will do the same. As soon as he is at your side, praise him and then let him go with the order, "Go."

With a hardheaded or very-sure-of-himself adult dog, you may need some help. You may set up a situation on a country road where the dog will have a negative encounter. Ask a helper, who in this case must not be someone that the dog knows, to hide at a turn or in the bushes. A few yards before our helper free the dog.

Before he reaches the place where the person is hiding, call him; if he should not obey he should see a rain of pebbles coming from the sky. As he advances he should see the stranger come toward him, menacing him with a leafy branch. The way toward the owner must be the only direction in which he can go. The dog will return to you, and you will have to seem like a protector and reassure and defend him. Be careful though: in no situation must one hit the dog once he returns. It is good to always release him after this exercise. Only once he is tired and lies down at your feet should you put the leash back on him.

Heel on the Leash (3 to 4 months)

This is a fundamental and essential exercise for the Newfoundland. Because of his great strength and resistance, this dog was used in his native land for pulling; thus it is instinctive. He thinks that he is helping his owner. While the dog weighs less than 30 kilograms (66.23 pounds), things will go smoothly, but what will happen when his 60 kilograms (132.45 pounds) of muscle drags you around the street, jerking on your arms? Not everyone has biceps and legs like the drivers of the Roman chariots and thus you will have to forget about taking your "bulldozer" with you. As long as you are stronger than him, however, it is not to hard to teach him the right habits.

First of all, absolutely no choker collars! As a collar, the ideal is a small, flat chain in one band, which does not rip the long hair even if one leaves it on his neck for several hours. It should have a leather leash, with two very strong clasps and two rings.

For the first few months, one must instead use a small leather collar. The exercise requires small jerks on the neck of the dog at short intervals. The choker collar absorbs the jerk and renders the exercise useless. Furthermore, one cannot be sure how much strength is needed and is afraid of hurting the animal.

The first reaction of a puppy on a leash is the same as that of a gelding with saddle and bridle: he starts bucking. One he has jumped a couple of times, he gets further way, pulling backward on the leash and looking at you with a questioning air. You must reassure him immediately, speaking to him tenderly. You then begin walking, pulling him along decisively. The moment he begins to understand that the collar does not represent anything more than a slight annoyance, he will follow you, at first stubbornly and then more confidently. It can even happen that once he begins to gain confidence, he will begin to precede you and pull you along.

Here the exercise begins.

The position of your hands on the leash is important.

The dog must always be held on your left side. This allows you to have him between you and the wall when you walk him, and leaves you a certain amount of space on the right. Both hands must be free, so you should not take the dog for his first walk if you are going shopping. The left hand should hold the leash near the collar; the right hand should hold the head and the remainder of the leash. If the dog should pull and manage to jerk the leash away from our left hand, you will still be able to hold him with the right because of the length of the leash. There must not be constant pressure on the leash, otherwise the dog will pull. At the first sign of disobedience say, "Heel," and win his

Swimming out with the harness.

resistance by bringing his head to the height of your knee, releasing immediately after the hold. The leash must hang next to the neck. If the dog is shy and moves away, by patting your leg encourage him to come closer. The exercise is properly done only when the dog is able to follow you in every direction. After having given the command, "Heel," quickly turn left or right. If the dog tends to go forward, he will hit against your knee; if he strays behind, he will feel the pull of the leash. Or, you can pass near a tree so that he must stay between it and you. If he does not do this, he will get tangled with the leash around the tree trunk. Soon he will learn to follow carefully. After about ten lessons you will be able to go on to the heel exercise without the leash. This will be easy to learn only if the previous lesson was learned perfectly. The dog will walk at your side. Your hand will move next to him. All you will need will be the command, "Heel," to have him come closer if he moves away.

Sit, Stand, Lay Down (5 to 6 months)

The dog has learned to observe you. He knows that obeying your commands provides him with praise and thus is a satisfaction for him and that, in substance, his freedom is not limited. At this point we can teach the "Sit," "Down " and "Stand" commands.

After having walked for a bit on the leash, stop, placing yourself in front of the dog. Give the command "Sit." Logically, he will not understand. Return to his side, holding the leash high, and push down on his behind. The dog will sit. Pet him, and scratch him under he throat. If he should try to get up, a decided, "No," and pressure on his behind will dissuade him. In order to have him lie down, give the command to an already sitting dog. Pull the anterior limbs forward and exert pressure on the withers. As soon as he is in the correct position, praise him as usual. The correct lying down position is that of the sphinx. The standing position is obtained by pulling on the collar after giving the, "Stand," command clearly.

All of the above exercises must be repeated daily for a few minutes, trying to work on them when the dog doesn't have other distractions and is not too excited. As soon as he has understood the meaning of the three commands, he must obey immediately; if not, catch his attention by saying in a severe tone, "What did I tell you?" One must not repeat the command several times, because he would get used to delaying the obedience.

Stay (7 to 8 months)

The puppy now knows how to correctly obey the command "Down." Now, unhook the leash, giving the command "Stay." His first instinct is to follow you. As soon as he tries to get up, say a severe, "No." If he gets up anyway, take him a few steps away from the place where he was lying down. Repeat the command. If he disobeys, take him a bit further. His love for you pushes him to follow you. If at every disobedience you place him further away from you, he will understand that it is not what he wants. He will be perplexed and watch you disconcertingly as you walk away. As you go further away, after just a few steps, quickly return to him and praise him. He will thus be very happy to wait, because every return will be an opportunity for praise.

Keep going further from him, without ever disappearing from his view, and always returning soon after. After this, call him. He must not move before the order, "Come." If he should move, repeat the exercise. Once you are more sure of your dog, hide, ready to stop him if he should disobey and thus obtain a training on which you can really depend.

Bark on Command (8 months)

This command is not too hard. The important thing is to understand when the dog is about to bark naturally. There are dogs who like to "chat;" it is enough for them to get impatient seeing their dinner on the table and they start asking for it, voicing their desire. With them it is easy to explain the meaning of the command, "Bark." It is enough to show them their food after preparing it. Usually though, even quieter dogs will bark when they hear strange noises outside the house, especially at night.

Consequently, give the command "Bark" right before the dog is about to do so.

Retrieving (9 months)

The Newfoundland puppy has a great instinct for retrieving. It is the blood of the retriever that emerges. Teaching him this command is not only fun for him, but also necessary. Some dogs, as I have said, like to take their owner by the hand and lead him. To these dogs you must give the utmost trust and opportunity, allowing them to guide you and showing yourself pleased. When your back begins to ache, give the command "Give," and open the dog's mouth, freeing your hand.

You must be very careful though not to confuse the dog and have him think about the retrieving work as play. When you throw your puppy a ball or a stick, he will almost always go and get it. He may bring it back to you; he may, with a move of the head, invite you to follow him or he may chew on it. In all of these cases, he is not working but playing. And it would be good if you showed little interest in this. It would be negative if you confused this with retrieving and continually tossed things for him to catch in the water. In the best case the dog would bring these things back, leaving them a few feet away from the water, depending on what he feels like doing. The purpose of this exercise would thus be useless. It is up to us to teach him the meaning of two important commands: "Fetch" and "Give."

The exercise is taught to a dog which already knows the command, "Sit." Once the dog is in this position, show him a wooden barbell and give the command "Retrieve." Then, open his mouth and place the object between his teeth and repeat "Good; Fetch." As soon as you have taught the dog to hold the object by himself for a couple of minutes, take it back in your hand and give the command, "Give."

The objects that you use for this work are of the utmost importance. It is not a good idea to use pieces of wood that were found on the ground. After finishing the exercise, you might leave them where you found them and the dog would learn to give no importance to them. Thus, begin with the classical barbell or so-called "manchon," a piece of tube covered in polyester that you can make yourself. Later, you will also use personal belongings for which the dog will pay the most attention. Once he knows the order, the time in which he holds the object should become longer and later, the weight of the object should become greater, without tiring the dog though. Later, you should bring the object

Pulling the inflatable boat.

156

away from the dog and give the command "Fetch," as soon as the dog has retrieved the object: then tell him to come and to give it to you.

The pleasure that you find in seeing this work done will be the best praise for your willing friend. At this point the dialogue is open. He will be able to concentrate better on the commands and will be more attentive than when he was younger.

Pulling (10 months)

The pulling of rope is a classic task for a Newfoundland. Many times while looking at a book about the breed, I have seen him drawn with all muscles in tension, as he holds a rope in his tightly clenched mouth. This exercise must be taught when the dog has already achieved proper muscle development.

After tying a large object to a rope, give the command, "Fetch;" Pull." If the dog does not like the rope, tie a barbell to it for the first few times. As soon as he has done what was asked, praise him.

If possible, apply the work learned by your friend for a useful purpose. He will be interested and you will be proud of such an able helper. You will teach him in this way to bring a lifebelt from or to land, to pull a dinghy. He will also learn to hold a rope during the tying of a boat.

Turn (6 months or at first swim)

The Newfoundland that goes to the beach for the first time feels a natural instinct to save swimmers and in particular those who are snorkeling. The problem is that these people have absolutely no desire of being saved. Many times, novice owners have asked me what to do to avoid the scratches that their dog gives when he is in the water for the first time.

Let us try to take his place.

Centuries of life on the coasts of Newfoundland have taught your friend that the water may be a friend but that it may also be an enemy. When the dog sees us in the water, he does not know that we are able to swim. Immediately he feels he must save us. As soon as he comes close to us, his strong paws will come into contact with our poor skin pushed by the swimming motions. The reaction of the owner combined with the counteraction of the dog who sees us in trouble, causes him to try even harder to grab us and save us. In order to avoid this unpleasant situation, take a few precautions. First of all, do not dive, but remain standing in the water up to your armpits. The dog will come close to

Rescuing the manequin.

you and you will keep him away with your arm and give the command "Turn." Because he is swimming and, sees you calm and safe, he will understand that you are able to swim as well.

Only after he has learned to stay near without jumping on you, will you be able to swim with him. And I assure you, it is incredible to watch the powerful movements of the limbs, the flexing of the body, the shining and wavy hair moving through the water, and to enjoy with your friend the pleasant and relaxing sensation that the water gives. Then, when you are tired and want to go back, you have your four legged friend ready for you, happy to help you. If your dog does not yet know how to retrieve, you may have him pull you by holding on to the hair on his sides. Never hang on to the tail, which, held rigidly at water level, is used to turn.

Water Retrieving (10 months)

Only after the dog has correctly learned to retrieve on land can you go on to teach him how to retrieve in water. Holding the dog at your side, throw the object that he is to retrieve into the water, after having first shown it to him. He must be attentive, but remain seated. Soon after give the command, "Go. Retrieve." The reaction should be immediate. The object should be brought back to the owner and released on command.

Water rescue.

An already well-trained dog, that knows how to retrieve on land will most likely have no trouble learning to do so in the water.

If he should drop the object in order to shake, immediately give the command "Retrieve" and "Give." Little by little, increase the weight and volume of the object, until you can use a dummy.

Rescue in the Water (12 months)

This is the goal of all of our work, where training and instinct come together to give the best results. Many Newfoundlands instinctively save those who are in danger, but a serious training program assures you of having help when necessary. Since he was small, you were always pleased when he took you by the hand, so you will accustom him to take your arm or that of a helper with the usual commands. If you are alone, have the dog stay on the edge of the water with the command, "Stay," while you swim far away, then call him. As soon as he is close to you, command him to take your arm. It is almost certain that your Newfoundland will obey and will quickly head toward land. While you let him pull you at his side, playing dead, you will find yourself being pulled with your head on his shoulder. Even if the dog grabs your arm carefully, he will have to exert some pressure on your arm because of your weight and the resistance of the water; it may occur that your arm will start hurting a bit. Be careful though, the "ride" is short and the pain minimal, don't give in to temptation and pull your arm away. You must reach land. Only in this way will the exercise be constructive. If you have a

Bringing the life preserver.

helper, you can give the order "Fetch" while staying on land. Later the dog will get used to coming not only when called but also when he sees a person in danger.

The exercises previously described constitute the basis for more intense training in water. As in other countries, the Club Italiano del Terranova in Italy has elaborate regulations that are presented in the following pages.

Extract of the Regulations for Attitude and Operative Trials for the Ability of Water Rescue for the Newfoundland, published by the Club Italiano O Del Terranova in June 1991

The Newfoundland is a utility dog. His attitude is based on an instinctive passion for swimming and retrieving, which along with his strength, intelligence, and courage, makes him capable of impressive exercises that include saving human life. The water trials have the purpose of highlighting the characteristics of the breed and to form the Canine Units trained for rescue in the water. Thus, handler and dog are inseparable.

The trials are divided into attitude and operation:

PART 1: ATTITUDE TRIALS

Article 18

The work trials are comprehensive of different levels depending on the preparation. The minimum age for taking the First degree trial is 12 months: the entry for the more advanced trials requires the passing of the previous level with points that are not less than 80 percent.

Article 19

The attitude trials, which can take place in a lake, in the sea, or in a river, are comprehensive of the following three exercises, and the points assigned to each:

First degree:	100 points
Second degree	100 points
Third degree	100 points
TOTAL	**300 points**

Every group of exercises is comprehensive of the following trials and the scoring of maximum points for each, the total of which is the highest score for that group.

Article 20

The Canine Units will pass the attitudinal trials and will be admitted to the second operative set of trials if they have scored at least 80 percent of the highest score for each of the three groups described in the above Art. 19.

Description of the trials

First degree
1.) Obedience on land:
      A. Walking on the leash   10 points
      B. Heel without leash   10 points
      C. Sit   10 points
      D. Stay   10 points
      E. Recall   10 points
2.) Swimming for 100 meters   10 points

3.) Retrieval of an object
   thrown in the water by the
   handler   20 points
4.) Retrieving of an object
   thrown in the water by the judge   20 points

Total Points: 100

1. Exercises of obedience on land

The exercises of obedience on land will take place on a field of 40 by 20 meters (or 43.76 by 21.88 yards), depending on the indicated course to follow.

The dog, initially held on the leash on the left side of the handler, must follow him naturally, willingly and spontaneously at a normal or fast speed. The handler may give the commands for the various gaits and positions that the dog must assume. Beginning at point A, he will reach point B following the indicated changes in direction. This must be done with maximum ease, avoiding any sign of submission. In particular, the dog must show a great love for his work. Once point B has been reached, the handler will unhook the leash and do the heel exercise without a leash, once again following the indicated pattern. Once he has reached the starting point, the handler, with his dog on his left side, will ask the dog to sit and then to stay; he then must go away at a normal speed for twenty steps, he will turn toward the dog and, after a short wait, he will call him. The dog must quickly return to the side of the handler.

At the end of this trial, and before going on to the water trials, the dog must pass while at the side of the handler, through a group of people without showing aggressiveness toward either people or dogs; he must allow the judge to touch him, and he will show no fear when an offshore motorboat is started.

2. Swimming for 100 meters (or 109.41 yards)

The dog, along with the handler and the judge is put on a dinghy that goes 100 meters (109.41 yards) from shore. Once the dinghy has stopped, the dog is given the command to go and must dive or be helped into the water (only in the first level); after this, the dinghy returns to shore and the dog must swim after it as the handler gives the command. The dog must show ability in swimming, remaining with his back parallel to the water line, and must not show fear or excessive tiredness.

3. Retrieving of an object thrown into the water by the handler

Handler and dog are on the shore. The handler must throw a barbell in the water and then give the command "Retrieve." The dog must go into the water, retrieve the barbell and bring it back to the handler.

4. Retrieving of an object thrown into the water by the judge

Handler and dog are on the shore. The judge is on the dinghy at about 25 meters (82 feet) from shore, and throws the object into the water. The handler must give the command to "Go. Fetch." The dog must retrieve and bring back the object.

Second degree
1. 150 meter (164.11 yards) swim   25 points
2. Bringing an oar back to the boat that fell from the boat   25 points
3. Bringing a dummy thrown from the boat to the shore   25 points

4. Saving, with the aid of rings, a person in the water   25 points

Total Points 100

1. 150 meter (164.11 yards) swim

The dog, along with the handler, and the judge ride in a dinghy that goes a distance of 150 meters (164.11 yards) from shore. Once the dinghy has stopped, the dog must be told to go; he must dive. After this, the dinghy returns to shore and the dog must follow it.

2. Bringing an oar that has fallen back to the boat

The dog is on the dinghy with the handler and the judge. While the dinghy moves at a slow speed, an oar is dropped into the water. The dinghy must stop. The handler gives the command to retrieve, the dog must dive, get the oar and bring it back to the boat.

3. Bringing a dummy thrown from the boat to the shore

Handler and dog are on land. The dinghy, with a 30 kilogram (66.23 pounds) dummy on board, goes 25 meters (82 feet) from shore, then the dummy is thrown in the water. The handler gives the order to retrieve; the dog must dive into the water and bring the dummy back to shore.

4. Saving, with the aid of rings, a person in the water

Handler and dog are on shore. From the dinghy, which is 25 meters (82 feet) away, a person falls in the water. The handler must give the command, the dog must dive, reach the person; he must allow the person to grab on to the rings and must pull him or her back to shore.

Third degree
1. Bringing back to the boat a person that has fallen from it,
with the aid of rings   25 points
2. Bringing a boat back to shore, beginning at the boat   25 points
3. Bringing a boat to shore, starting from shore   25 points
4. Retrieving, by the arm, a person fallen from the boat   25 points

Total Points: 100

1. Bringing back to the boat a person that has fallen from it, with the aid of rings

The handler and dog board the boat along with the judge and a fourth person; they go to a distance of 50 meters (54.70 yards) from shore, the dinghy slows and the person falls into the water. The dinghy stops after about 20 meters (21.88 yards). The handler must give the retrieve command; the dog must dive, reach the person, who must grab the rings, and the dog must bring him or her back to the dinghy.

2. Bringing a boat back to shore beginning from the boat

Handler and dog go on the dinghy that stops about 25 meters (82 feet) from shore. The handler must throw a pulling rope into the water; he must give the retrieve command; the dog must dive and pull the dinghy to shore.

3. Bringing a boat back to shore beginning from the shore

The dinghy, with the judge and the captain, leaves the shore and stops at about 5 meters (5.47 yards) from shore. The judge must throw a tow rope into the water; on shore the handler must give the retrieve command to the dog, who must dive, reach the dinghy and pull it back to the beach.

4. Retrieving, by the arm, a person fallen from the boat

A person, who is on a dinghy 25 meters (82 feet) from shore, falls into the water. The handler must give the retrieve command, the dog must dive, reach the person, grab him or her by the wrist and bring him or her back to shore.

PART 2. OPERATIONAL TRIALS

Article 1
The operative trials are the exercises of the fourth level that must show the ability of the canine unit in performing a water rescue.

Article 2
Only the canine units which have passed the attitude trials are allowed to participate.

Article 3
The operation trials must be held on the sea.

Article 4
The operation trials include the following:
-A demonstration of acquired swimming resistance by the dog
-Three trials of water rescue performed by the dog, the last of which must include a practical and theoretical trial of CPR done by the handler.

Article 5
At the end of the successful trials, the jury will award the canine unit a certificate enabling it to perform water rescues.

Description of Exercises:

Fourth degree
1. 300 meter (328.23 yards) swim
2. Carrying of a connecting rope
3. Bringing a lifesaver
4. Saving of two persons and CPR trial for the handler

1. 300 meter (328.23 yards) swim
The dog, handler and judge, board the dinghy, which goes a distance of 300 meters (328.23 yards) from shore. The handler must give the retrieve command, the dog must dive, the dinghy must return to shore with the dog swimming after it.

2. Carrying of a connecting rope
This trial simulates a situation in which one or more people are in the water because of currents, high tide or floods. Handler and dog are on shore, one or more people are on a boat or floating dock anchored at about 25 meters (27.35 yards) from shore. The handler gives the rope to the dog and commands him to go. The dog enters the water and reaches

the people in danger. These people unroll the rope, hold one end and give the other to the dog, which, when returning to the handler on shore, creates the connection.

3. Bringing a life saver

Handler and dog are on shore, a person 25 meters (27.35 yards) away simulates drowning because of current or high seas. The handler throws the lifesaver further away than the break point and gives the command to the dog. The dog dives, grabs the lifesaver and brings it to the person in danger; he allows the person to grab it and begins to pull him or her back to shore. The handler has time to put the boat in the water and reach the dog and help him and the person on board.

4. Saving of two people and CPR trial by the handler

Handler and dog are on the dinghy about 25 meters (27.35 yards) away from shore. Two people are on a dingy not too far away. The dinghy turns over, the people fall into the water, one grabs the dingy, the other goes underwater feigning risk of drowning. Handler and dog dive and reach the drowning people. The handler grabs the drowning person and with the free hand grabs the rings on the dog. The dog grabs a rope of the dingy, and pulls at the same time: handler, dingy and persons to shore. Once on the beach, the handler will describe and demonstrate the CPR techniques on the "drowning" person.

A moment during the water trials of the Italian Newfoundland Club.

VIII. CLUB ITALIANO DEL TERRANOVA

by Adelio Seveso, C.I.T. Secretary

The Newsletter Number 6, year III of May 1932 announced the imminent dissolution of the S.I.T. (Societá Italiana Terranova). It was necessary to wait until the 1970s for the breed to grow enough to justify the formation of another association.

It was thus on October 2, 1976, that forty-two founders met at the Astor Hotel in Genova Nevi. After having discussed plans and possible further developments, the reading of the constitution took place and successively it was signed, thus forming the Club Italiano del Terranova.

The constituent assembly nominated the first board of directors: Emmy Bruno (president), Renata Rovera (Vice President), Adelio Seveso (Secretary), Paola Barbante and Paolo Trevisi.

The first initiative taken by the board was that of organizing a show during the International dog show taking place at Villa Reale in Monza on may 7, 1977. It was a great success: thirty-five subjects participated, compared to the three or four that had been present at the shows in the past.

On October 15, 1978, the first meeting of the Club took place at the sporting Club of Garbagnate Milanese, with the participation of thirty-four subjects, which is quite a good number if one keeps in mind the number of Newfoundlands present in Italy at the time. At this meeting there was also the first photographic competition.

Meanwhile, the ENCI, after having accepted the constitution of the Club in December 1976, accepted our request to become a recognized specialized society, nominating in 1980, Mrs. Angela Cipolla as ENCI delegate for the Club, a very important event that also meant a further commitment for the breed that we represented.

In June 1980, the first newsletter of the Club appeared: a publication which in the beginning was not too professional, but was a means of holding together all of those interested. It represented a further means for "discussing" the breed: the talk about standards began, about water work, about diet, and the information for the members became more precise and complete through the publication of the minutes of the assemblies and meetings. In addition, this newsletter, which was now becoming more professional also from a graphic point of view, was given and maintained a semester printing schedule.

On November 27, 1982, the first meeting with judges was organized, and from this the responsibility of the specialized society in giving information and orientation based on the breed was born. This was followed by the formation of a Standard Commission, formed by members of the club and three judges, with the task of monitoring the evolution of the breed.

The work in the water also began to take some importance; on occasion of the meeting in Aenzano in 1984, the first work trials took place, a beginning that would open the door to important character evaluations and useful alternative activities. Further work trials were organized at Angillara, Verbania, Marta, and at every meeting that followed.

In 1984, the regulations for the winning of the title of Social Champion, reserved to the members of the Club Italiano del Terranova, was made official.

Meanwhile, the number of the members kept growing.: from 104 in 1980 to 172 in 1984, to 235 in 1988 and to about 400 today; with this the importance of being careful and better organized grew as well. Along with the growth in the number of members, the number of breeders also grew from two in 1976 to eight today.

Coinciding with the period of maximum growth, in 1986, there also began the regional meetings that have represented a reference and meeting point for the members in the various regions. It was at first a group of six people to which others later joined to become ten today.

1986 was also the tenth anniversary of the foundation of the club: an important event, significant for the continuity and vitality that had been met in the various activities. The parties for the anniversary took place during the meeting organized in Bellagio on October 11 and 12 with the participation of the American judge Kitty Maynard Drury and of Doctor Antonio Morsiani.

The activity of the regional dog fanciers continued to become more specialized: the various tasks were being redesigned, in order to obtain the most, a person responsible for coordinating the initiatives and following the single events was nominated. The regional meetings organized by the Newfoundland lovers kept growing along with the annual meeting, which were both moments for exchanging information and fertile ground for the positive evolution of the breed.

In June 1989, at St. Vincent-Col de Joux, the first meeting of large dogs was organized at which there were the St. Bernards, the Great Pyrenees, and the Leonbergers along with the Newfoundlands. This turned out to be a positive experience that required quite a bit of effort for its organization.

In the meanwhile, a series of other initiatives were taking place, with the goal of preparing a program of water work that was accepted definitely in 1991.

Another important initiative found consideration after a considerable verification activity: on June 30, 1990, the board put out a series of operative rules regarding the research for hip dysplasia.

But, this is a story of our days. And the future? It is full of programs. The growth of the breed, which is becoming quite large, unites us in the responsibility that we have toward it. Being part of the club signifies participation in this guardianship, imposing on ourselves precise rules that we must follow and respect, and the more we do this, the greater will be the strength with which we will be able to sustain the programs that need to be brought to completion.

GLOSSARY

AKC-American Kennel Club.

Barbet-This French breed, ancestor of the Poodle, was once quite common and frequently used for hunting ducks. A great swimmer and very adept at bringing back the hunted prey, the Barbet was often kept on board ships. He was described as an animal with a wide and rounded cranium, a strongly developed forehead and a woolly coat.

Black wolf-This breed of wolf from America, which is unfortunately extinct, presented very particular traits. It was different from other wolves in color, position of eyes, quality of coat, and a greater predisposition for being domesticated. Typical and unique to the female was a white star on the chest.

Bloodhound-This member of the Hound group is used for tracking.

Borzoi-Formerly known as a Russian Wolfhound, this member of the Hound group is used for hunting game much in the same way as is the Saluki.

Canton-A female Newfoundland known to have survived the shipwreck of an English frigate in 1807.

Chesapeake Bay Retriever-A thick, water-resistant coat is the hallmark of this bird dog, which is a member of the Sporting group.

Chromosomes-Although a man has 46 chromosomes, a dog has 78. Chromosomes are presented in couples in every cell of the organism except for the reproductive cells.

Conjunctivas-The mucous membrane that covers the forepart of the eyeball.

Coon dog-This name is used for a number of hunting-dog varieties primarily used to hunt raccoon and opossum.

Cryptorchidism-The failure of both testicles to descend into the scrotum.

Curly Coated Retriever-A water-retrieving breed known for its unique coat.

Dewclaw-A double spur on the hindquarters. The presence of a single dewclaw is uncommon enough in young Newfoundlands that the standard requires it must be removed. The fifth toe, or rear dewclaw, which may appear rudimental, is situated at the level of the metacarpal. It must be removed in the first days of life because it is useless and may cause distortions or traumas if it hooks onto something.

Dewlap-The soft and elastic skin of the neck; in a Newfoundland, it must never hang as in the Mastiff. A pronounced dewlap usually results from both general cutaneous relaxation and relaxation of the ligaments.

DNA-Deoxyribonucleic acid comprises the building blocks of physical characteristics and specific traits.

Dogue de Bordeaux-A French breed not currently recognized by the American Kennel Club.

Dominant homozygotes-Like genes that dominate all others.

Dystocia-Uterine inertia

Ectropian-This defect is one in which the eyelid is turned outward from the orbital cavity. It can involve a portion of or the whole eyelid.

ENCI-National Italian Kennel Club

English Mastiff-A member of the Mastiff family of dogs.

Entropion-This term indicates introflexion of one or both of the eyelids toward the orbital cavity. It can be limited to the lateral angle or it can involve the whole eyelid.

Epagneul-An early name for the Brittany Spaniel.

European show classifications-AB (fairly good), B (good), MB (very good), ECC (Excellent). If there are various subjects they are then compared in order to create a qualification. In the national shows, the judge can assign CAC (Attitudinal Championship Certificate) to the male and female qualified as first; in the Open Class, ECC is assigned; in the international shows, aside from the CAC, the CACIB (International Beauty Championship Attitude Certificate) may be assigned.

F.C.I.-Federation Cynologique International or the International Cinological Foundation.

Flat Coated Retriever-A member of the Sporting group, this dog is generally used for hunting.

Flews-The pendulous outside part of the upper lip; pronounced flews are not desirable in a Newfoundland.

French Pyrenees Mountain Dog-Although similar to the Burnese Mountain Dog, this dog is not a breed recognized by the American Kennel Club Registry.

Golden Retriever-This quite popular dog belongs to the Sporting group.

Great Dane-This dog, belonging to the Working group, is remarkable for its large size.

Heterozygotes-Has genes for dominant and recessive characteristics.

Hound-This general term is used for breeds that hunt by smell or sight.

Indian dog-This is not a term recognized by the American Kennel Club; it is a general term for those dogs found in the New World by the colonists.

International Champion-A dog must have obtained four CACIBs in three different countries and with at least three different judges. One of the CACIBs must be obtained in the country of residence.

Irish Water Spaniel-This member of the Sporting group is noted for its curly hair.

Italian Champion-The Newfoundland must obtain four CACs, two awarded in international shows and two ECC Firsts in the Open Class in a show organized by the Italian Newfoundland Club. The titles must be given by at least five different judges.

Labrador Retriever-This member of the Sporting group is one of the most popular dog breeds in the United States.

Landseer-A white and black version of the Newfoundland named for Edwin Landseer, a noted painter.

Leonberger-A rare European breed not listed in the American Kennel Club Registry.

Lordosis-A downward curvature of the lumbar spine; also called a weak topline.

Mastiff-A member of the Working group, this breed is both powerful and sturdy.

Meiosis-Procedure that leads to the formation of the sperm in the male and of the ovule in the female in which the pairs of chromosomes do not duplicate but instead divide.

Mitosis-Normal multiplication process of the cells

Molossus-A classification formulated by Pierre Megnin in 1897; it includes the Newfoundland, as well as other breeds demonstrating a massive head structure.

Monorchidism-The failure of one of the testicles to descend into the scrotum.

Montagna-A rare European breed not listed in the American Kennel Club Registry.

Occiput-The back part of the head.

Pastern-A vertical line dropped from the center of the humero-radial articulation must divide the forearm and metacarpal into two almost equal parts, touching the ground just behind the foot; in relation to this line, if the carpal is arched forward it is said to be "knuckling over;" if it is arched backward it is said to be "down in pastern."

Pedigree-Antecedents of a dog.

Pelshound-A rare European breed not listed in the American Kennel Club Registry.

Perdiguero-A rare European breed not listed in the American Kennel Club Registry.

Pluripara-A bitch who has already had two or more litters.

Pointer-A general term for a Sporting group breed, such as the English Pointer.

Poodle-This breed comes in toy, miniature, and standard sizes.

Ptosis-Associated with the eyelid, it is usually caused by too much skin on the head.

Recessive homozygotes-Recessive gene characteristics.

Retriever-A general term for water dogs who primarily retrieve birds.

Rottweiler-This breed belongs to the Working group.

S.I.T.-Societá Italiana Terranova, or Italian Newfoundland Society

Sailor-A Newfoundland known to have survived the shipwreck of an English frigate in 1807.

Scissors bite-This is the preferred bite structure for a Newfoundland; the top teeth are superposed and adherent to the lower ones and well squared with the jaw.

Scottish Sheepdog-This breed is also known as the Collie.

Setter-A general term for a group of dogs used to hunt birds.

Spanish Pyrenean Mastiff-A member of the Mastiff family of dogs.

St. Bernard-A mountain dog of the Working group often used for rescue.

Stop-The depression in the face at the junction of the forehead and foreface; in a Newfoundland, it should not be too emphasized.

Tibetan Mastiff-Another member of the Mastiff family.

Ticking-Black dots on a Landseer are considered a defect in varying degrees by the different standards.

Viking Bear Dog-A rare breed not registered in the United States.

Water Spaniel-A generalized term for some of the Spaniel breed, such as the American Water Spaniel.

White and black-see Landseer

Wolf-A member of the Lupus family, a wild canidid.

USEFUL ADDRESSES

Ente Nazionale Cinofilia Italiana
Viale Premuda 21 - 20129 Milano MI
02/760.21.706-7-8-9; FAX 02/783.127

NEWFOUNDLAND CLUBS OF THE WORLD
Italy: Club Italiano del Terranova
Viale Silvio Amico 18 - 17025 Loano (SV)
019/66.84.46

Austria: Osterr. Neufundlander Klub
Simmeringer Huaptstr. 252/1/2
Geschafrsstelle 1110 Wien

Belgium: Belgische Newfoundlander Club
Tupenlaan 6
9080 Moerbeke-Wass

Canada: Newfoundland Club of Canada
c/o Margo Brown
PO Box 5
Carlisle, Ontario. LOR 1HO

Denmark: Newfoundland Klubben I Danemark
c/o Inge Artsoe
Graftebjerg, Lonholtvej 14
DK-3480 Fredensborg

Finland: Suomen Newfoundlandinraydhistys Finska
Newfoundlandsshund foreningen Tampere Keso
3620 Kangasala

France: Club Français du Chien Terreneuve
16, impasse Saint Jean
02290 Vic Sur Aisne

Germany: Deutscher Neufundlander Klub
Kaiser-Wilhelm-Ring 38
5000 Koln

Great Britain: Newfoundland Club
c/o Miss J. Davies
Old Shelve Farm
Lenham, Maidstone, Kent. ME17 2DT

Luxembourg: Luxembourg Newfoundland Club
Millegassel 18
2156 Luxembourg

Norway: Norweigian Newfoundland Club
c/o Rigmor Ulstad
P.A. Hdmsvei 26
N 1164 Olso 11

Spain: Club Espanol del Terranova
C. Torre de Pisa 34
Colmenar Viejo - 28770 Madrid

Sweden: Svenska Newfoundlandklubben
c/o Edor Westerlund
Besebacksstigen 2
S-433 31 Partille

Switzerland: Schweizerischer Neufundlander Klub
c/o Bodo Elbert
Gerbergasse 20
4001 Basel

United States: Newfoundland Club of America
Mrs. Robert M. Price
4908 Rolling Green Parkway
Edina MN 55436

BIBLIOGRAPHY

Alferink-Lerche, Renate, *De Neufundlander een hand om van te houden*, 1981.

Barbieri, Ignazio, *Lezioni di cinognostica*, 1975.

Bernet, Charles, Tesi di laurea Scuola Veterinaria di Lione, 1971.

Bonetti and Gorrieri, *Il cane si muove*.

Booth Chern, Margaret, *The Complete Newfoundland*, 1976.

Cooper, Carol, *The Newfoundland*, 1978 and 1989.

Darcillon, Christine, Tesi di laurea Scuola Veterinaria di Alfort, 1978.

Drury, Maynard K., *This is the Newfoundland*, 1971.

Fatio, A., *Manuale pratico di addestramento*, 1966.

Fehringer, Otto, *Der Neufundlander*, 1953.

Fiorone, Fiorenzo, *Le razze canine*, 1961.

Goerttler, Victor, *Neufundlander und Landseer*, 1978.

Gothen Christensen, Birgitte, *Newfoundlandshunden*, 1985.

Heim, Albert, *Der Neufundlanderhund*, 1928.

Ippen, Heinrich, *Neufundlander*, 1978.

Nutbeem, Megan, *Book of Newfoundland*.

Riley, Jo Ann and Betty McDonnel, *The Newfoundland*, 1985.

Solaro, Giuseppe, *Sunto delle lezioni di zoognostica c.*, 1974.

van der Molen, Robert, *De Neufundlander en De Landseer*, 1980.

Wolter, R., *L'alimentazione del cane e del gatto*, 1983.

Index